A Guide to Animal Tracking and Behavior

Stokes Nature Guides

by Donald Stokes

A Guide to Nature in Winter
A Guide to Observing Insect Lives
A Guide to Bird Behavior, Volume I

by Donald and Lillian Stokes

A Guide to Bird Behavior, Volume II
A Guide to Bird Behavior, Volume III
A Guide to Enjoying Wildflowers
A Guide to Animal Tracking and Behavior

by Thomas F. Tyning

A Guide to Amphibians and Reptiles

ALSO BY DONALD STOKES

The Natural History of Wild Shrubs and Vines

ALSO BY DONALD AND LILLIAN STOKES

The Bird Feeder Book
The Hummingbird Book
The Complete Birdhouse Book

A Guide to Animal Tracking and Behavior

DONALD W. STOKES AND
LILLIAN Q. STOKES

ILLUSTRATIONS BY LESLIE HOLT MORRILL
RANGE MAPS BY LESLIE COWPERTHWAITE
TRACKS BY DONALD W. STOKES

LITTLE, BROWN AND COMPANY
BOSTON   NEW YORK   TORONTO   LONDON

Illustrations by Leslie Holt Morrill
Copyright © 1986 by Leslie Holt Morrill

Range Maps by Leslie Cowperthwaite
Copyright © 1986 by Leslie Cowperthwaite

Library of Congress Cataloging-in-Publication Data

Stokes, Donald W.
  A guide to animal tracking and behavior.

  Bibliography: p.
  Includes index.
  1. Animal tracks.   2. Animal behavior.   3. Tracking
and trailing.   I. Stokes, Lillian Q.   II. Title.
QL768.S76   1986   599'.051   85-23994
ISBN 0-316-81730-9
ISBN 0-316-81734-1 (pbk.)

HC: 10   9   8   7   6   5   4   3   2   1
PB: 10   9   8   7   6   5

BP

Published simultaneously in Canada
by Little, Brown & Company (Canada) Limited

PRINTED IN THE UNITED STATES OF AMERICA

CONTENTS

A Guide to Animal Tracking and Behavior

GETTING STARTED

W E ONCE HEARD a young boy who was about to follow a nature trail ask, "Will I see lots of wild animals along the path?" We knew that he wouldn't, since mammals are secretive and often hard to see, but there are several good reasons he might expect to. One is that other features of nature, such as birds, insects, trees, and wildflowers, are often obvious, so why not mammals? Another is that books, magazines, and films often portray mammals as conspicuous and interacting with one another — wild bears with cubs crawl out of trees, deer bucks lock antlers in battle, raccoons catch crayfish out of streams, and deer mice peer charmingly out of their nests.

Mammals are rarely seen because of certain features of their behavior. Many mammals, such as raccoons and rabbits, come out only at night or in the crepuscular hours of dawn and dusk; some mammals live underground, like the woodchuck, or in water, like the beaver; others, such as the bobcat and moose, shy away from human presence and tend to live in more remote areas; and some, like mice and shrews, are just so small that they escape our notice.

Because people do not actually see any mammals in a given area, they usually assume there are no mammals there. And yet, all kinds of mammals live around us and in almost every habitat. They are actually far more common than people believe. The reason that *we* know this is that we have become skillful at reading the many clues that mammals leave behind. In fact, to discover the presence and lives of our native mammals, you need to be like a detective involved in solving a marvelous mystery.

For example, the other day we went to a nearby state park. Our

3

walk took us behind a barn, across the edge of a large field, and into an area piled with old logs. From there we went in among some hemlocks and then down to a small stream. Throughout the walk there were no mammals in sight. Nevertheless, we discovered many clues to their presence and secrets of their lives.

Our first clue was some small diggings in the short grass of the meadow. These we knew were evidence of a skunk that had been searching for insects and other small animals in the surface of the earth. We looked for more evidence and found some dark scats (animal droppings) about an inch and a half long, which were additional signs of the skunk's visit to the area.

Adjacent to this area were some taller grass and a pile of logs. Suspecting mammals might live there, we went over to explore. By gently pulling apart the tall grass, we found narrow runways along the ground, neatly trimmed of grasses. These were the work of voles, for they are the only mammal that makes tunnels like this. There was also a crease through the grasses, showing that a mammal had walked through, and at the base of the crease were small matted spots of grass, showing where its feet had stepped. From the pattern of steps and the distance between each step, we guessed that a fox had made the sign. This guess was backed up by our knowledge that foxes regularly hunt for voles.

Next to some weeds in the same area was a collection of small circular scats that we knew belonged to a cottontail. We pulled apart the taller grasses nearby and found a larger runway, about four inches in diameter. Rabbits use runways like this. The rabbit runway went through a wire fence, and we looked for bits of hair that might have caught on the wire but saw none. While following the runway we came across a hole dug out under a large board; we were not sure whose hole it was, but a possible user might have been the skunk.

A huge flock of juncos flew up as we went into the adjacent hemlock grove. We had seen a porcupine up in one of the hemlocks several months before but could not spot it this day. Instead, we looked for clues to its presence. There were several. One was its scats inside a hollow portion of an old log, but they were not fresh. Then we saw the tips of hemlock branches scattered on the ground under one of the trees and recognized this as a sign of porcupine feeding. As we looked closely at the lower limbs of this tree, we could also see the claw marks that the porcupine had left as it climbed.

In another twenty yards we crossed a stream that was channeled through a culvert covered by earth and noticed a subtle trail going over the earth from one end of the culvert to the other. It was clearly made by some type of animal, but we were puzzled as to what kind. A little farther on we encountered some burrows dug into the hillside in the woods. From the location, size of the hole, and the mounds of earth in front of them, we knew they were originally made by wood-chucks. Since the entrance of the burrow was free of cobwebs and debris, we knew it had recently been used. But since there was no odor to the den and no fresh earth in front, we figured that the woodchuck had left. Perhaps a skunk or raccoon had recently used it for shelter. Finally, as we started back, we heard the distant scolding of a red squirrel.

Our walk had taken us no more that two hundred yards and, although we had not seen a single mammal, we had discovered numerous clues, some we could solve and others that would remain mysteries. Best of all, we were able to enter part of the mammals' lives and feel as though we had almost seen the mammals whose clues we had found. This is the reward that awaits you when you learn to read animal signs. The signs are your key to recognizing the animals' presence and discovering facts about their lives and behavior. Once you know them, any simple walk becomes a challenge worthy of the best Sherlock Holmes. So head outdoors equipped with this guide and search for the evidence. Mysteries abound; the case is afoot!

How to Use This Book

This guide is designed to help you discover and identify animal tracks, trails, scats, and signs and also to help you understand and enjoy animal behavior throughout the year. These two go together: The better you are at finding animal signs, the more you can learn about their behavior; and the more you know about their behavior, the easier it is to find their signs.

The first half of the book is a guide to the identification of mammal tracks, scats, and other signs. If you find a track that has a clear footprint, you can identify it in "A Guide to Tracks." If you find a track that is not very clear, then you can identify it through "Track Learning."

Scats are often so distinctive that you can know what animal made them. "A Guide to Scats" has life-size illustrations of scats from each of our common mammals, as well as descriptions and helpful clues to their identity.

Following is "A Guide to Signs"; this includes all other evidence of mammals besides their tracks and scats, such as dens, nests, trails, chewing, claw marks, et cetera. For easy reference, the signs are grouped under several headings, such as injury to trees or shrubs; digging, scraping, and tunneling in the ground; constructed nests, homes, and dams; disturbed vegetation; natural cavities; and food remains and caches.

The second half of the book contains complete descriptions of each mammal's life and behavior. For each species there is an introduction, followed by three sections — Getting Around, Food and Feeding Habits, and Family Life — as well as a Quick Reference chart offering at a glance the facts about each mammal.

In the introductions we share a few of our own experiences with mammals. They will help you see what kinds of everyday experiences you also can have as you seek out mammal signs and behavior.

We describe in Getting Around the mammal's use of space — how and when it moves about, how large an area it lives in, whether it is territorial, and whether it uses trails, tunnels, or burrows in its everyday life.

In Food and Feeding Habits you will learn what the animal eats and how its diet changes with the seasons. You will also learn how animals catch prey, how they store food, and how you can recognize the signs of their feeding.

The social structure of the mammal and any social behavior that you may see are discussed in Family Life. We also tell about the relationship between male and female throughout the year, about mating, and about how and when the young are raised.

A *Guide to Animal Tracking and Behavior* is unique in a number of ways. It is the first guide to picture all tracks and scats at their actual size, and not only does it contain more signs than any other guide to North American mammals, but it also is the only guide to present an easy way to identify these signs in the field. All of the most recent scientific research has been used for the writing of the behavioral descriptions and, as a result, no other guide to signs also presents such complete information on the life and behavior of the individual mammals.

We have carefully chosen the mammals in this guide to include all of people's favorites as well as those whose signs are most commonly seen. Due to limitations of space, we could not include all species and had to make some choices. Because this is a guide to behavior as well as signs, we have chosen to include the domestic cat and dog since their behavior is the most easily seen, and because understanding their behavior sheds light on the behavior of all other mammals.

You can use this guide in a number of ways. You can take it into the field with you to identify tracks, scats, and signs. Or you might look over the various scats, tracks, and signs before you go out, so that you are familiar with what to look for. After finding and identifying a track, scat, or sign, you can turn to the description of the mammal's behavior and read about what it may have been doing and why it was at that spot. The descriptions of the mammals can also be used as enjoyable reading at home or as a handy reference when a question comes up about a particular mammal.

However you use A *Guide to Animal Tracking and Behavior*, we hope that you enjoy it and that it leads you to a greater awareness of the lives and presence of mammals right around you.

Part One

TRACKS AND SIGNS

HOW TO IDENTIFY TRACKS

Finding Tracks

Searching for tracks is one of the most exciting things to do in all of nature, for tracks are a direct link to an animal's presence, and you never know beforehand whose track you may discover.

To find tracks requires looking in places where animals live and on surfaces where their feet will leave impressions. There are four good surfaces that register tracks — snow, mud, dust, and sand.

Snow is one of the best, for it usually provides a large, continuous surface that enables you to track an animal over a long distance and learn more about its behavior. Not all snows are good for tracking. Snow with a hard crust does not show tracks, snow that drifts can obscure tracks, and a wet snow that later blows off the trees makes the surface below so pockmarked that it is hard to distinguish tracks. The best snow is slightly moist and just a few inches deep; this does not inhibit the animals' movements, and it retains perfect impressions.

Mud is also good for track impressions. But there is usually only a small amount of mud in a given area, so that just a few tracks show and you cannot follow a long trail. Look for tracks in mud along rivers and ponds, on old roads, and at the edges of puddles. You can also sometimes find tracks in old dried mud.

Dust is a very sensitive recorder of tracks and shows the most detail; it can even show the trails of insects that crawled across it. Like mud, it is usually found only in limited areas and will not record a long trail. Look for tracks in dust in summer and fall along the sides of old roads and paths.

Sand is the fourth good medium for tracking. The advantage of tracking on sand at areas like a beach or a dune is that you can follow a trail for long distances. Sand does not record tracks in much detail, especially when it is dry and drifting. Therefore, the best times to find tracks in sand are after a rainstorm or in the morning, when moisture from the cooler night air is still on the sand's surface.

Identifying Tracks

When trying to identify a track, always do these three things:

1. Look for a clear, individual track.
2. Follow the trail of the animal to discover its track pattern and gain additional information.
3. Use as many clues as you can from other signs and from your knowledge of the animal's behavior.

When clear, individual tracks are found, identification is easy. Just notice the size of the track and count the number of toes that show in it. Then turn to "A Guide to Tracks," where the tracks are all pictured life-size and grouped by the number of toes that show. By comparing your track with the pictures, you will soon know what animal made it.

When individual tracks are unclear or confusing, which is often the case, turn to "Track Learning" to identify the maker. In this chapter you will find a different way to identify tracks, one based primarily on track patterns.

Even after years of experience, we find many tracks and track patterns that we cannot readily identify. Most of these are simply unclear, or the animal has stepped on the same spot too many times. So when you are beginning to identify tracks, start with the ones in which the details seem clear. This way you will have the greatest initial success.

The following is a short list of tracking terms:

Track: The impression of a single foot.

Track pattern: A series of tracks showing the sequence of the animal's steps.

Trail: A long line of tracks showing the animal's movements and behavior.

Stride: The distance between two consecutive tracks.

Straddle: The width of a track pattern or trail.

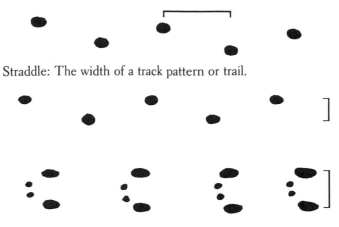

A GUIDE TO TRACKS

IF YOU FIND a clear track that shows the size of the foot and the number and pattern of the toes, then use this chapter to identify the track's maker. The tracks are arranged by the number of toes that show. Here are the categories:

Tracks with 2 toes
Tracks with 4 toes
Tracks with 5 toes
Tracks with 5 hind toes and 4 front toes

In each category the tracks are arranged with the smallest first. All tracks are illustrated life-size.

If you find a track that is not clear, turn to "Track Learning" to help you identify it.

Tracks with 2 Toes

Deer

Behavior, page 383

Deer tracks show 2 *toes*. Length varies from 1½ to 3 *inches*; the smallest prints belong to fawns and the largest to mature bucks. With intermediate lengths, there is no way to distinguish the sex, for older does may have larger prints than young bucks. A print made in snow or soft mud may have 2 marks behind the cloven hoof. These are from the dewclaws, 2 small toes farther up on the deer's foot. They are large and close to the hooves on the forefeet, and small and farther from the hooves on the hind feet. When walking, deer place their hind feet in or near the prints of their forefeet, so prints often overlap.

See "Track Learning," page 44

Moose

Behavior, page 395

Moose tracks show 2 *large toes*. They range in length from about 2½ *inches* in a young calf to about 6½ *inches* in a large bull. The track of a moose calf may be similar to that of a large deer, but the moose calf would be accompanied by its mother, and her tracks would be unmistakable. By the time young moose are on their own, their tracks are more than 3 inches long and larger than those of the largest deer. Like deer, moose have dewclaws, which show when the track is in soft mud or snow.

See "Track Learning," page 44

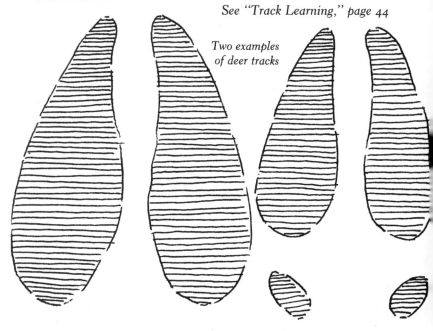

*Two examples
of deer tracks*

Tracks with 2 Toes

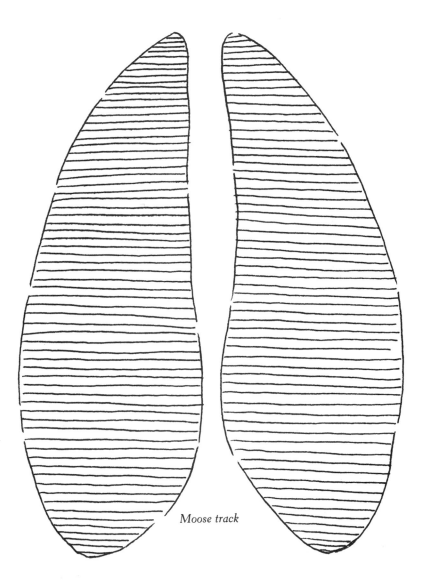

Moose track

Tracks with 4 Toes

Cottontail
Behavior, page 161

Cottontail tracks have *4 toes, with claws occasionally showing.* The front tracks are *oval* and about *1 inch long.* The hind tracks are *oblong* and when fully shown are about *3 inches long.* Cottontail tracks are small even when adult size. The hind foot may have just the toes placed on the ground, and then the resulting track looks exactly like the front track. A single track could look like that of a cat except that claws are visible.

See "Track Learning," page 34

Snowshoe Hare
Behavior, page 171

Snowshoe-hare tracks have *4 toes, occasionally with claws showing.* The front tracks are *round* and about *1¾ inches long.* The hind tracks are *triangular* and *very large,* up to *5 inches long.* A small snowshoe-hare track could be mistaken for that of a rabbit, but in general, once you see a snowshoe-hare track you will recognize it thereafter by its distinctive hind print.

See "Track Learning," page 34

Cat
Behavior, page 373

A *small round print with 4 toes* and *no claws* belongs to a house cat. It is about *1 inch in diameter.* The only other print this small with 4 toes is the front print of the cottontail, but the galloping pattern of the cottontail and the claw marks on its toes distinguish it from the cat. Sometimes more than 4 toes show in a cat print, and this is caused in two ways: Occasionally cats are born with extra toes; and, when cats *perfect-step* — put their hind feet directly in the track of their front feet — they sometimes overlap the prints in such a way that another toe imprint is created.

See "Track Learning," page 37

Bobcat
Behavior, page 365

A *large round print with 4 toes* and *no claws* is a good indication of a bobcat. It is about *2 inches in diameter* and similar to that of a house cat but about twice its size. A distinctive feature seen in clear tracks is a small indentation at the front of the heel pad, which distinguishes it from the prints of canines.

See "Track Learning," page 37

Tracks with 4 Toes

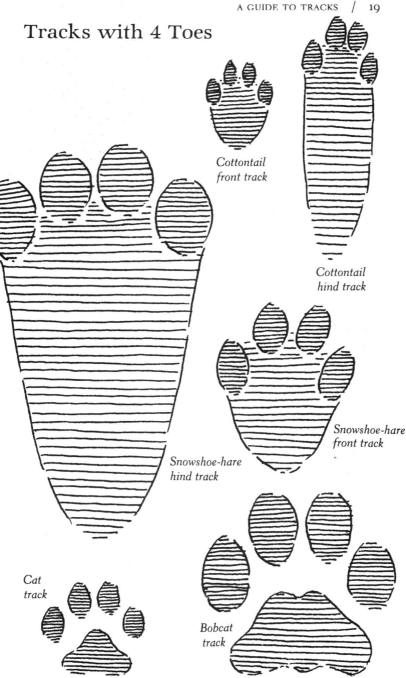

*Cottontail
front track*

*Cottontail
hind track*

*Snowshoe-hare
front track*

*Snowshoe-hare
hind track*

*Cat
track*

*Bobcat
track*

Fox   *Behavior, page 277*

Fox tracks are *oval* and have *4 toes with claws* in front of a small heel pad. The larger front track is about *2½ inches long* and rounder than the hind track, which is about *2 inches long*. Fox tracks can be hard to distinguish from those of a small dog or coyote. They can be distinguished from dog tracks by evidence of perfect-stepping, the lack of foot drag, and the purposefulness of the trail. Distinguishing a fox track from a coyote track is more difficult, though these clues may help: A fox straddle measures 4 inches or less, while a coyote straddle is 4 to 6 inches; in winter, fox toes are so heavily covered with hair that the toe pads show indistinctly; the heel pad of a fox's forefoot is shaped like a thin inverted **V**, but this shows up only in mud or dust.

See "Track Learning," page 37

Coyote   *Behavior, page 267*

Coyote tracks are *oval* and have *4 toes with claws* in front of a triangular heel pad. The larger front track is *2¼ to 2¾ inches long* in adults. It is very similar to that of a fox or small dog, such as a cocker spaniel, and cannot be identified without using other clues. Coyotes have more of a tendency to perfect-step than dogs do and their trail expresses more cunning and awareness of their environment. Another difference between a coyote and a small dog is stride: A small dog's stride will be about 10 to 12 inches, while that of a coyote will be closer to 14 to 16 inches.

See "Track Learning," page 37

Dog   *Behavior, page 289*

Dog tracks are *oval* and have *4 large toes with claws* in front of a triangular heel pad. Dog tracks vary greatly in size, depending upon the breed of dog. In general, they are larger than those of a fox or coyote. Small dogs, such as cocker spaniels, have prints the size of a fox's, about *2 to 2½ inches long*; whereas medium-size or large dogs have prints *3 to 4 inches long*. Still, it is often difficult to distinguish between the tracks of a dog and its wild relatives. You need to use other clues; for instance, dog hind prints are not perfectly placed in the front prints but tend to overlap to the side or behind; dogs frequently drag their feet between steps; dog trails wander more and are less purposeful than those of a fox or coyote.

See "Track Learning," page 37

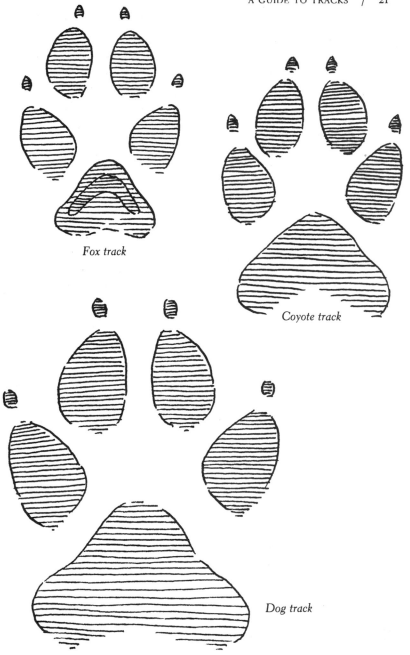

Fox track

Coyote track

Dog track

Tracks with 5 Toes

Weasel *Behavior, page 329*

Weasels make *tiny tracks* consisting of *5 toes with claws* in front of a pattern of heel pads. The tracks of the largest weasel — the long-tailed weasel — are about *1½ inches long* and *¾ inch wide*. Those of the smallest weasel — the least weasel — are only *¾ inch long* and *⅜ inch wide*. So think small when you are identifying weasel tracks. The tracks tend to leave *diamond shapes in snow*, and the toe pads are so small they are rarely seen. The best clues to identifying this animal are the track pattern and print size.

See "Track Learning," page 46

Mink *Behavior, page 339*

Mink tracks have *5 pointed toes* in front of a semicircular heel pad. They are about *1¼ inches wide* and *1¼ inches long*. The toes appear pointed because of the closeness of the claw to the pad. Like weasel tracks, mink tracks can appear diamond-shaped in loose snow.

See "Track Learning," page 46

Skunk *Behavior, page 347*

Skunk tracks have *5 toes with claw marks* in front of each pad. The *toe pads* are *elongated* and *not round*. The hind tracks are about *1½ inches long* and *1 inch wide*; the front tracks are about *1 inch long* and *1 inch wide*. The heel pad is larger on the hind foot and is divided into two parts. The size, number of toes, and position of the claws make this print distinctive.

See "Track Learning," page 46

Fisher *Behavior, page 321*

A fisher track has *5 pointed toes* around a thin, semicircular heel pad. It is about *2½ inches long* and *2½ inches wide*. It resembles that of the mink but is about twice as big. The toes appear pointed because of the closeness of the claw to the pad.

See "Track Learning," page 46

Otter *Behavior, page 355*

Otter tracks are *large with 5 pointed toes* around a small heel pad. The size of the track is distinctive — *3 to 3½ inches wide* and *3 to 4 inches long*. You may also see webbing between the toe pads in the track.

See "Track Learning," page 46

Tracks with 5 Toes

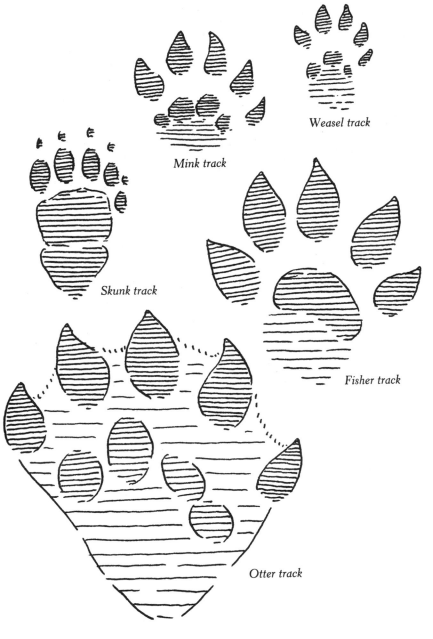

Mink track

Weasel track

Skunk track

Fisher track

Otter track

Raccoon *Behavior, page 311*

Raccoon prints look like *miniature human hands, with long, finger-like toes.* The front prints have shorter heel marks and are *2 to 3 inches long*; the hind tracks have longer heel prints and are *3 to 4 inches long.* The large size and 5 long toes on both hind feet and forefeet are distinctive.

See "Track Learning," page 42

Opossum *Behavior, page 137*

The front track of the opossum is similar to that of the raccoon in size and shape, but the *hind print is distinctive* because of a *thumb-like toe* that *projects to the side and back* of the print. This is the toe that enables the opossum to grasp with its hind feet. Front tracks are about *2 inches long* and *2 inches wide*; hind tracks are about *3 inches long.*

See "Track Learning," page 42

Muskrat *Behavior, page 247*

These tracks are *small, hand-like prints,* with long, finger-like toes. The hind print is about *2 to 3 inches long* and is like a smaller version of a raccoon track. The *front print is distinctive,* for the *inner toe is extremely small* and *barely shows* in the track. Thus this track may appear four-toed.

See "Track Learning," page 42

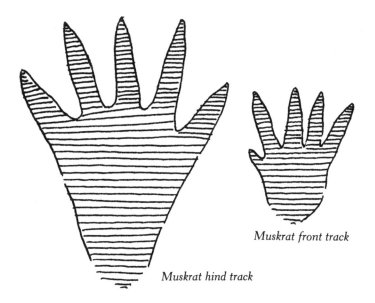

Muskrat front track

Muskrat hind track

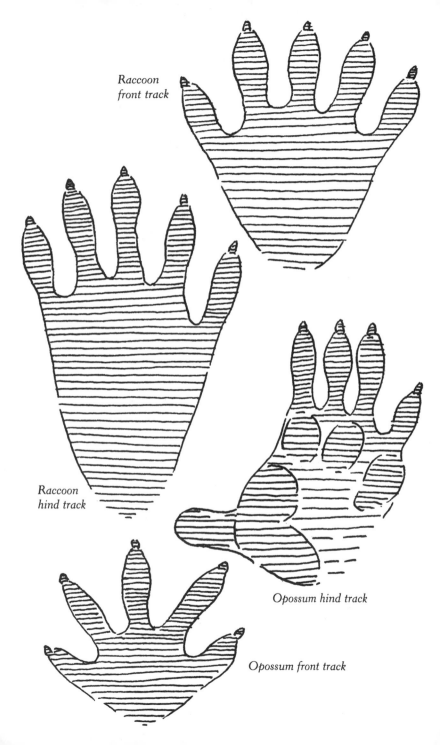

Raccoon front track

Raccoon hind track

Opossum hind track

Opossum front track

Beaver

Behavior, page 219

The beaver track is not often seen, possibly because the tail may drag over it. When it does occur, the front track looks like a *small hand with 5 long fingers*, though sometimes only 3 or 4 fingers are visible. It is about *3 inches long*. The *hind track is distinctive*, for it is *large with very long toes* and *webbing between the toes*, not all of which may show. The hind track is *5 to 6½ inches long* and *4 to 5 inches wide* at the front.

See "Track Learning," page 50

Porcupine

Behavior, page 257

Porcupine tracks are *medium-size* and *oval, with very large heel pads, 5 small toes*, and *long claws*. The tracks are about *2½ to 3½ inches long* and about *1½ inches wide*. They usually appear to be slightly pigeon-toed in the track pattern.

See "Track Learning," page 50

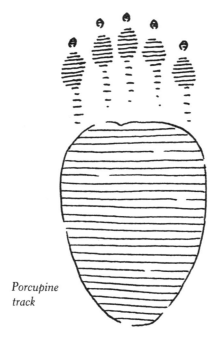

Porcupine track

Black Bear   *Behavior, page 301*

This is a *large track with 5 toes, claws,* and a *large heel pad.* The inner toe is smallest in bear tracks and may not always show up, so the track may look four-toed. The long heel pad of the hind foot makes the track look like a human footprint. The track is *6 to 7 inches long* and *3 to 4 inches wide.* The front heel pad is divided into two: an oval part just behind the toes and a small round dot behind that. The dot does not always appear in the track. Front tracks are about *4 inches wide* and *4 inches long.* The claws of black bears extend about ½ inch in front of the toe pads. Those of grizzly bears extend about 1 inch.

See "Track Learning," page 49

Bear front track

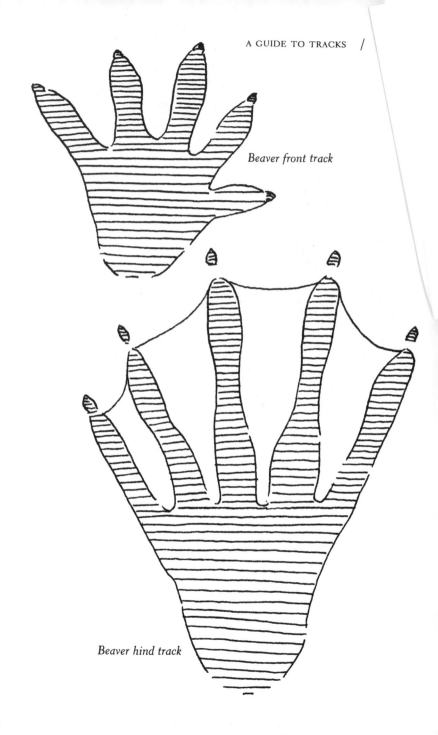

Beaver front track

Beaver hind track

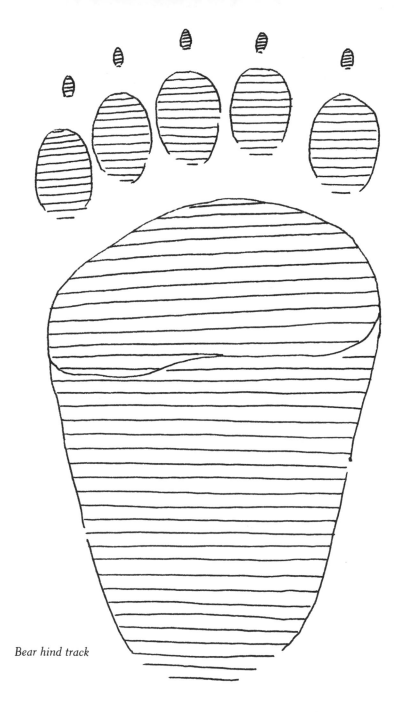

Bear hind track

Tracks with 5 Hind Toes and 4 Front Toes

Mouse, Vole, Shrew   *Behavior, pages 229, 239, 145*

If you find *tiny tracks* about *¼ to ⅜ inch wide with 5 toes on the hind feet*, and *4 toes on the forefeet*, then you have come across the track of a mouse or vole. There is no clear way to distinguish between the tracks of these two animals without using other clues, such as track pattern and behavior. A *shrew* has an even *smaller track with 5 toes on each foot*, which would show up only in mud or dust.

See "Track Learning," page 40

Chipmunk   *Behavior, page 179*

Like the tracks of the mouse and vole, the chipmunk track shows *4 toes* in the front track and *5 toes* in the hind track; its front track, however, is *twice the size of that of a mouse or vole*. It is *½ to ⅝ inch wide*, while the hind track can be up to *1 inch long* if the whole heel pad is showing.

See "Track Learning," page 34

Red Squirrel   *Behavior, page 209*

The red-squirrel track is *similar to the chipmunk track but a little larger*. It is about *¾ inch wide* and *¾ to 1½ inches long*, depending on how much of the hind heel pads shows. Like the tracks of all of our common squirrels and mice, it shows *4 toes* on the front track and *5 toes* on the hind track. Since chipmunks are often dormant in winter, most small squirrel-like tracks in snow will belong to red squirrels.

See "Track Learning," page 34

Gray Squirrel   *Behavior, page 199*

The gray-squirrel track is *similar to the track of the red squirrel but considerably larger*. The hind track is about *1 inch wide* and *2¼ to 2½ inches long* when the whole heel pad is showing. It also has *5 toes* in the hind track and *4 toes* in the front track. To distinguish among various squirrel tracks, you should use other clues besides just the track, such as the straddle of the track pattern and the habitat.

See "Track Learning," page 34

Tracks with 5 Hind Toes and 4 Front Toes

*Mouse
front track*

*Mouse
hind track*

*Chipmunk
front track*

*Chipmunk
hind track*

*Red-squirrel
front track*

*Red-squirrel
hind track*

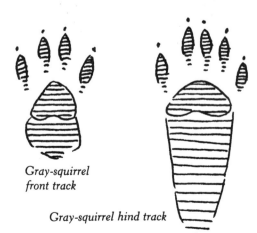

*Gray-squirrel
front track*

Gray-squirrel hind track

Woodchuck

Behavior, page 191

Woodchuck tracks look like small hands. Because woodchucks hibernate, you will find their tracks and trails on snow only in late winter and on dirt or sand in spring through fall. Their tracks are *similar to* those of the *muskrat, raccoon,* and *opossum, but* unlike them, they *have only 4 toes on the front feet* and *5 toes on the hind feet.* The front print is about *1¾ inches wide* and *2 inches long;* the hind print is slightly larger.

See "Track Learning," page 50

Woodchuck front track

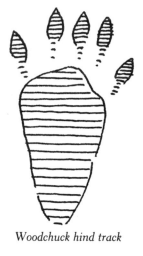

Woodchuck hind track

TRACK LEARNING

W HEN YOU FIND a track in which the impression of the animal's foot is clear, then it is easy to identify with the previous chapter. Tracks are often not clear, however, in which case you need to use a variety of other clues for identification. This chapter is designed to help you identify these unclear or indistinct tracks. It groups together animals whose tracks share certain obvious features. Then it gives simple clues for distinguishing the different tracks within the group.

To use this method, just scan through the various groups to see which one fits the track you have found. Then use the additional clues to discover the exact identity of the animal. The groups have been arranged with the most common appearing first. In fact, 90 percent of the tracks you find will fit into one of the first three groups.

After years of experience in tracking, we have discovered that the method presented in this chapter is the easiest way to identify all tracks, and it is the one we use most often. It is very helpful to take a moment to familiarize yourself with the various groups presented in this chapter, especially the first three or four, before you go out.

Good luck and good tracking!

Squirrel-Rabbit Group

Look for groups of prints in these patterns:

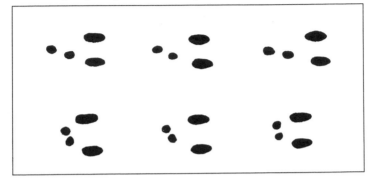

When you find these track patterns, chances are they were made by rabbits or squirrels. The hind feet of these animals are larger than their forefeet. When they move, their hind feet land in front of their forefeet. This type of movement is called *galloping*. In the track pattern below, the animal was moving from left to right.

Squirrel pattern showing direction of travel

DISTINGUISHING RABBITS FROM SQUIRRELS

The first thing to learn when you see one of these patterns is how to distinguish rabbit-like animals (cottontails, snowshoe hares) from squirrel-like animals (chipmunks, squirrels). This is easy. Look at the placement of the forefeet. Rabbits tend to place one forefoot behind the other; squirrels tend to place the forefeet next to each other.

Rabbit track pattern   *Squirrel track pattern*

Some other clues: Squirrel tracks often start and end at trees, but rabbit tracks never do; rabbit tracks tend to be in the underbrush and often have scats near them.

DISTINGUISHING COTTONTAIL FROM SNOWSHOE HARE

Cottontail track pattern   *Snowshoe-hare track pattern*

This is easy since the snowshoe hare has large and distinctive hind feet. See "A Guide to Tracks," page 18.

DISTINGUISHING CHIPMUNK, RED SQUIRREL, AND GRAY SQUIRREL

The tracks and track patterns of these three mammals are very similar except for their size. The best way to distinguish between them is to measure the straddle, or width, of the track pattern, which reflects the size of the mammal. The straddles of the three mammals are:

Chipmunk: 2 to 3 inches
Red squirrel: 3 to 4 inches
Gray squirrel: 4 to 5 inches

Clearly, there may be some overlap, so that it is not always possible to make a positive identification from the track pattern alone. If this is the case, check the track sizes (see "A Guide to Tracks," page 30) and use other clues, such as habitat and behavior. For example, gray squirrels prefer deciduous woods; red squirrels prefer coniferous woods; and chipmunk tracks are rarely seen in snow, since these animals are usually dormant in winter.

OTHER FEATURES AND VARIATIONS

The Speed of Movement

As rabbits or squirrels speed up, their hind feet land farther in front of their forefeet, and as they slow down, their hind feet may land behind their forefeet. You can also tell the speed of the animal by the distance between groups of tracks.

Squirrel tracks showing change from slow to fast pace

Tracks in Deep Snow

When an animal in this group gallops in deep snow, its whole body tends to make an impression in the snow. This is especially true of the red squirrel, the gray squirrel, and the cottontail. The cottontail imprint shows the tail behind as well, and the squirrel imprint shows two diamond-like shapes where its legs have dragged in and out of the snow. As we mentioned before, the chipmunk is not usually active in winter, so its tracks are scarce, and the large feet of the snowshoe hare support it on the snow's surface.

Cottontail tracks in deep snow

Squirrel tracks in deep snow

Hind Feet Looking Small

Sometimes, especially in the case of the cottontail, the mammal places only the tip of the hind foot on the ground, making the track appear small, like the forefeet, as in the following example:

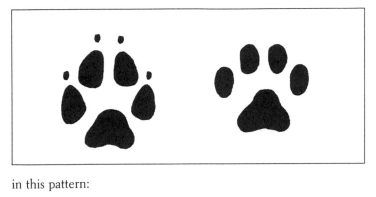

Dog-Cat Group

Look for 4-toed tracks like these:

in this pattern:

Dog or cat track pattern

When you find these tracks or this track pattern, they were probably made by a member of the dog family or cat family. These include the domestic dog, the fox, and the coyote in the first group, and the house cat and the bobcat in the second. Most of the time these animals practice perfect-stepping, placing the hind feet exactly into the track of the front feet.

DISTINGUISHING THE DOG FAMILY FROM THE CAT FAMILY

When you find tracks like these, the first thing to do is decide whether you have a cat-like animal or a dog-like animal. To do this, look at the individual tracks. Cat-like animals have round tracks with no claws showing at the tips of their toe pads. Dog-like animals have oval tracks with a claw mark showing at the end of each toe.

Cat track   *Dog track*

DISTINGUISHING DOG, FOX, AND COYOTE

This is not always easy to do since there are various sizes of dogs, and fox and coyote tracks are very similar. But there are a few good clues.

Domestic Dog

The track pattern of the domestic dog is often distinctive for three reasons. First, dogs rarely perfect-step; usually their hind feet land a little to the side or behind the tracks of their forefeet. Second, dogs often drag their hind feet slightly, and the drag mark shows, especially in the snow.

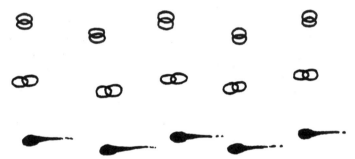

Domestic dog patterns: faulty perfect-step (top and middle), hind feet dragging (bottom)

Third, you may also see a difference in the character of the whole trail. The dog's trail often meanders, revealing an incautious curiosity that its wild relatives cannot afford. It is also true that most dog tracks are larger than those of foxes or coyotes. See "A Guide to Tracks," page 20.

Fox and Coyote

The track pattern of these animals is a nearly straight line of neat prints in which the hind feet step exactly into the track of the forefeet. The tracks and strides of the two animals are so similar that distinguishing them may be difficult. In general, the fox is a more delicate animal with a narrow straddle, 3 to 4 inches; being light, it makes a shallower impression. The heavier coyote has a larger straddle, 4 to 6 inches, and makes deeper impressions.

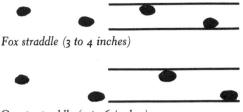

Fox straddle (3 to 4 inches)

Coyote straddle (4 to 6 inches)

The trails of the fox and coyote also generally portray a keen awareness of environment, a directness of intent, and no wasted energy.

DISTINGUISHING CAT AND BOBCAT

These two animals differ in both stride and track size. Cat tracks are 1 inch in diameter and their average stride is 6 to 8 inches. Bobcat tracks are 2 inches in diameter and their average stride is 10 to 16 inches. See "A Guide to Tracks," page 18.

OTHER FEATURES AND VARIATIONS

Fox and Cat

Red-fox and house-cat tracks are often found in the same suburban and rural areas. At first they may look similar, but an easy way to distinguish them is by stride: The stride of a cat is usually less than a foot, while that of a red fox is usually more than a foot.

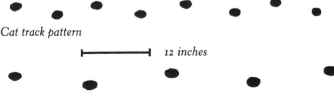

Cat track pattern

12 inches

Fox track pattern

Patterns from Different Gaits

About 90 percent of the time these mammals walk or trot, creating the perfect-stepping patterns shown before. Occasionally they move faster or in ways that create different track patterns. Below are some of the variations in track patterns typical of all animals in the dog-cat group:

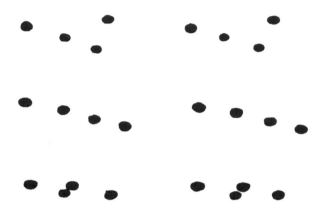

Tiny-Track Group

Look for tiny sets or lines of tracks, like these:

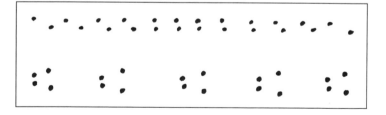

When you find such tracks, chances are they belong to mice, shrews, or voles. These animals have such tiny feet that you cannot see the details of their tracks, only little dots in various patterns on the surface of the snow.

Shrews

These are the smallest of the three tiny-track makers, and size distinguishes their trail from the others'. The width of their trail is 1 inch or less, whereas the trail width of the mouse and vole is about 1½ inches or slightly more.

Track pattern for shrew

The trail of a shrew often resembles a little trough in the surface of the snow or a tunnel underneath the snow. The track patterns in this tunnel or trough vary as shown above. Sometimes the shrew's tail makes a line down the center of its trail.

Voles

Vole trails and tracks are similar in most respects to those of shrews. Voles also tend to tunnel in deep snow and/or make small troughs through shallow snow. Their trails can be distinguished from shrews' by the width of the trail, which tends to be about 1½ inches or more. Also, their tails do not usually leave drag marks in their trails.

Track pattern for vole

Mice

Mice can be distinguished from shrews and voles by their track patterns. Mice generally gallop over the surface of the snow, often for long distances, and each gallop may take them from a few inches to more than 4 feet. Their track patterns look like miniature versions of squirrel track patterns, except that often their long tails make drag marks in the pattern. Mice generally do not tunnel through the snow or leave troughs in shallow snow.

Track pattern for mouse

Other Features and Variations

Small birds, such as sparrows and juncos, leave little pairs of tracks in the snow around sources of food. Their tracks are distinctive because of their long hind toes.

Track pattern for bird

Fingered-Track Group

Look for medium-size tracks with long, finger-like toes:

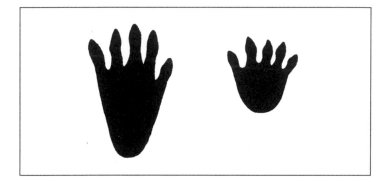

When you find tracks like these, they probably belong to an opossum, raccoon, or muskrat. These mammals make 2- to 3-inch-long tracks that look like a series of small handprints. The long, finger-like toes on their tracks are their most recognizable and distinctive feature. The tracks of all three are often found in the mud along streams, swamps, and lakes, especially those of the muskrat and raccoon.

Opossum

The easiest track to decide about is the opossum's, for its distinctive hind foot quickly distinguishes it from the raccoon and muskrat. Its hind foot has a large, backward-pointing thumb that is always obvious in the track.

Opossum hind track

Even when the individual toes are unclear in the track pattern, the thumb is distinct.

Opossum track pattern

DISTINGUISHING RACCOON TRACKS FROM MUSKRAT TRACKS

The tracks of these two animals are similar, except that the forefoot of the muskrat is smaller and shows 4 long toes, while that of the raccoon is larger and shows 5 long toes. See "A Guide to Tracks," page 24.

Muskrat front track   *Raccoon front track*

When the tracks are indistinct, you can use the track patterns to tell the two mammals apart. The track pattern of the raccoon shows the large hind track placed next to the smaller front track of the opposite side.

Raccoon track pattern

The track pattern of the muskrat shows the hind track placed behind the front track of the same side.

Muskrat track pattern

Hooved-Mammal Group

Look for deep impressions made with single or cloven hooves:

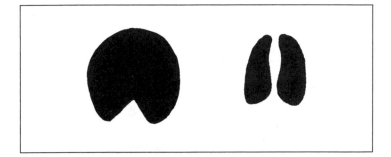

If you find deep tracks made by single or cloven hooves, they have probably been made by horses, moose, or deer. We mention horses simply because people often ride horses in areas where you may be tracking. The horse's hoof is a single semicircle with a triangular indentation in the back. The moose and deer have two-part hooves and can be differentiated on the basis of size. See "A Guide to Tracks," page 16.

| Horse | Moose | Deer |

The track patterns of these animals are similar to those of the Cat-Dog Group, for they also use perfect-stepping.

Hooved-mammal track pattern

OTHER FEATURES AND VARIATIONS

Deer Trails in Deep Snow

White-tailed deer may continually use the same trail through deep snow. In these cases the deer travel single file, each stepping in the tracks of the deer before it. This may result in a trough through the snow with deeper alternating tracks within it.

Deer trail in deep snow

Other Track Patterns of Deer

Also, deer may gallop for short distances. Then their track pattern looks like this:

Deer galloping

WEASEL-FAMILY GROUP

Look for track patterns like these:

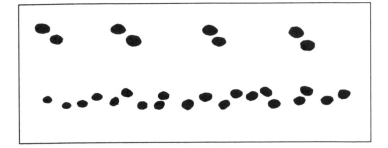

If you find diagonally placed pairs of tracks or a long, meandering trail of medium-size tracks, they were probably made by a member of the weasel family, which includes the weasel, mink, skunk, fisher, and otter. (The marten is another member of this family, but it is very uncommon and lives only in the far North.)

The skunk produces a meandering trail when it walks, and this is distinctive, for no other animal makes a pattern quite like it. When the skunk moves at faster speeds it may produce any of the three variations of track patterns illustrated, but it never goes at these faster speeds for very long, since it would much rather waddle about at its slower speed.

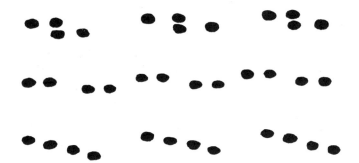

Variations in weasel-family track patterns

The diagonal pairs of tracks are the major track pattern of all other members of the weasel family — the weasel, mink, fisher, and otter. Seeing this pattern should instantly make you think of these animals, for no other common mammals make it. Like the skunk, the others also move at different speeds and can create the same three variations in track patterns as the skunk does. Distinguishing among the tracks of the four mammals is done primarily through the size of their tracks. See "A Guide to Tracks," page 22.

OTHER CLUES TO THESE ANIMALS

Skunk

Skunks spend the day and a good deal of the winter resting in ground dens, so you often find their tracks coming in and out of holes. When they come out of a hole, they frequently track fresh earth from the burrow out onto the snow surface. In northern areas, skunks do not come out of their burrows except on warmer winter nights. Their tracks are particularly common on the snow in late winter when they are becoming fully active.

Skunk track pattern

Weasel

Weasels are the one member of the family that almost always creates the diagonally paired track pattern and not the variations. Weasels are also the smallest member of this family. Even the largest weasel's tracks are only $\frac{3}{4}$ inch wide.

Weasel track pattern

Mink

Look for mink tracks along the edges of streams and lakes, where it hunts for its food. Mink usually create the diagonally paired track pattern, and the rest of the time they can show any of the variations. Their track size and habitat preference afford good ways to distinguish their tracks from those of weasels. Occasionally mink slide in snow like otters, but the resulting trough is narrower — 4 to 6 inches wide.

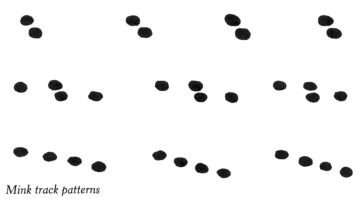

Mink track patterns

Fisher

Look for fisher tracks in deep woods in the North. Of all the members of the weasel family, fishers vary their track pattern the most. A track that is fairly large and shows two or three of the above variations within 20 or 30 yards is a pretty good sign of a fisher.

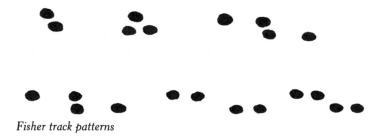

Fisher track patterns

Otter

Look for otter tracks near streams, rivers, and lakes because the otter lives and hunts for food in water. Otters create the diagonally paired track pattern as well as all of the variations. They also often slide both up and down hills and on level areas. The slides look as if someone pulled a small toboggan about 8 to 10 inches wide along the snow. Otter tracks are very large, for they are by far the largest of the mammals in this group.

OTHER FEATURES AND VARIATIONS

The diagonally paired track pattern of these animals is created by a movement called *bounding*, in which the forefeet move forward together and the hind feet land exactly in the tracks made by the forefeet. When the hind feet land a little behind the tracks of the forefeet, these track patterns may be seen:

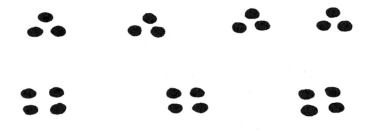

Bear Group

Look for a very large track with 5 toes and claw marks like this:

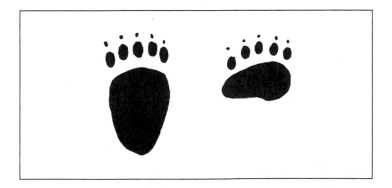

in track patterns like this:

Bear track pattern

No other pattern like this has as large a track, and this makes the bear trail unique. In most northern areas, black bears hibernate throughout much of the winter, and thus you will not see their tracks in the snow, except perhaps late in the season.

Porcupine Group

Look for medium-size oval prints in a pigeon-toed pattern like this:

Porcupine track pattern

In snow more than 2 inches deep, the porcupine's low-slung body and quills make a wide trough about 6 to 8 inches wide through the snow. In the trough you will see the 3-inch-long, slightly pigeon-toed tracks. The tail of the animal often drags over the tracks, obscuring them slightly. The trail usually ends at either a den or a tree.

Woodchuck and Beaver

The tracks of the woodchuck and beaver are rarely seen even though the animals are common. The woodchuck hibernates throughout the winter and does not venture out onto the snow except in late winter, and the beaver remains in its lodge or under the ice for most of the winter and does not often come up on land. Also, the beaver's broad, flat tail often obscures its tracks.

Woodchuck

Late in winter, woodchuck tracks will be seen going from one den to another and often trailing fresh earth from the burrows onto the snow surface. The track pattern looks like this:

Woodchuck track pattern

Beaver

Look for beaver tracks at the edges of ponds or rivers where there are other signs of the animal. At some point they must come out from under the ice or out of the open water, so look for these spots. Beavers also will bring water up with them onto the snow surface. Their tracks should also lead to signs of feeding, such as gnawed trees, since this is the main reason they come onto land in winter. Their track pattern looks like this:

Beaver track pattern

A GUIDE TO SCATS

Although identifying scats is not an exact science, scats are an important clue to the presence of an animal, and you should look carefully for them as you walk through woods and fields or along streams and lakes. Some scats are very distinctive in color and/or shape and enable you easily to identify the animal they belong to. Other scats are less distinctive or resemble those of other animals.

The guide that follows presents the best accumulated knowledge on distinguishing the scats of different animals. Use the descriptions and drawings only as guidelines toward identification, for scats, even from the same species, vary greatly according to the size of the animal and the type of food eaten. In the case of the scats of coyote, fox, and bobcat, which are similar, researchers have been able to distinguish them only through chemical analysis; visually there is no sure way to know. As with all animal signs, you need to gather a variety of clues that then add up to the identification of the animal.

Why some animals' scats are more commonly found than others is a result of several factors, such as whether the animal is rare or common, whether it uses scats in scent-marking, whether it buries its scats, whether it lives in an environment where we would not see its scats (trees or water, for example), and how long the scats remain whole before decomposing.

The scats for all of the animals in this guide are described in this chapter, but if you start by learning the most common ones, you will quickly be able to identify almost 95 percent of those you find. The most commonly found scats come from vole, mouse, muskrat, cottontail, snowshoe hare, deer, porcupine, skunk, raccoon, fox, and dog.

The scats are arranged in two groups. First are the scats of herbivores — those animals that eat only plants. These scats tend to be small and uniform in texture. The second group includes the carnivores and omnivores — those animals that eat only meat and those that eat both meat and plants. These scats tend to be larger and contain hair, bones, fish scales, and seeds. In both groups the scats are arranged in order of size, with the smallest first.

Herbivores

Shrew, Mouse, Vole   *Behavior, pages 145, 229, 239*

These animals all make *tiny, cylindrical scats* about ¼ *inch long.*
They are all so small that there is no way to distinguish among them.
Vole and shrew scats are most often found in these animals' tunnels
in grass and leaf litter, and often at the crossroads of tunnels. Mouse
scats are found in their nests or other areas they frequent.

Chipmunk   *Behavior, page 179*

Chipmunk scats are only *slightly larger* than those of *voles, shrews,*
and *mice.* They are about ¼ to ½ *inch long* and ⅛ *inch in diameter.*
Since the chipmunk is so active and often in its underground tunnels,
its scats *are rarely found.* There is no sure way to distinguish them
from the scats of smaller animals, but bear in mind that chipmunk
scats will not be found in mouse nests or shrew and vole tunnels. You
may find them at a spot where a chipmunk regularly perches to feed.

Red Squirrel   *Behavior, page 209*

Red-squirrel scats *are rarely found.* They are *small, cylindrical* scats
about the size of *chipmunk* scats, about ¼ to ½ *inch long* and ⅛ *inch
in diameter.* There is no sure way to distinguish them from those of
chipmunks.

Gray Squirrel   *Behavior, page 199*

Gray-squirrel scats are distinctive, for they are *twice the diameter of
chipmunk* and *red-squirrel* scats and are more *oval.* They are about ½
inch long and ¼ *inch in diameter.* They are not normally found in
the wild, but you can find them around places where the animals
regularly feed, such as bird feeders.

Muskrat   *Behavior, page 247*

Muskrats produce *brown, slightly curved, cylindrical* scats about ½
inch long and ⅜ *inch in diameter.* They are usually placed on prominent objects, such as a rock or log, at the edge of water. At these
spots you will usually find small accumulations of several scats
lumped together.

Herbivores

Shrew, mouse, or vole scats

Chipmunk scats

Red-squirrel scats

Gray-squirrel scats

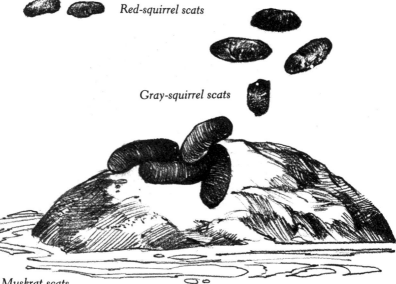

Muskrat scats

Cottontail   *Behavior, page 161*

Rabbit and hare scats are distinctive, for they are *slightly flattened spheres composed of light brown, sawdust-like material.* The animals always void them at their feeding places, where you will find 5 to 10 of them scattered on the ground. The scats of cottontails are about ⅜ *inch in diameter.*

Snowshoe Hare   *Behavior, page 171*

Snowshoe-hare scats are *similar* to those of *cottontails* but *are slightly larger,* about ½ *inch in diameter.* There is no sure way to distinguish them from those of cottontails; you must use other clues, such as tracks or the different ranges of the two animals.

Deer   *Behavior, page 383*

Deer droppings vary greatly in shape, yet they are always fairly easy to recognize. Their scats for most of the year are a *large number of dark cylindrical pellets with one flat or concave end* and *one pointed end.* They are usually about ¾ to 1 *inch long* and about ⅜ *inch in diameter.* There tend to be 20 to 30 pellets in a spot. During late spring and early summer, when deer are feeding on very succulent vegetation, these pellets are softer and may stick together or even coalesce into one large, soft dropping. Still, the size and shape are distinctive. Deer scats are commonly seen in areas that deer frequent.

Porcupine   *Behavior, page 257*

Porcupine scats are usually *oblong* and *yellowish brown,* and are deposited in *large numbers of pellets.* Each scat is about ¾ to 1 *inch long,* about ⅜ *inch in diameter,* and sometimes *slightly curved.* They often have a rather sweet, resinous odor, which sometimes can be smelled several yards away since there tend to be such large accumulations of them. Look for the scats at the base of trees in which the porcupine is feeding or in hollow logs, caves, or burrows in which the porcupine has been resting. In summer, when more succulent vegetation is available, the pellets may be joined together by thin strands.

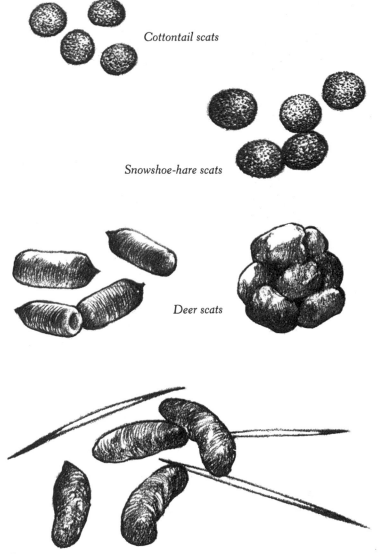

Cottontail scats

Snowshoe-hare scats

Deer scats

Porcupine scats and quills

Moose *Behavior, page 395*

Moose scats, like those of deer, are usually deposited in large numbers of pellets in one spot. Moose pellets can look like those of *deer* or even those of *porcupine* but *are much bigger*. They are usually about *1½ inches long* and *¾ inch in diameter*. Their size makes them distinctive. Like deer, moose eat more succulent vegetation in summer, causing their pellets to form a clump or even a cow-pie shape if they are very loose.

Moose scats, winter

Moose scats, summer

Carnivores and Omnivores

Weasel   *Behavior, page 329*

Weasel scats are *long, thin,* and *pointed at the ends.* They are *1 to 2 inches long* and about *⅛ to ¼ inch in diameter.* The scats are not often seen, but those that are, are usually placed along a trail on some prominent object, such as a rock or log.

Skunk   *Behavior, page 347*

Skunk scats are *medium-size, long,* and *usually have blunt ends.* They contain all types of food, from insect skeletons to seeds to hair. They are *1½ to 2 inches long* and about *½ inch in diameter.* Often they are found near spots where the animals have been feeding or digging small holes in the earth looking for insects. The scats may also be near a den where the skunks spend the night. Skunk scats are fairly common.

Mink   *Behavior, page 339*

Mink scats are *slightly larger versions of weasel* scats, about *2 to 3 inches long* and about *⅜ inch in diameter.* They overlap in size with those of larger weasels. The scats are rarely seen, but when found are *likely to be on such noticeable objects* as rocks or logs *near water.* Mink eat animals, birds, and fish, and their scats take the following forms: Those from animal prey have fur, those from birds have feathers and are lighter-colored, and those from fish have scales and are very dark. This last example is a good clue to a mink, along with size and the placement of the scat near water.

Fisher   *Behavior, page 321*

The scats of fishers are *rarely seen.* They are about *3 to 4 inches long* and about *½ inch in diameter.* They may contain fur, bits of porcupine quills, and occasionally fruit seeds. There is no positive way to distinguish them from coyote or fox scats without considering other clues like track prints and patterns.

Cat   *Behavior, page 373*

Because cats usually scrape away a depression, void their scat in it, and then cover it up, their scats are rarely seen. They are about *2 to 2½ inches long* and about *⅝ inch wide.* They contain fur or feathers only if the cat is eating on its own or supplements its home diet with wild fare.

Carnivores and Omnivores

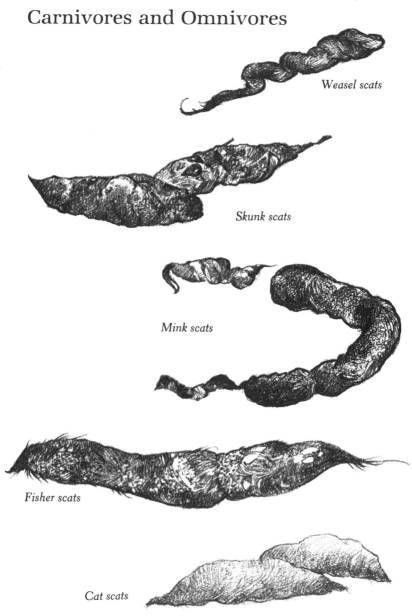

Weasel scats

Skunk scats

Mink scats

Fisher scats

Cat scats

Otter   *Behavior, page 355*

Otters chew their food extremely well, so their scats contain only fine bits of food remains, such as fish scales. The scats are about *6 to 7 inches long, ¾ inch in diameter,* and are divided into *2 or 3 segments.* They are *black* and have a *heavy mucus* mixed in among the food remains. With exposure to sun and weather, they become bleached, lighter in color, and may disintegrate rapidly.

Winter scats contain mostly fish remains, while summer scats contain the remains of fish, frogs, insects, snakes, turtles, and cray-fish. Scats are left on prominent spots at the water's edge, often repeatedly at the same spot.

Opossum   *Behavior, page 137*

Opossum scats are *not commonly found.* Some observers believe that opossums digest their food so well that the scats are seldom solid and so disintegrate quickly. They are usually found *in segments 1 to 3 inches long* and may *contain practically any type of food,* for the animals are general feeders.

Raccoon   *Behavior, page 311*

Raccoon scats are *large, crumbly,* and *flat-ended,* and usually *contain a wide variety of food items,* from seeds, insects, and mammals to trash. The total length of the scat may be *3 to 6 inches,* but it is *usually broken into segments.* It is about *¾ inch in diameter.* The scats are often left at prominent spots, such as rock lookouts or fallen logs. They are also very common at the base of trees where the raccoon may have rested for the day. Where we live, they are often at the base of white pines.

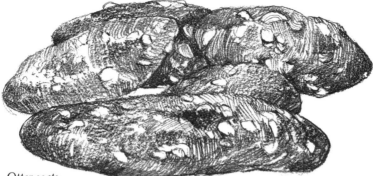

Otter scats

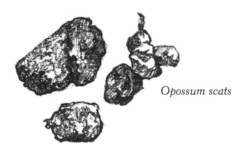

Opossum scats

Raccoon scats

Fox   *Behavior, page 277*

Fox scats in fall, winter, and spring are *2 to 4 inches long*, and about ½ *inch in diameter*, and usually have *pointed ends*. At these times of year the scats usually *contain hair* from prey and sometimes bits of insect skeletons or pieces of fruit. In summer, when foxes eat more insects and berries, the scats are shorter, with blunt ends, and usually crumble apart in a few days. Chemical analyses have found some slight differences between fox scats and coyote scats, but through sight or smell alone there is no way to make a positive distinction. The best you can do is compare the diameters of the scats. Scats ¾ inch or more in diameter are *probably* coyote or one of its hybrids; scats less than ⁷⁄₁₆ inch in diameter are *probably* fox.

Coyote   *Behavior, page 267*

Coyote scats, like those of foxes, are left along the sides of trails or at other important spots. They are *2 to 5 inches long* and *¾ inch or more in diameter*. In areas where both fox and coyote live, only careful measurement of the diameter of the scats can give you a clue to the animal's identity. Scats ¾ inch or more in diameter are *probably* coyote or one of its hybrids; scats less than ⁷⁄₁₆ inch in diameter are *probably* fox.

Bobcat   *Behavior, page 365*

The scats of bobcats are very *similar in shape and size* to those of the *fox* and *coyote*, so much so that it is impossible to identify them positively. You must use other clues. Sometimes bobcats scratch earth over their scats with their front feet, but not always. If the soil is too hard, it is impossible for the animal to scratch it up. In general, bobcats digest the bones of their prey more thoroughly than do the fox or coyote, so there are fewer bone remains in the scat. Also, sometimes there is a cat-like odor to the scat. Scats are often left on some slightly elevated spot and are *2 to 5 inches long* and about *½ to ¾ inch in diameter*. Even though the scats of the mountain lion are generally larger than bobcat scats, the sizes of these animals' scats overlap a good deal.

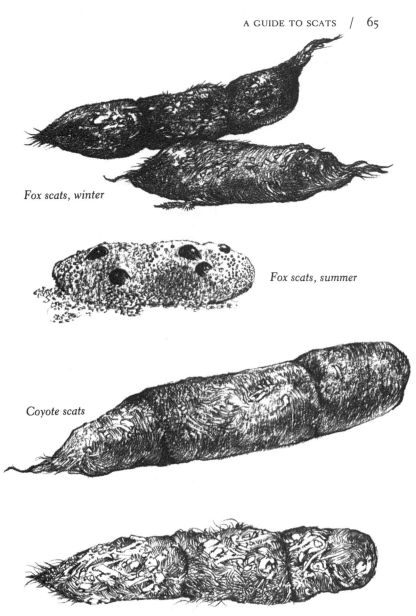

Fox scats, winter

Fox scats, summer

Coyote scats

Bobcat scats

Dog   *Behavior, page 289*

Dog scats vary in size with the size of the dog and often have the color and consistency of the dog food the animal has been eating. If the dog eats at home, there is a *lack of animal hair or other remains of wild prey* or wild vegetation. Dog scats have *flat ends*, unlike the scats of fox and coyote, which have pointed ends.

Black Bear   *Behavior, page 301*

Bear scats are distinctive because of either their *large size* or their contents. They are *cylindrical, with flat ends*, and are *often broken into segments*. Segments are *2 to 3 inches long* and *1¼ to 1½ inches in diameter*. Scats contain insects, bits of grass, leaf litter, wood, berries, and hair, in any combination. When the bear eats primarily berries, as in midsummer, the scat will be a loose, cow-pie–like mass. In this case, it can be distinguished from moose scats by the fact that it contains berry seeds.

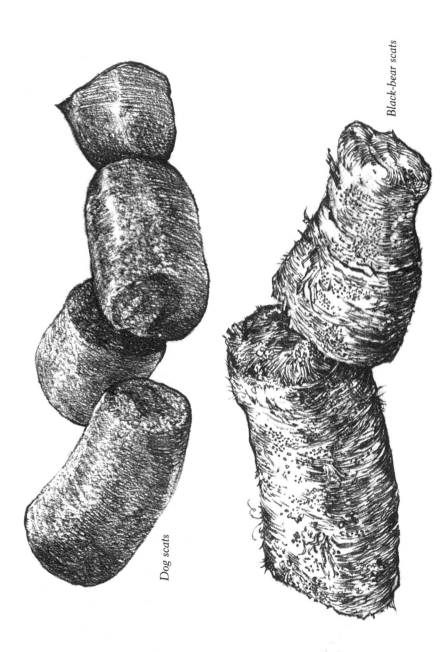

Dog scats

Black-bear scats

A GUIDE TO SIGNS

An animal sign is any disturbance or change in the environment caused by the animal's activity. Signs range from those as small as the nibbling of grass to those as large as the building of dams across streams. They can be found in all habitats, from city streets to suburban backyards to country woods and meadows. They are exciting to find, for they always reveal something about the animal's behavior — what it eats, where it lives, how it travels, how it communicates.

Some animal signs, such as squirrel nests, muskrat lodges, or mole hills, are obvious even to the untrained eye, for they are large-scale changes in the environment. But most animal signs are more subtle and require care and skill to recognize and identify.

For easy reference, the signs in this chapter have been grouped into several categories:

Injury to trees or shrubs (page 70): chewed or scraped bark or gnawed wood.

Digging, scraping, and tunneling in the ground (page 84): evidence of burrows or dens in the ground, or any scraping done for marking purposes.

Constructed nests, homes, and dams (page 98): collected and arranged plant material forming a shelter or home, such as squirrel nests, mouse nests, beaver lodges, et cetera.

Disturbed vegetation — trails, runways, tunnels, beds, rolling places (page 104): often subtle signs; may involve just the matting of vegetation or the parting of grasses. These are the result of animals' movements, sleeping, and marking.

Natural cavities (page 112): rock crevices, spaces under fallen logs, or areas in human-built structures — in a chimney or culvert or under a porch. These cavities are not created by animals but are often used by them as homes and for shelter. Only other signs near the cavities will identify the animals that are using them.

Food remains and caches (page 120): signs of animal feeding such as a pile of nuts stored under a log or a dead animal cached for later feeding.

The best way to learn about animal signs is to know what to look for and where to look for it even before you go out on a walk. To do this, become familiar with the illustrations of the signs and look over the specific text at your leisure. Then when you go out, it will be easier to find signs, and you can identify them with the help of the guide.

Injury to Trees or Shrubs

BARK SCRATCHED OR PEELED: Bobcat, Cat, Red Squirrel

Bobcat, Cat   *Behavior, pages 365, 373*

Bobcats and house cats both have the habit of reaching up with their forefeet and scratching at the bark of certain trees. This is usually done on trees with fairly rough bark and makes the outer bark look worn down. The injury does not expose the inner bark. Bobcat scratching occurs 2½ to 3½ feet high on the tree, while cat scratching occurs at about 1½ to 2 feet high. These *scratching posts* may serve several functions, including maintaining the fitness of the claws and advertising the animal's presence.

Red Squirrel   *Behavior, page 209*

On trees whose bark can be pulled off in long shreds, such as cedar and juniper, you may find sections that look scratched or worn away. This may be the work of red squirrels, which peel off strips of the bark and use it as insulation in their nests. The worn-down section usually occurs on the middle or lower portion of the tree. Occasionally gray squirrels also do this.

BARK SCRAPED OFF: Deer, Black Bear

Deer   *Behavior, page 383*

Large portions of bark may be scraped or peeled (as opposed to chewed) off trees by deer or bears. The most common sign of this type is the *buck rub*, caused by the male deer's scraping its antlers against the bark of a young tree. In one study, the average buck rub occurred on trees about 6 feet tall and 1 inch in diameter. The section of exposed wood averages 10 inches and covers half the circumference of the trunk. Rubs often occur on trees with aromatic bark, such as cedar, juniper, pine, cherry, shining sumac, and sweet gum. Rubs are made during the mating season, from September through November. The earliest rubs may break small saplings in half and may show traces of velvet rubbed from the buck's antlers. The later rubs will not contain velvet and are more conspicuous because more bark has been rubbed off. Several rubs may occur in the same area.

Injury to Trees or Shrubs

Cat scratching post

Bark peeled by red squirrel

Deer rub

Black Bear   *Behavior, page 301*

Two different signs indicate how black bears scrape the bark off trees. One occurs at the base of coniferous trees, such as pines, spruces, and firs. The bear rips off strips of bark with its teeth and then chews at the inner bark underneath. You may see teeth marks on the inner wood of the tree.

The other sign of bear activity occurs 4 to 7 feet above the ground and on large coniferous or deciduous trees that are often by the side of a major path. At these *mark trees* the bear gets up on its hind legs and reaches up with its forepaws to scratch at the bark and possibly also bite at it. These trees are injured repeatedly, perhaps by more than one bear. The scraped area may be up to 3 feet long and 1 foot wide. The bear may also rub its back against the spot, and hairs may adhere to sap that has oozed from the injury. These marks are most frequently made in midsummer, but the results of the injury may be seen all year.

BARK CHEWED OFF: Porcupine, Beaver, Deer, Moose, Cottontail, Snowshoe Hare, Vole, Mouse, Woodchuck, Gray Squirrel

Many animals chew bark off the sides of branches or the trunks of trees. Some eat the bark, especially in winter when other foods are not available. A few animals chew away small portions of bark to leave a marking. The way to distinguish the various animals' chewings is to notice the appearance and location of the chewed section and the size of the teeth marks.

Porcupine   *Behavior, page 257*

Porcupines chew bark most often from the upper portions of tree trunks, next to a limb where the animal sits while eating. The bark is neatly chewed away, leaving large patches of exposed wood.

Bear feeding

Bear marking tree

Porcupine chewing

Beaver   *Behavior, page 219*

Besides the porcupine, the only other animal that neatly chews away large portions of the bark is the beaver. Since beavers cannot climb, their chewing is always found at the base of a tree or on trunks and on branches on the ground. Beavers often cut up trunks, branches, and twigs into smaller lengths and gnaw all the bark off them. This type of work is a sure sign of beavers.

While many animals chew at the bark, the beaver can actually chew away large chips of wood. Beavers do not eat the wood; they chip at it to fell trees so they can feed on the leaves and thinner young bark of the upper branches. They also chip the wood when cutting up branches into smaller pieces for use in building their lodges and dams. Piles of large, light-colored wood chips are signs of these activities.

Deer, Moose   *Behavior, pages 383, 395*

Deer and moose also eat bark in winter when other foods are not available. Moose often chew bits of bark off the trunks of trees such as aspen or balsam poplar. The teeth marks will be large and placed rather high since the animal is tall. Deer often eat the bark off the branches of fruit trees and may rip it off in strips.

Cottontail, Snowshoe Hare   *Behavior, pages 161, 171*

Cottontails and hares eat the bark off branches. You may see individual teeth marks on the branches, or small pieces of bark may have been ripped off. This often occurs on fruit trees or willow shrubs. Look for other signs, such as scats or diagonally cut twig ends, to confirm that cottontails and hares have been chewing.

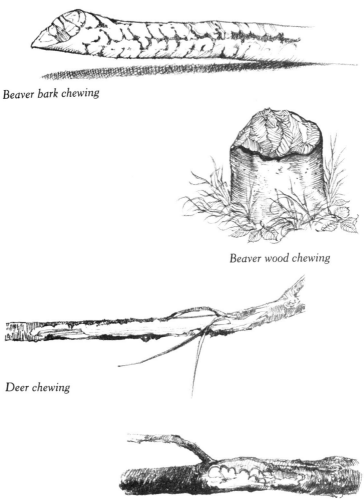

Beaver bark chewing

Beaver wood chewing

Deer chewing

Cottontail chewing

Vole, Mouse   *Behavior, pages 239, 229*

At the very base of such shrubs as rose, sumac, and crabapple you may find the bark eaten away. In most cases, this is the work of voles during the winter, although mice may do it to a much lesser extent. The teeth marks of the mice are minute; those of voles, though still tiny, are about twice as big.

Woodchuck, Gray Squirrel   *Behavior, pages 191, 199*

Woodchucks are known to chew bark from trees near their dens when they emerge in spring. There will be signs of only slight gnawing, and teeth marks may not be evident. Proximity to a den is the best clue to gnawing by woodchucks. Gray squirrels similarly gnaw bark, usually at the base of trees, and possibly also as a marking system.

Teeth Sizes:

The comparative widths of bark-chewing animals' two central incisors are listed below. These measurements are only approximate guidelines, since individuals within a species vary in size. The measurements are for the combined width of both front teeth and are arranged in order of size, from the smallest to the largest.

Mouse: less than 1/16 inch
Vole: slightly more than 1/16 inch
Gray squirrel: about 1/8 inch
Cottontail: about 1/4 inch
Snowshoe hare: about 1/4 inch
Woodchuck: about 1/4 inch
Porcupine: about 3/8 inch
Beaver: about 3/8 to 1/2 inch
Deer: about 1/2 inch
Moose: about 1/2 to 1 inch

Mouse or vole chewing

Woodchuck chewing

CLAW MARKS ON TREES: Gray Squirrel, Porcupine, Opossum, Raccoon, Bear

When animals climb trees, they use their claws to hold onto the bark. Where the bark is smooth or missing, the animal's claws scrape along the tree as it tries to find a foothold. These claw marks are a good clue, and the number of claws and the distance between them can actually enable you to identify the animal. Trees with smooth bark, such as birch, beech, cherry, and aspen, show claw marks best. On other trees, such as maple, pine, and spruce, look at the upper portions where the bark is smoother. You might also examine old, dead trees without bark.

Gray Squirrel
Behavior, page 199

Gray squirrels have 5 claws on their hind feet and 4 claws on their front feet. The claw patterns are about ¾ to 1 inch wide. Red-squirrel claw patterns, when visible, will be narrower, but these animals are so light that their claws do not slip as much and so do not leave marks.

Porcupine
Behavior, page 257

The next widest claw pattern is that of the porcupine, which has 5 claws in a pattern about 1¼ to 1½ inches wide.

Opossum
Behavior, page 137

Opossums also climb trees. They have 5 toes on each foot, but on their hind feet only 4 of them have claws. The 4 hind claws make a pattern about 1½ inches wide, and the 5 front claws make one about 2 inches wide.

Raccoon
Behavior, page 311

The 5-claw pattern of the opossum's forefoot might be confused with the 5-claw pattern of the raccoon, for they are similar in size. However, adult raccoons have a wider pattern, about 2½ inches wide, and they have 5 claws on their hind feet as well.

Black Bear
Behavior, page 301

The largest claw pattern is that of the black bear. Not only is it much wider than all of the others, but also it is the deepest scratch because of the bear's weight. There are 5 claws per foot, and they create a pattern 3½ to 4½ inches wide.

Tree with various claw marks

TWIGS ON THE GROUND: Red Squirrel, Porcupine

If you are walking under evergreens and find a number of green branch tips lying on the ground, you may be looking at a sign of either a red squirrel or a porcupine. We have found these nipped branches most often under hemlocks, but they appear under other conifers and deciduous trees as well.

Red Squirrel
Behavior, page 209

The red squirrel chews off branches about ¼ inch in diameter so that it can feed on cones or buds at the tips.

Porcupine
Behavior, page 257

Porcupines chew off branches up to ½ inch in diameter. The chewed twig end is distinctive; it is cut at a diagonal and shows tiny parallel rows of bites. If a porcupine is in the area, there should also be other evidence, such as the animal's scats on the ground under the tree.

TWIG ENDS BITTEN: Cottontail, Snowshoe Hare, Deer, Moose

Cottontail, Snowshoe Hare
Behavior, pages 161, 171

Deer, moose, cottontails, and hares all feed on the tips of woody twigs in winter. Cottontails and hares have both upper and lower incisors, and when they nip off a twig it leaves a neat 45-degree-angle cut. To distinguish between cottontail and hare feeding signs, you must use other clues such as scats and tracks.

Deer, Moose
Behavior, pages 383, 395

Deer and moose have only lower incisors, which bite against the hard palate in the upper jaw. When they eat twigs, they close down on the twig and then, by jerking their heads up, break it. As a result, the twig end is ripped rather than neatly cut. To distinguish between signs of moose and deer feeding, you must use additional clues, such as scats and tracks.

Twigs on ground

Deer twig end

Cottontail twig end

FRUIT-TREE LIMBS BROKEN:
Black Bear   *Behavior, page 301*

Apple or other fruit-tree limbs may be broken off by bears as they try to get at the ripened fruit. Also look for half-eaten pieces of fruit and claw marks on the bark of the broken limb.

ROTTED LOGS BROKEN APART:
Black Bear   *Behavior, page 301*

Bears commonly rip apart rotted logs to feed on insects and small animals that live in the soft wood. You will see bits of wood torn off the log and scattered about. To a much lesser extent, a raccoon may do the same thing. Look for substantial tearing and possible claw marks to suggest the work of a bear.

Rotted log torn apart

Digging, Scraping, and Tunneling in the Ground

HOLES IN THE GROUND: Shrew, Vole, Mole, Mouse, Chipmunk, Red Squirrel, Muskrat, Woodchuck, Skunk, Opossum, Raccoon, Cottontail, Fox, Coyote, Bear

Holes in the earth are some of the most commonly seen signs of animal activity. Almost everyone at some time has wondered who or what made a particular hole. This cannot always be answered with assurance, but there are some guidelines that will help you narrow down the choices and perhaps even determine the burrower and/or user. Size is the first and most important consideration, and thus the following examples are arranged from the smallest hole to the largest. You must then take into account the structure and placement of the hole and the behavior of the animal.

Various terms are used for holes in the ground, such as "den" or "burrow." They mean the same thing. Which terms are used with which animal is mainly a matter of tradition.

1-Inch-Diameter Holes: Shrew   *Behavior, page 145*

Since they are our smallest mammals, *shrews* make the smallest holes. Shrews usually just tunnel on the surface of the ground through leaf litter, but they may also dig holes in soft soil. Some shrews are so small that their holes or tunnels may be only ½ inch or less in diameter. Our largest shrew, the short-tailed shrew, makes a hole or tunnel 1 inch in diameter.

1½-Inch-Diameter Holes: Vole, Mole, Mouse
Behavior, pages 239, 153, 229

Voles, which are extremely common, do some tunneling in the soil and create extensive runways through the grass.

Moles live in the same size tunnels as voles, but you rarely see the entrances to their tunnels since they are often plugged with earth. Holes this size in the banks of streams may be the tunnels of star-nosed moles, for their tunnels often exit near water where the moles swim and catch food under the water. There is often some excavated earth beneath the hole in these cases.

Mice may occasionally use a vole or mole tunnel, but they do not usually dig their own.

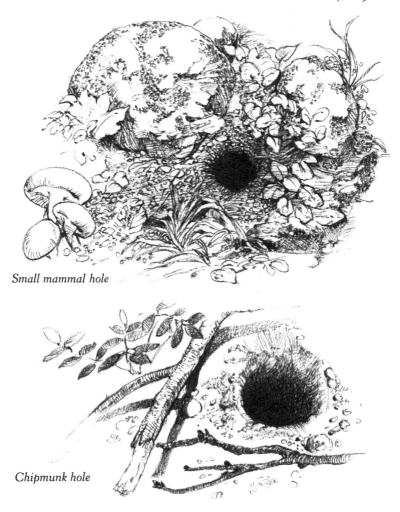

Small mammal hole

Chipmunk hole

2-Inch-Diameter Holes: Chipmunk   *Behavior, page 179*

Holes about 2 inches in diameter going directly into the earth and without any sign of excavation are often those of *chipmunks*. These are usually in or near woods. Entrances to chipmunk burrows can be hard to find, for the animals may not enter the burrow when they are being watched.

2½- to 3-Inch-Diameter Holes: Red Squirrel

Behavior, page 209

Red squirrels dig tunnels most often in coniferous woods, where the ground is soft and there are plenty of cones to eat. They may even cache their food underground. There may also be signs of eaten cones near the tunnel entrance.

5- to 6-Inch-Diameter Holes near Water: Muskrat

Behavior, page 247

Tunnels 5 to 6 inches in diameter and near water are usually the work of *muskrats*. Muskrats excavate dens in the banks of streams, lakes, ponds, irrigation ditches, or dikes. If you are walking along the bank, look for channels through the vegetation in shallow water, for the muskrat usually makes these to the entrance of the den. Also look for old, caved-in tunnels, a fairly common occurrence. As the tunnels get longer, muskrats open up ventilation holes to the surface. These vary in size but can be distinguished from other animal holes by their connection to the 6-inch-diameter tunnel beneath.

5- to 6-Inch-Diameter Holes away from Water: Woodchuck, Skunk, Opossum, Raccoon, Cottontail

Behavior, pages 191, 347, 137, 311, 161

Woodchucks are the major hole-diggers away from water. They make most of the large burrows you find in fields or woods. The typical woodchuck burrow has one or more entrances with a large mound of earth in front. The burrows are dug in well-drained soil and often on a slope. The mound of earth is the most conspicuous feature of the burrow and will alert you to the presence of the hole. Besides openings with mounds, there may be others without mounds, which have been excavated from underneath. These are sometimes called *plunge holes*, for the woodchuck can plunge into them for safety when out feeding.

Active woodchuck dens are always being renovated during the warmer months, and so freshly excavated earth will appear on the mound several times a week. We have found that burrows have a distinct odor in spring when inhabited by woodchucks, something like the smell of chicken stock.

Muskrat hole

Woodchuck hole

Skunks will readily use old woodchuck burrows when they are available, but when there are none, they will dig their own. Their dens are similar to those of woodchucks, except that they usually have only one or two entrances and are not as large at the beginning of the tunnel. Skunks may leave their scats at or near the entrance, whereas you never find woodchuck scats. Most digging occurs in late summer and fall, when the skunks are looking for a place to spend the winter.

Without seeing the tracks, it is hard to know if a skunk is in a woodchuck hole. One clue could be the skunk's use of bedding material, another its habit of putting a plug of leaves in the den during cold weather. The bedding material of leaves and grasses is usually gathered from around the entrance, and there may be evidence of its being scraped up or dragged down the burrow.

Opossums do not dig their own burrows but primarily use those of woodchucks. As in the case of the skunk, there is no sure way to know if an opossum is in a woodchuck burrow without seeing its tracks. In fact, it is hard to determine whether a hole is being used by a skunk or opossum since both carry in bedding materials and plug up the entrance with leaves during cold weather.

Raccoons use woodchuck burrows for shelter in bad weather, but in general they prefer tree holes when they are available. There are no outward signs that a raccoon is using a hole, except possibly scats or tracks near the entrance.

Cottontails do not dig their own burrows but use those of woodchucks and skunks. They use them for shelter during bad weather and usually venture only a short way into the tunnel.

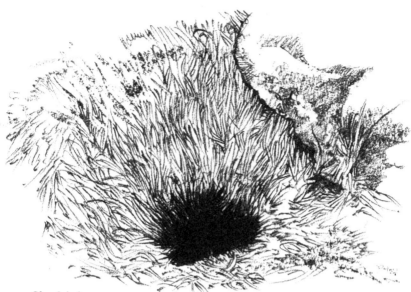

Skunk hole

9- to 12-Inch-Diameter Holes: Fox   *Behavior, page 277*

If there were as many *fox* dens as people have claimed to have found, we would be overrun by these lovely animals. Most of what people call fox dens are just woodchuck burrows. Many people are also quick to assume they have found an active fox den when in fact the den may not be in use.

Foxes may dig their own dens, but they are more likely to renovate an existing woodchuck burrow when one is available. Thus, the difficulty when you find a woodchuck burrow is determining whether it has been occupied or is being actively used by a fox. Start by checking the diameter of the burrow, for the first thing the foxes do to a woodchuck den is to make its diameter larger by several inches. Most fox dens have entrances of about 10 to 11 inches in diameter.

To decide if you have found an active fox den, you need to consider a number of things: (1) Foxes use dens only to raise pups, and this occurs in late winter and spring; after that they abandon the dens. (2) Foxes begin to excavate or renovate several den sites in late winter, when the woodchucks are usually still in hibernation. (3) The young are born in the den, and prey is brought for them to feed on. Remains of prey, such as fur, bones, and flesh, are almost always around the entrance of an active den. Old dens do not have prey remains, for other animals carry the bones and remains away. (4) The den may or may not smell strongly of fox. (5) The parents may move the cubs to new dens one or more times during their rearing, especially if they are disturbed.

Short of seeing fox tracks going into the den, all you can do is consider all the clues and make an educated guess. Also remember, fox dens are uncommon.

1- to 2-Foot-Diameter Holes: Coyote   *Behavior, page 267*

Except for the size of the hole, there are not many other clues to a *coyote* den — partly because so few of them have been studied. Some report the entrances to be higher than wide, with roughly oval dimensions of 10 by 20 inches. Coyotes may dig their own burrows, or they may use and renovate those of other animals, such as badgers, foxes, skunks, and woodchucks.

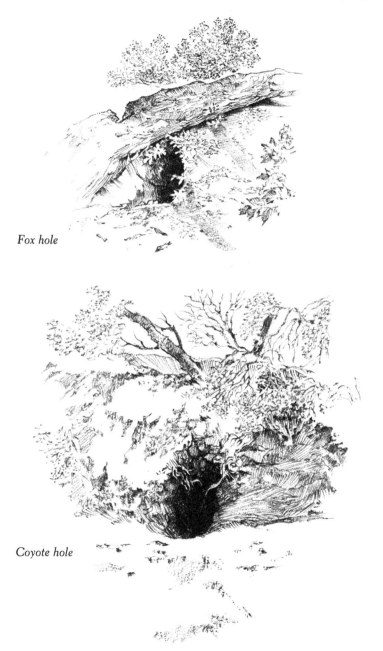

Fox hole

Coyote hole

3-Foot-Diameter or Larger Holes: Black Bear

Behavior, page 301

Black bears may dig out the entrance to an existing cavity in order to use it as a winter den. You may find a large space inside the entrance that may be lined with tree boughs. If it is midwinter, you may also find the bear.

SHALLOW DIGGING IN THE EARTH: Skunk, Squirrel

Skunk
Behavior, page 347

Skunks make small holes about 1 to 2 inches in diameter and 1 to 2 inches deep when they are looking for insects to feed on. They most commonly dig in grassy or lawn areas, and usually several holes appear in the same few square yards. Sometimes the skunk leaves scats in the vicinity of the holes.

Squirrel
Behavior, pages 199, 209

Squirrels, especially gray squirrels, make shallow holes in the ground when they retrieve nuts they have buried singly in forest litter or on lawns. These holes usually appear in winter and spring. They are slightly larger than skunk diggings, and the excavated earth is usually scattered to one side of the hole. There are often bits of the stored nut at the hole since the squirrel usually eats it at the spot.

SCRAPED DEPRESSIONS: Moose, Deer, Cottontail, Bobcat

Moose
Behavior, page 395

During the mating season for moose, in September and October, the male moose may urinate on a spot and then paw at the earth, making a muddy area in which he or the female he is courting may wallow. Such areas are called *moose wallows*. They can be 10 or more square feet large and may smell of the moose's urine.

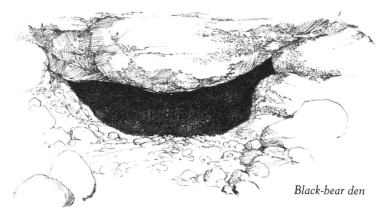

Black-bear den

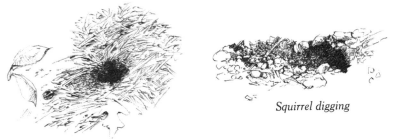

Squirrel digging

Skunk digging

Moose wallow

Deer   *Behavior, page 383*

During the mating season for deer, from September through November, male and occasionally female deer may scrape out an area in the earth. The depression is 1 to 2½ feet in diameter and can be rectangular or circular. After making the scrape, the deer may urinate or defecate in it. *Deer scrapes* are usually found in an area clear of underbrush and are also often located under a limb where the deer may rub its forehead and leave scent. Several scrapes may occur in the same area.

Cottontail   *Behavior, page 161*

Cottontails may repeatedly use a small area of cleared earth for rolling in, possibly to alleviate problems with external parasites. This area is about a foot in diameter and is called a *dust bath*. Birds also use areas like this, and it may be difficult to distinguish between the two, unless there are either feathers or rabbit fur in the dust area.

Bobcat   *Behavior, page 365*

Occasionally a bobcat makes a *scrape* by digging up an area that is a rough rectangle about 4 by 10 inches. You may find a scat in the middle of the scrape.

SMALL RIDGES OF EARTH: Mole   *Behavior, page 153*

Meandering ridges of earth about 3 inches wide and 1½ to 2 inches high are a good sign of a mole. You may see the ridges or feel them with your feet as you walk over them. These are surface tunnels of moles, usually found in rich soil. The eastern mole tends to inhabit lawns and meadows, the star-nosed mole wet areas or the edges of swamps.

Deer scrape

Cottontail dust bath

Bobcat scrape

Mole ridge

MOUNDS OF EARTH: Mole, Beaver, Otter

Mole *Behavior, page 153*

A small mound of fresh earth about 6 to 12 inches in diameter and 2 to 4 inches high is probably a *molehill,* the excavated earth from the mole's deeper tunnels. Molehills usually occur in rich, loose earth but may also be found in woods, fields, or lawns.

Beaver *Behavior, page 219*

Piles of mud placed near the water's edge, ranging in size from just a few inches to 2 feet high, may have been made by beavers. The beavers carry mud and rotted vegetation in their front paws while walking on their hind feet and place the mud on the spot. They then mark it with castoreum, a strong scent. New mud may be added each time the mound is marked, or the mound may be scratched after marking. Most *scent mounds* are made and used in spring, and, to a much lesser extent, in fall. They are also made at other times of year if a beaver family is establishing itself in a new area. One study showed beaver scent mounds occurring at a frequency of about eight per hundred yards of shoreline. But this was with very careful observation; most observers find fewer mounds.

Otter *Behavior, page 355*

A small mound of earth about 4 inches high and topped with scats may be the *scent mound* of an otter. The mounds are usually located within a few feet of water and on a prominent land feature, such as a point or clearing. The mounds tend to be visited regularly by otters, who leave more scats on top each time.

Molehill

Beaver scent mound

Constructed Nests, Homes, and Dams

CONSTRUCTIONS IN WATER: Beaver, Muskrat

Beaver   *Behavior, page 219*

A linear pile of branches and mud at right angles to the flow of a stream or river is a *beaver dam*. New beaver dams are hard to mistake, but old ones may have all kinds of plants growing over them, hiding them from view. A perfect clue to beaver construction is that the twigs and branches used are totally free of bark because the beavers have chewed it off. Dams can range in size from 2 to 10 feet high and from a few yards to hundreds of yards long. An actively used dam will have the water level behind it right at its top. When the water level is quite a bit lower than the dam, you can conclude that the dam is not maintained and that beavers are no longer there.

A mound of sticks and mud 4 or more feet high and 10 or more feet in diameter is a *beaver lodge*. It may be built in the still water behind a beaver dam, in a slow-moving river, or in a lake. It may be located next to the shore or surrounded by water. Sometimes lodges are overgrown with plants. A good clue is that the branches forming the lodge are peeled of bark and chewed at the ends.

Muskrat   *Behavior, page 247*

A *feeding platform* is a spot where the muskrat sits and feeds. Found in marshy areas, it is an accumulation of water plants arranged into a roughly circular platform about 2 feet in diameter. There may be channels through the mud leading to the platform.

Muskrat lodges are rounded mounds of mud and vegetation generally found out in the open water, occasionally in among cattails or rushes. They are usually about 2 feet high and 3 feet in diameter, but can be as large as 6 feet high and 8 feet in diameter. They look like small beaver lodges but can be identified by the material they are made from: cattail leaves, rushes, other water vegetation, and mud. Beaver lodges are made only from peeled branches and mud.

Feeding shelters look like small lodges about 1 foot high. They are made of mud and reeds in areas where muskrats are active and there is a good deal of water vegetation. They may be built near lodges, and there may be channels through the mud leading to them. They are hollow inside, and the muskrat uses them to feed in safety.

Push-ups are found only in winter when there is ice. They are made from vegetation that is pushed up through a hole in the ice and

Beaver dam

Beaver lodge

Muskrat lodge; muskrat feeding shelter in foreground

then rests on the ice. In late winter they may be covered with snow, and they become visible as the snow begins to melt. They collapse as the ice melts. The muskrat uses them as temporary shelter when swimming about in winter.

CONSTRUCTION IN OR ON THE GROUND: Mole, Deer
Mouse, Vole, Shrew, Cottontail, Weasel

Mole   *Behavior, page 153*

Mole *nests* are located in tunnels near the surface or several inches
below and are made of grasses and leaves that the mole collects from
the surface of the ground. They are about 10 inches long and 4 inches
wide. A given mole may use several nests.

Deer Mouse   *Behavior, page 229*

Deer mice and white-footed mice build *nests* on the ground or in
trees. When on the ground, the nest is usually in a little cavity under a
tree root or fallen log and consists of a 6-inch sphere of shredded
grasses and other downy materials. There is no easy way to distinguish these ground nests from those of voles, especially those species
that live in the woods. Mice tend to leave their droppings in the nest.

Vole   *Behavior, page 239*

Meadow vole *nests* are usually found in fields with lush grasses. In an
area that offers some protection, such as fallen grasses or at the base of
a tuft of grass, you may find a loose aggregation of shredded grasses.
The shredding is what distinguishes nest material from grasses that
might have just blown into a pocket. It will be about 6 to 8 inches in
diameter, and there will be vole runways leading to the nest.

Shrew   *Behavior, page 145*

This *nest* is similar to the nests of voles and mice, being composed of
shredded grass and leaves and measuring about 6 to 8 inches in
diameter. It may be located along tunnels or under discarded boards,
logs, tree roots, or rocks. The shrew's droppings tend to be left
outside the nest. A good clue to a shrew's nest can be the small
diameter — about 1 inch or less — of the tunnels leading to it.

Cottontail   *Behavior, page 161*

Cottontail *nests* are made in shallow depressions about 4 inches
deep, 5 inches wide, and 6 to 7 inches long. They are lined with fine
grasses and dried weeds and then filled with cottontail fur from the
mother cottontail. The young are covered in the nest with fur and
grasses whenever the mother leaves them.

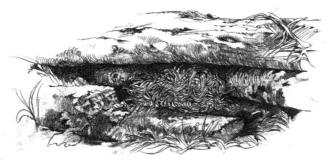

Deer-mouse nest

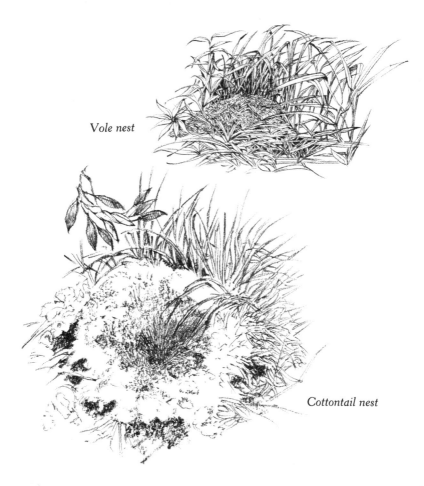

Vole nest

Cottontail nest

Weasel *Behavior, page 329*

Smaller weasels may take over the nests of mice, voles, moles, or shrews, and of course these may be underground or on the surface. There are no obvious indications that a nest may have been used by a weasel, except possibly the presence of fur from prey. In nests of the long-tailed weasel, the largest weasel, there may be larger remains of prey items brought to the nest, such as bones.

CONSTRUCTION IN TREES: Gray Squirrel, Red Squirrel, Deer Mouse

Gray Squirrel *Behavior, page 199*

Spherical collections of twigs and leaves 1 to 1½ feet in diameter are usually gray-squirrel *nests*. They are often built in the tops of deciduous trees and are conspicuous in winter.

Red Squirrel *Behavior, page 209*

Spherical collections of leaves, grasses, bark strips, and other fibrous material about 1 to 1½ feet in diameter are usually the *nests* of red squirrels. Red-squirrel nests are more dense than those of gray squirrels because the materials used are finer. They are often placed in the tops of evergreens.

Deer Mouse *Behavior, page 229*

Spherical collections about 6 inches in diameter made of shredded grasses, cattail fluff, and other soft materials are usually the *nests* of white-footed or deer mice. They can be placed in tree holes or more commonly among the branches of shrubs. Often a mouse uses a bird's nest as a base, covering it over with a dome of material. Check birds' nests in winter to see if they are still cup-shaped, the way the bird made them, or have been covered by a dome and thus renovated by a mouse.

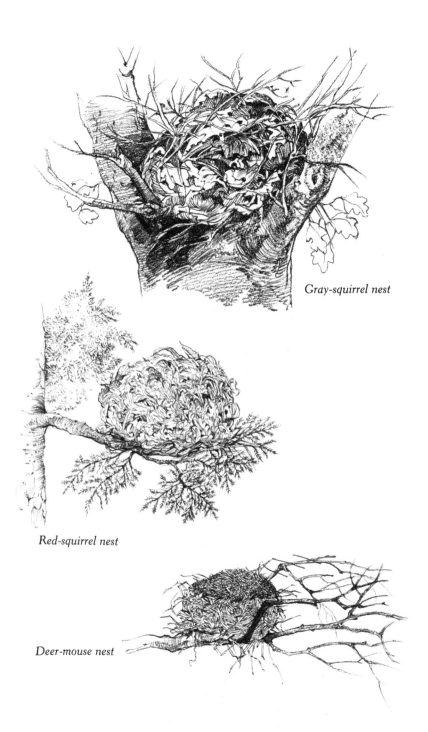

Gray-squirrel nest

Red-squirrel nest

Deer-mouse nest

Disturbed Vegetation: Trails, Runways, Tunnels, Beds, Rolling Places

MATTED VEGETATION: Cottontail, Snowshoe Hare, Deer, Otter

Cottontail, Snowshoe Hare   *Behavior, pages 161, 171*

A small oval depression in the vegetation approximately 6 to 8 inches by 4 to 6 inches may be the *form*, or resting place, of a cottontail or snowshoe hare. The most common way to find a form is by accidentally scaring a rabbit or hare from it. Forms are often located next to some natural feature that offers protection, such as a log, rock, or grass tuft.

Deer   *Behavior, page 383*

A matted area of vegetation 3 to 4 feet long and 2 to 3 feet wide may be the *bedding area* of a white-tailed deer. The deer usually bed in areas of dense cover and may return to the same spot over many days. Since the deer often travel in small groups, there may be several bedding areas in the same vicinity.

Otter   *Behavior, page 355*

Rolling spots are areas about 3 feet in diameter at the water's edge where otters come out and roll, possibly to dry or groom themselves or mark the spot in some way. There is often a trail from the water's edge to the rolling spot. Frequently found on islands in lakes or in clearings under bushes, the rolling spots may be rubbed free of vegetation and show bare earth. There may be up to ten rolling spots in one otter home range. In winter, they occur in the snow.

TORN-UP GRASSES: Skunk   *Behavior, page 347*

When skunks are looking for insects, they frequently explore at the base of grasses, often pulling the grasses apart. They may also do this when going after voles. The area can be several yards in diameter or a good deal smaller. You may also see skunk digging nearby.

Cottontail form

Deer bedding area

Rolling spot for otter

Grasses torn up by skunk

TRAILS AND RUNWAYS: Deer, Beaver, Woodchuck, Cottontail, Snowshoe Hare

Deer   *Behavior, page 383*

Deer often use regular routes through their home range that become worn-down *trails* which look a little like narrow human footpaths. The trails are usually clear of shrubs and low vegetation but are not bare earth. Sometimes a trail is barely discernible, and you must be in a position to survey the whole of the trail to get a sense of it. Other animals may use these trails. They often go through woods.

Beaver   *Behavior, page 219*

Beaver *trails* are a foot or more wide, starting at the water's edge and leading to a feeding spot up to 100 yards away. The trail may have small shrubs nipped off it to keep it clear. The beaver will probably have dragged branches along it to feed on near the water. Evidence of beaver chewing along the trail is a sure sign.

Woodchuck   *Behavior, page 191*

Woodchucks make regular *trails* between one burrow entrance and another and from their entrances to good feeding areas. These trails are about 6 inches wide and may consist of matted-down vegetation in fields or a slight matting of leaves in the woods. A woodchuck burrow at either end of the trail is a sure clue. Other animals, such as skunks and opossums, may also use the trails and the burrows.

Cottontail, Snowshoe Hare   *Behavior, pages 161, 171*

Within their home range, cottontails and snowshoe hares move about on a network of *runways*, which are about 4 to 6 inches wide. The runways of the snowshoe hare occur mostly in brushy areas and may be quite matted down. Those of cottontails may be in fields as well; if the grass is long, the runway will actually form a tunnel about 6 inches in diameter under overarching grasses. In winter the runways of snowshoe hares may become packed trails through the snow.

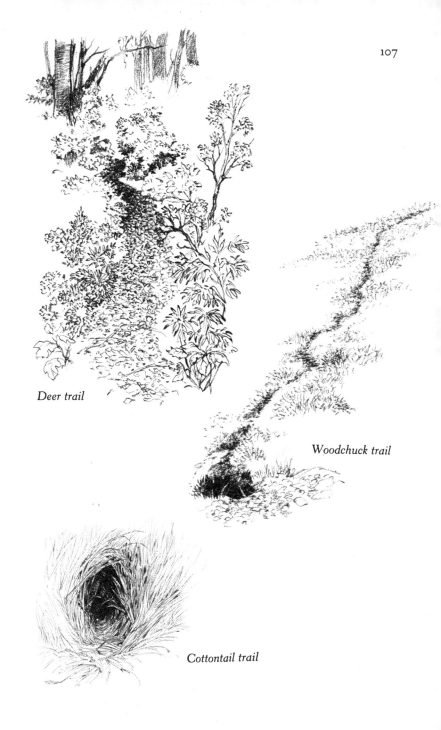

Deer trail

Woodchuck trail

Cottontail trail

TUNNELS THROUGH GRASSES AND LEAF LITTER: Vole, Shrew

Vole   *Behavior, page 239*

Voles make neat *tunnels* through grasses. They nip off the vegetation at the bottom and along the sides of the tunnel so that there is usually bare earth showing on the path. The tunnels, about 1½ inches in diameter, meander and often intersect. Vole scats are frequently found in the tunnels, especially at the intersections. In practically any lush meadow you can dig down among the grasses and find these tunnels. Shrews and mice also use them.

Shrew   *Behavior, page 145*

Shrew *tunnels* are similar to those of voles but are about an inch or less in diameter. The vegetation is not nipped clean but rather is pressed to the side. Shrew tunnels are common in leaf litter just above the soil surface. Shrews may also use vole tunnels.

TUNNELS THROUGH SNOW: Cottontail, Weasel, Red Squirrel, Vole, Mouse, Shrew

Cottontail   *Behavior, page 161*

In deep snow, cottontails may dig *tunnels* under the snow. They are about 6 inches in diameter.

Weasel   *Behavior, page 329*

Weasels tunnel through snow to prey on the small rodents living under the snow. The *tunnel* may be 1 to 3 inches in diameter, depending on the size of the weasel. Look for tracks on the surface of the snow near the tunnel entrance to confirm that the maker is a weasel.

Red Squirrel   *Behavior, page 209*

When there are 6 or more inches of snow, red squirrels may make a network of *tunnels* connecting their caches of food to resting and eating places. The tunnels will be about 3 inches in diameter. To confirm that they belong to red squirrels, you would have to see other signs of feeding, or nests in nearby trees.

Vole tunnel

Shrew tunnel

Vole   *Behavior, page 239*

When the snow is 4 or more inches deep, voles will begin to *tunnel* through it. The tunnels are most often seen when the surface snow starts to melt off the top of the tunnels, revealing a winding path through a meadow or woods. The melting snow often widens the existing tunnel, so look for tunnels 1½ to 2 inches wide. Sometimes voles also dig holes from their tunnels to the snow surface; these are commonly seen, especially in meadow areas.

Mouse   *Behavior, page 229*

Mouse *tunnels* are similar to vole tunnels, except that mice tend to move over the surface of the snow rather than tunnel through it. However, they do dig holes down through the snow to their burrows or to sources of food. The tunnel entrances will be about 1½ inches in diameter. Look for the mouse's galloping track pattern on the snow surface leading to or from these holes.

Shrew   *Behavior, page 145*

Shrews *tunnel* through the snow in the same manner as voles. The only way to distinguish between shrew and vole tunnels is by size. Shrew tunnels will be about an inch or less in diameter unless melting has occurred. Shrew tunnels, like vole tunnels, also show up as meandering trails when the snow begins to melt.

SLIDES IN THE SNOW: Mink, Otter   *Behavior, pages 339, 355*

Both the mink and the otter occasionally slide on their bellies through the snow. This can be done either uphill or downhill, but mostly the latter, and the slide may end in water. The animals may repeatedly slide over the same spot, and this results in a trough through the snow. Otters more commonly use slides, and their slides are at least 8 inches wide. The slides of mink are less common but, when found, can be distinguished by their smaller width of about 4 to 6 inches.

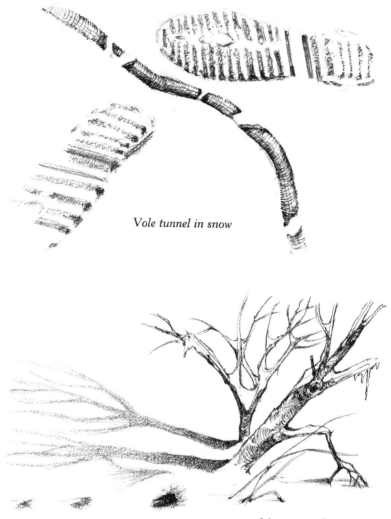

Vole tunnel in snow

Mouse tunnel in snow

Natural Cavities: Tree Holes, Hollow Logs, Rock Caves, Upturned Stumps, Buildings

Many mammals do not construct homes or dig burrows but rather use existing cavities in which to rest, hibernate, or raise young. When you find such a cavity, you first may want to know whether animals have ever used it. To determine this you should look for scats, shed hairs, tracks, teeth or claw marks, food remains, and check for odors or any evidence of trails to and from the spot.

If a cavity has been occupied, you may want to know how recently. To do this, use commonsense clues, such as the presence or absence of cobwebs, the presence of debris such as leaves in the entrance, general wear and tear in the cavity, and also the age of any scats you may find, or the strength of any odor.

Finally, you may want to determine the cavity's user or users, for more than one animal may have lived in the spot at different times. Obviously, tracks, scats, odor, hairs, teeth and claw marks, and food remains will be your best clues. After that you must resort to a process of elimination, taking into account the size of the cavity, the habitat, the time of year, and the likelihood of a given animal being in the area and using it. It is frequently impossible to make an exact identification, but it is possible to narrow down the field.

Here are the animals that use natural cavities and the clues they are likely to leave behind.

Black Bear
Behavior, page 301

Black bears use natural cavities only in winter when they hibernate. These *dens* can be above ground in hollow portions of trees, in rock cavities, or in brush piles. Occasionally they may excavate their own dens. The trees bears use are generally 3 to 4 feet in diameter, and the hollow portion used may be anywhere from about 20 to 75 feet above ground. You should be able to see some scratch marks on the tree trunk where the bear climbed.

Bears often use rock crevices as well. The average crevice is about 2 feet high, 3 feet wide, and 6 to 7 feet deep. Entrances can be smaller than one would imagine necessary for such a large animal, averaging about 2 feet by 1½ feet. Some vegetation, such as evergreen boughs, leaves, branches, and rotting wood, may be dragged into the den.

Natural Cavities: Tree Holes, Hollow Logs, Rock Caves, Upturned Stumps, Buildings

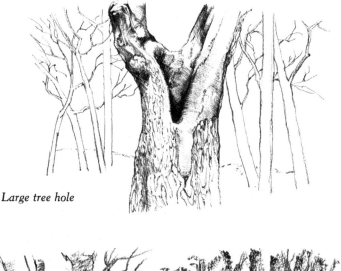

Large tree hole

Rock crevice

Bobcat
Behavior, page 365

Bobcat *dens* are rarely found. Bobcats use dens throughout the year for resting, avoiding bad weather, and raising young. The dens are often located in rock crevices but may also be found in the spaces beneath fallen logs or in other similarly protected spots. There are few signs that the dens are being used, although in some cases piles of scats may be left near the entrance, or the inedible remains of prey, such as bones, feet, or tails. Remember that the bobcat is only about 2 feet tall and can use a fairly small space.

Otter
Behavior, page 355

Otters use *dens* for raising their young, and this most often occurs in the months of February to June. Their dens are often located near large bodies of water. They may den in the lodges or bank dens of muskrat or beavers, or they may use another natural cavity such as an upturned stump or the space beneath a fallen log. The den is usually lined with shredded vegetation. There are no other clues to otters' use of a den, so you must rely on tracks, trails, and other signs.

Fisher
Behavior, page 321

Fishers have two types of *dens*: temporary dens used for cover and sleeping, and breeding dens used for raising their young. The temporary dens are occupied only for one to several days at a time and can be in any protected place, such as a hollow log, brush pile, rock pile, burrow, or even a tunnel in deep snow. There is no way to recognize one of these sites without seeing tracks leading to it.

Breeding dens are used in spring when the young are born. The few that have been discovered have been 20 to 30 feet up in the hollow portions of trees. In some cases there have been signs of prey and scats at the bases of the den trees; in other cases the den has been absolutely clean. This is why so few fisher breeding dens have been discovered.

Mink
Behavior, page 339

Mink use *dens* in late spring and early summer to raise young, and throughout the rest of the year they use them as protected resting spots. Dens can be located in any natural crevice but are almost always near water. Frequently mink use muskrat bank dens. To determine if a mink is using a cavity, you must see its tracks, although mink have been known to leave piles of scats outside dens that are used for extended periods of time. Resting dens may be used for only a day or for several weeks.

Hole under fallen log

Hollow log

Weasel
Behavior, page 329

Weasels are small animals and will use the burrows of other animals as well as natural cavities. They will also readily nest in spaces under human constructions or in woodpiles. There are very few clues to confirm that a den belongs to a weasel. You might check for the remains of prey around the area in midspring to midsummer, when weasels are raising young.

Opossum
Behavior, page 137

Opossums use a wide variety of sites for resting during the day and for long periods of sleep throughout winter. They may use hollow logs, hollow trees, rock crevices, burrows, and the spaces under buildings. There is no sure way of identifying a den as belonging to an opossum unless you see the animal's tracks or the animal itself go into it.

Porcupine
Behavior, page 257

A porcupine *den* is easy to recognize because the porcupine always leaves its scats in the den, and over time they accumulate into a thick layer in the bottom of the den. Porcupines will den in rock crevices, hollow logs, other animal burrows, under buildings, and in hollow trees. Besides the scats, you may also see shed quills or signs of porcupine feeding in the area. The freshness of the scats can give you some clue as to how recently the den has been used.

Raccoon
Behavior, page 311

Raccoons prefer hollow trees as den sites but have also adapted to culverts, spaces under buildings, and chimneys. They occasionally use the burrows of woodchucks. There are not too many clues to raccoons' use of a spot, but they do have the habit of leaving their scats in the area, especially at the base of a tree or a building that they are about to climb.

Skunk
Behavior, page 347

Like raccoons, skunks are comfortable in suburban areas and will den in spaces under houses and porches. Skunks are often disturbed in suburban areas and are forced to spray. As a result, the skunk's smell in the vicinity may be a good clue to its use of a den site. You may also see evidence of feeding on your lawn.

Hole under house porch

House chimney

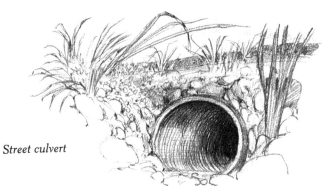

Street culvert

Gray and Red Squirrels   *Behavior, pages 199, 209*

Squirrels often use tree holes and may line them with leaves or other soft material for added warmth in winter. The signs of current use, other than seeing the animal go in the hole, are claw marks on the tree trunk or gnawing around the entrance hole, done to make it somehow more suitable. Mice also may use these holes and stuff them with shredded grasses.

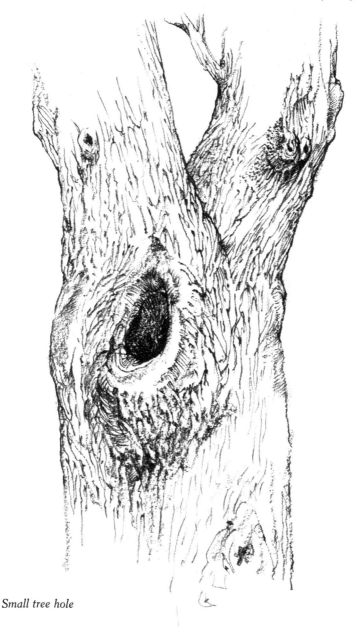

Small tree hole

Food Remains and Caches

There are numerous signs of mammals' feeding on both vegetable and animal matter. While most of them are listed under the feeding habits of each species, here are a few that are very common.

MUSHROOMS HALF-EATEN OR FOUND IN TREES:
Red Squirrel, Gray Squirrel, Mouse, Vole

Behavior, pages 209, 199, 229, 239

Red squirrels eat a great many mushrooms. One of the things they do is to place mushrooms up among the twigs of trees and let them dry. After the mushroom has dried, the red squirrel may eat or store it.

You may find mushrooms still in the ground with bites taken out of them. This may be the work of mice, voles, or squirrels; the size of teeth marks will help determine the eater. For the measurements of the front teeth of these animals, refer to page 76.

BRANCHES PILED IN THE WATER: Beaver

Behavior, page 219

In the fall, beavers begin to build up a store of food for the winter. They do this by cutting off branches and securing them in the mud at the base of their ponds. You will see only the tops of the branches sticking above the water and filling an area anywhere from 10 to 30 feet in diameter. These branches are used gradually over the course of the winter. Caches like this are often located near the lodge.

Food Remains and Caches

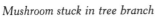

Mushroom stuck in tree branch

Mushroom with bites taken out of it

Beaver cache in water

COLLECTIONS OF NUTS, SEEDS, OR CONES: Red
Squirrel, Chipmunk, Mouse

Red Squirrel, Chipmunk   *Behavior, pages 209, 179*

Red squirrels and chipmunks cache nuts, cones, and seeds in protected spots. Both animals usually store them underground in cavities or burrows under tree roots, or in log piles. Caches of squirrels are occasionally located within large *middens*, piles of refuse from cones and nuts formed when an animal eats its food at the same spot week after week. Middens made by red squirrels are commonly found and can either be just a few inches high or several feet or more in diameter and 3 to 4 feet high. Middens often appear at the base of a tree where a squirrel sits on a favorite branch to feed.

Mouse   *Behavior, page 229*

Deer mice and white-footed mice make small caches, usually consisting of nuts or seeds only. These are placed above or just below the ground surface. They may be under a fallen log or a rock, or in a hole. These are more commonly encountered than the caches of red squirrels.

CHEWED NUTS OR CONES:
Gray Squirrel, Red Squirrel, Chipmunk, Mouse
                                  Behavior, pages 199, 209, 179, 229

Cones are often eaten by squirrels. Both red and gray squirrels eat them in the same way, chewing off the scales at the bottom of the cone first to get at the seeds underneath. They turn the cone as they eat, for the scales are arranged in a spiral around the stalk of the cone. The stalk and scales are all that are left after feeding.

Gray squirrels eat cones near where they find them. Red squirrels tend to cache the cones first and then gradually bring them out one at a time. They often eat at the same spot repeatedly, so that the scales and cone stalks begin to accumulate into a midden. Over the months and even years, this midden can grow to several feet high and is a conspicuous sign of red-squirrel activity.

Nuts stored in log pile

Red-squirrel midden

Chewed pine cones

Mice generally eat smaller cones, such as those of hemlock, fir, or spruce. Like the gray squirrel, they usually eat them where they find them. Since mice are smaller and closer to the ground, the small pile of scales they leave is not as scattered as that left by the larger gray squirrel.

Squirrels, chipmunks, and mice also eat nuts. They usually eat acorns by ripping off the outer coating in little bits. Harder nuts, such as hickory nuts and walnuts, require more work. The animals gnaw a hole in either side of the nut before chewing out the meat inside. The result is an empty shell with a gnawed hole in either side. Occasionally animals may gnaw four holes in the shell. There is no sure way to tell which animal did which gnawing, for the patterns of gnawing may vary among individuals and the different sizes of nuts. However, you can look at the teeth marks and use their relative sizes to some extent.

HORNET'S NESTS TORN OPEN: Skunk, Raccoon, Fox, Black Bear

Behavior, pages 347, 311, 277, 301

By the end of summer, the nests of social wasps are at their largest and contain both adults and developing larvae. Skunks, raccoons, foxes, and black bears may dig up these nests or tear apart those close to the ground to eat the insects inside. This often occurs in fall, when the social order of the hive is breaking up and the insects have been slowed down by the cold.

DUG-UP TURTLE EGGS: Skunk, Raccoon, Fox

Behavior, pages 347, 311, 277

Turtles lay their eggs on land, digging a hole in sandy soil, depositing the eggs in the hole, and then covering it up. Skunks, raccoons, and foxes can detect these eggs in some way, dig them up, and eat them. The sign you will find is the dug-up hole and the soft turtle eggshells scattered about the area and curled up after drying.

GNAWED BONES: Mouse, Vole, Squirrel, Chipmunk

Behavior, pages 229, 239, 199, 209, 179

Bones from dead animals seldom last very long in the wild because smaller rodents find them and gnaw on them for their nutrients. Anytime that you find a bone or skull, check it for the teeth marks of these animals.

Various chewed nuts

Hornet's nest chewed apart

Dug-up turtle eggs

Gnawed bones

Part Two

MAMMAL LIVES AND BEHAVIOR

INTRODUCTION TO MAMMAL BEHAVIOR

In the process of writing this book and researching mammal behavior, we soon became aware of two interesting facts. The first was that most mammals' lives still remain a mystery to both the scientist and nature lover. Of the four thousand species of mammals in the world, only about 1 percent have been thoroughly studied. Some of our most common mammals, such as shrews and moles, possess social systems and means of courtship almost totally unknown to us. Even mammals that have been well studied, such as the red fox and white-tailed deer, have aspects of their behavior that are just being discovered.

The second thing we realized was that, even though we are also mammals, many features of wild mammals' lives are strikingly different from our own. For example, most mammals are nocturnal; they live in a world of scent communication that is totally unknown to us; they have a variety of ways of digesting and storing food; they are only rarely monogamous; and their sexual cycles are complex and extremely varied. Thus, we thought that it might be helpful to provide a brief review of some of the basic features of mammals' lives.

Reproductive Behavior

One of the most intricate parts of mammals' lives is their reproductive cycle. In the vast majority of our common mammals, males and females remain separate through most of the year and meet only during the time that mating occurs. This means that when it is time to mate, the first thing a male and female must do is locate each other. This is usually accomplished through scent or sound or a combination of the two. Often the female gives off the scent. It may be excreted in her urine or feces or from other special scent glands on her body. At the same time, the male of the species may roam more widely in search of females and their scent. These beginning stages of the breeding cycle are probably triggered by changes in photoperiod — the length of daylight.

At the start of the breeding season, the male's testes begin actively to produce sperm; outside the breeding season they may regress and become inactive. At the same time, the female sexual organs start a series of progressive stages called the *estrous cycle*. In the first stage, *proestrus*, the female's sexual organs become active and prepare for ovulation, mating, and fertilization. She may begin to give off scents or give calls at this time, but if a male shows up she will not yet let him mate with her.

The second stage is called *estrus*, or "heat." This is defined as the stage in which she will accept the male and mate with him and in which ovulation usually occurs. The length of estrus varies from several hours to several days. In some cases, the female shows external signs of being in estrus, such as the changed behavior of the house cat, but most female mammals show no signs at all except for the fact that they will accept the male for mating. During estrus the female may ovulate regardless of what else happens; this is called spontaneous ovulation. In many other cases, she will ovulate only after the stimulation of mating; this is called induced ovulation.

After mating, the male and female usually separate and go their own ways, for in the majority of our mammals, there is no lasting bond between the adult pair, and the female raises the young alone. Once mating has occurred, the female's eggs are fertilized. The period between fertilization and birth is called *gestation*. The length of gestation varies greatly among our mammals, from several weeks in the smaller species to several months in the larger ones. The longest gestation among our native mammals occurs in the fisher and lasts about eleven months. This extremely long time is due to delayed implantation, in which the fertilized egg stops further development and remains in a dormant state. Later, the egg implants itself in the wall of the uterus and continues its development; in the fisher this implantation occurs about a month before birth. Several other members of the weasel family, such as the weasel, mink, and otter, also have delayed implantation; it occurs in the black bear as well.

The third stage of the estrous cycle is *metestrus*. This occurs if a female does not mate during her estrus stage. During metestrus the female's uterus gradually returns to normal. Following this is the fourth stage of the estrous cycle, *diestrus*, in which the female's sexual organs are inactive.

The human sexual cycle consists of the menstrual cycle. In this cycle, if the egg is not fertilized, there are marked changes in the uterus involving a discharge of blood. This cycle occurs only in humans and other primates.

Scent-marking

Most mammals live in a world rich with scents that not only help them locate food but also enable them to communicate with each other. This part of their lives is very difficult for us to know and understand since our own ability to smell is so limited compared with that of other mammals. Mammals are constantly marking their environment with scents, and every mammal has several scent glands that it uses. Scent is often in urine or scats, but it also may be rubbed on objects from glands on the head, the feet, the sides of the body, the tail, or the anal region. Mammal scent may change with the season or situation and is used for a variety of purposes, from indicating sexual or emotional states to marking food, homes, and the area in which the mammals live.

Home Range and Territory

An individual mammal tends to stay within a given area throughout its life. This is called its *home range*. It becomes very familiar with this area and will often mark it with scent and use certain trails through it regularly. The sizes of home ranges vary greatly both among species and within species. Carnivores tend to have larger home ranges than herbivores, for their food items are more dispersed. Larger mammals also usually have larger home ranges both because they need more food and because they can more easily travel long distances. But the size of the home range depends in addition on the availability of food (abundant food enables an animal to remain within a smaller area) and the sexual cycle (many mammals expand their home ranges when looking for mates).

In most North American species, individuals remain solitary through most of the year. In these species each individual has its own home range. For some, like the gray squirrel, the home ranges of individuals may broadly overlap. In others, such as mink or bobcat, the home ranges of males may overlap those of females, but home ranges of individuals of the same sex do not overlap.

When an individual mammal actively defends an area of its home range against an intruder, this area is called its *territory*. In most of our species home ranges are not actively defended; rather, neighboring individuals just seem to avoid each other's presence.

Feeding Behavior

The most common activity of mammals is feeding. Each species has evolved a slightly different strategy for acquiring the food it needs to survive throughout the year. There are basically three types of feeders: herbivores, which eat only plants; carnivores, which eat only other animals, including insects, fish, snakes, et cetera; and omnivores, which eat both plants and animals.

Plant leaves and stems contain cellulose, which is difficult to digest, and herbivores have adapted to this by spending more time breaking down their food than do carnivores. Deer and moose have four different chambers in their stomachs. After their food goes into one chamber for a while, it is regurgitated and chewed again. Then it is swallowed and goes on through the other chambers. Another solution to extracting nutrients from leaves and stems occurs in rabbits and many of the rodents, such as voles and beavers. These animals excrete two kinds of feces. One kind is greenish, a result of the first passage of the food through the system. These feces are eaten, often right from the anus, and redigested. The next feces are dark and are not eaten.

Adaptations to Winter

Herbivores have also had to adapt to the lack of green leaves and other plant parts in winter. In the case of the rabbit, hare, vole, and deer, the animals switch to eating more of the buds and bark of trees and shrubs. Another adaptation, exemplified in squirrels and mice, is to store large quantities of the abundant nuts and seeds that mature in fall and then feed on them through winter. A third adaptation, practiced by the woodchuck as well as by many omnivores, such as raccoons, skunks, and opossums, is to store the plentiful food of summer and fall inside the body in the form of fat.

Still another way to overcome the lack of certain food in winter is to lower the consumption of food energy by becoming less active. Raccoons, skunks, and opossums may sleep in dens for days or weeks at a time in winter. Other animals, such as chipmunks and bears, not only sleep but also slow their metabolism, resulting in a reduced body temperature and slower heartbeat and breathing rates. Among the mammals in this guide, the woodchuck exhibits the most extreme change of this kind. Its body temperature falls to between 38 and 57 degrees Fahrenheit, and its breathing rate slows to once every 6 minutes. This is often referred to as true hibernation as opposed to the less extreme changes that occur in the chipmunk, bear, raccoon, and others. But in reality, these various states should be seen as a continuum of various levels of dormancy or torpor. Interestingly, most carnivores are active throughout the winter, probably because their food source is not significantly changed.

These are just a few of the fascinating features of mammals' lives that are described in detail for each species in the following section. Science is just beginning to understand mammal behavior, and so much more still needs to be discovered. Through the combined knowledge of animal signs and animal behavior, we hope that you can add to this process of discovery and at the same time develop a greater appreciation and awareness of the exciting lives of our native mammals.

Adult opossum

OPOSSUM /
Didelphus virginianus

Opossums are truly amazing animals. They have a prehensile tail and opposable big toe, both unique among our native mammals. Their young are born only 13 days after fertilization, crawl into the mother's pouch where they latch onto nipples, and continue their development for another 2 months. They have 50 teeth, more than twice the number of most other mammals. They also have nomadic habits, constantly changing sleeping dens, and almost comical mating behavior. Many of these traits are due to the opossum's being a very different mammal from all the others in this guide. It is the only member of the marsupial order in North America, and thus a closer relative to kangaroos and koala bears than to its neighbors the squirrels, foxes, and rabbits.

Probably the first thing that comes to mind when people think of opossums is their habit of feigning death when disturbed, or playing possum. It is amazing how much attention this gets when you consider that it rarely occurs in the wild. When an opossum is in danger, it will first hiss and growl, lunge at a predator, and then try to escape through running or climbing a tree. In those few cases where it is trapped, the animal instinctively falls down on its side with its mouth slightly open; it may also drool, defecate, and give off a bad smell. In short, the animal makes itself very unattractive to a predator. This state may last a few minutes or several hours, but the animal seems to snap out of it as rapidly as it fell into it. Since the action is an instinctive response, the animal is not consciously controlling it, as the words "playing possum" might suggest.

The opossum is a medium-size animal, grayish in the North and almost black in the South. It has a hairless, rat-like tail that is black at the base and whitish at the tip. Its ears are also hairless and dark at the base with white tips. Opossums are about 15 to 20 inches long, excluding tail, and weigh from 4 to 14 pounds. The scientific name is *Didelphus virginianus*. The animals are in the opossum family, Didelphidae, which is in the order Marsupialia.

Getting Around

Opossums are active at night, especially just after sunset and just before dawn; during the day they sleep in dens or other protected spots.

Radio tracking of opossums has shown that the animals tend to shift dens frequently. In fact, 75 percent of the time they use a den for only one night before moving on, though there are times when an opossum may use the same den over a period of 20 to 30 days. These longer periods may occur in winter when the animal is holed up for several days at a time. Because of its preference for keeping on the move, an opossum's home range — which overlaps broadly with the ranges of neighboring opossums — is constantly shifting. Some scientists believe opossums have no home range or territory at all but instead are nomadic. In any case, their movements seem to center around their most recent choice of den. If you followed a single night's ramblings by an opossum in the snow, you might cover ½ to 2 miles of trail, yet you would rarely move more than ¼ mile away from the den.

Opossums do not dig their own dens but instead use a wide variety of sites for protection: old buildings, hollow logs or trees, rock crevices, brush tangles, abandoned crow or squirrel nests, and burrows excavated by woodchucks. Winter dens in the North are usually underground to afford greater protection from the cold. Opossums may even share dens with other animals such as rabbits, skunks, and woodchucks.

The dens are usually lined with leaves or other soft material. When collecting the lining, an opossum takes mouthfuls of vegetation, passes them under its body, and holds them in its coiled tail. The material is carried this way to the nest, where the animal arranges it with its mouth and forefeet. Nest building often takes place in the middle of the night. Ground nests in burrows may have an additional plug of leaves in their entrance; in winter, this plug can be very dense and can act as insulation against the cold.

The real nature of opossum social structure is still not understood. In general, males are aggressive toward other males but not toward females; also, nonestrous females are generally aggressive toward estrous females. Male opossums have been observed to scent-mark by licking or rubbing the sides of their faces on chosen objects. When other males pick up the scent, they too mark the same spot and even display some aggression, doing a shuffling walk in which they kick their hind feet laterally, as if another male were present. Females also respond to scent marks. Scent-marking occurs all year but is most common during breeding periods and seems to be stimulated in a male by the scent of another male or of an estrous female. How these markings are used by opossums in the wild is still not known, but they may help males and estrous females keep track of each other's whereabouts.

Opossums will leave their scats anywhere, even in their nests. It is not known whether scats are used as a scent mark. Opossum scats are usually semiliquid and do not last very long.

Clues:	Tracks	Common	See page 24
	Holes in the ground	Common	See page 88
	Natural cavities	Common	See page 116
	Claw marks on trees	Common	See page 78
	Scats	Uncommon	See page 62

Opossum range map

Food and Feeding Habits

Opossums are slow-moving animals and are comfortable both in trees and on land. Because they are slow, they are limited to eating plants and small animals. They are omnivores, eating whatever is available seasonally in plant and animal matter.

One study indicated that the food eaten by opossums by volume was mammals, 22 percent; fruits, 14 percent; earthworms, 10 percent; amphibians, 9 percent; green vegetation, 8 percent; insects, 8 percent; birds, 7 percent; carrion, 6 percent; reptiles, 5 percent. The remaining percentage included small invertebrates not listed above and grains and nuts. These ratios were found to vary with seasonal availability. In winter, mammals, such as the meadow vole and short-tailed shrew, were the items most frequently consumed by opossums. In spring, green vegetation and earthworms were most prominent. In summer, insects, like grasshoppers and beetles, and amphibians, such as toads, were popular. And in fall, fruits and nuts were the most common food items. Throughout the year, carrion and the maggots on it were eaten.

Opossums spend a great deal of time foraging, especially in fall and early winter. They put on a lot of fat in these seasons, and this helps them survive, especially in cold climates, where they hole up in their dens during the winter months. As they hunt for food, they meander about, often stopping to sniff the air. They have a good sense of smell and probably use scent to locate their food.

There are very few signs of feeding that can be positively identified as those of opossums, for their food habits overlap those of other animals such as raccoons and skunks.

Family Life

Adult opossums generally lead solitary lives, with the exception of the female when she is raising young. Breeding occurs between January and November. During this time there are three periods when mating tends to take place. The first is in January, the second in May, and the third in August. Most females breed only once or twice a year. All adult females at least attempt to breed in the first period, which extends from December to January in the South and from January to February in the North.

It is not known exactly how the male and female locate each other in order to mate, but there is evidence that males scent-mark and that females in estrus may urine-mark and actively seek out males. A female is in estrus for about 36 hours, but successful fertilization usually occurs only in the first 12 hours of this period. When a male finds a female, he will approach, nuzzle with her, and then follow her. If she is not receptive, she will react aggressively with hissing, tooth clicking, or biting threats.

There are several curious aspects of opossum reproduction. During mating the male bites the fur on the female's neck and then climbs onto her back. At this point both topple over to the right, and copulation takes place. It has been found that they almost always fall to their right. If for some reason they fall to the left or remain standing, copulation is less likely to be successful. Copulation lasts for about 20 minutes.

Another amazing feature is that the female has a vagina split in two and the male has a branched penis that enters both parts of the vagina. After mating, a temporary plug is formed in the female's vagina that prevents any other males from mating with her. The plug is shed about 36 hours later, after the female is no longer in estrus.

Gestation of the young lasts only 12 to 13 days, at which point each baby is about ½ inch long and weighs the merest fraction of an ounce.

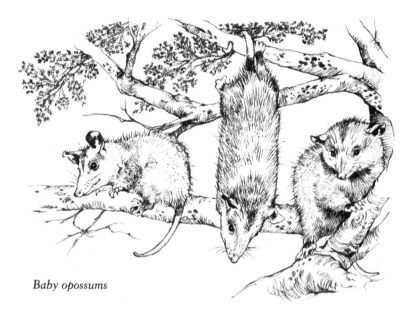

Baby opossums

The mother sits upright during the birth of the young, which takes slightly more than 10 minutes. As soon as the infants are born, they begin to crawl up the mother's belly to her pouch. They are believed to locate the pouch through scent. When they get to the pouch, they crawl in, find the nipples, and latch onto them with their mouths. They have special structures to hold on with, and the nipples also swell to fill their mouths. The young have separate breathing and drinking passages, so they do not drown or suffocate. There are an average of 6 to 10 young in a litter and 13 nipples to feed from. When there are more than 13 young, the ones that do not get nipples die.

The young stay attached to the nipples for 2 months. At the end of this time they are about 2 inches long (excluding their tails), they have a covering of fur, and their eyes are open. They let go of the nipples at this point, leave the pouch for brief periods, and then return to feed. They may stay in the pouch or ride about on their mother's back, holding onto her fur. They may also be left in the den while she goes out and feeds. When the young emerge from the pouch, the mother begins to pay more attention to them; before this point all she did was lick the pouch to keep it clean. Whenever she gives a clicking sound, the young come toward her.

In about 2 weeks they are weaned, and in another 3 to 4 weeks they are independent. All in all, it takes about 3½ months from birth to independence. Young opossums are first seen on their own in April and May. At this time, especially in the South, the female may have already mated again and produced another brood. The final period of mating, in August, may be taken advantage of by females that were unsuccessful before or by young females born the previous spring, for female opossums are believed to be sexually mature by 6 to 7 months. Males are mature by 8 to 9 months.

When the young are independent, they disperse but do not venture far away. In some cases, young females have been found to settle less than a quarter-mile from where they were raised. Young males tend to go a little farther.

Although opossums may live as long as 7 years in captivity, few seem to survive to an age of more than 1½ years in the wild.

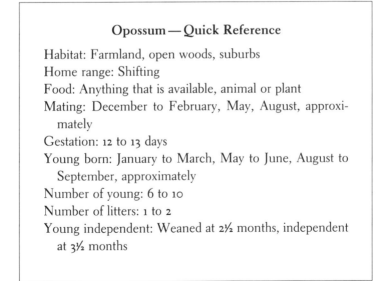

Opossum — Quick Reference

Habitat: Farmland, open woods, suburbs

Home range: Shifting

Food: Anything that is available, animal or plant

Mating: December to February, May, August, approximately

Gestation: 12 to 13 days

Young born: January to March, May to June, August to September, approximately

Number of young: 6 to 10

Number of litters: 1 to 2

Young independent: Weaned at 2½ months, independent at 3½ months

Adult shrew

SHORT-TAILED SHREW /
Blarina brevicauda

LEAST SHREW /
Cryptotis parva

MASKED SHREW /
Sorex cinereus

From the tracks we were following that winter morning, we could tell that the fox had been moving purposefully around the edge of the swamp. Then something changed in its gait — the stride shortened, showing that the animal had slowed, and then there was a leap. We looked ahead and spotted a torn-up patch of snow with a small animal to one side. It was a short-tailed shrew, clearly killed by the fox but then left, for the fox's trail continued on. We inspected the spot more closely and noticed that a house cat had also been there after the fox and had stopped by the shrew; it too had left the shrew. We had heard that shrews are often caught and then left, possibly because of their odor, but this was the first example we had seen. Some say the smell of the shrew is a predator defense, but if so, it is not a very good one, for it was obvious from the story in the snow that the fox killed first and sniffed later.

Shrews are definitely our smallest mammal; in fact, the least shrew is no bigger than your thumb. Shrews are also one of our most common mammals and live in an incredible variety of habitats. Being such a ubiquitous mammal, it is, amazingly, one of the least often seen or well known. To start to know the shrew, we recommend that you go into your nearest woods and carefully lift up some of the fallen leaves. If you notice any tiny, meandering tunnels about an inch in diameter, they probably were made by shrews. They are surprisingly common. If you don't find any in one spot, choose a new spot about 30 feet away and try again.

You can also see shrew tunnels in the snow during a thaw when the upper layer of snow starts to melt. The tunnels will look like someone dragged a thick stick in a meandering pattern across the snow. You may see the trails right across your lawn, for shrews live in both the suburbs and the country.

Recently we had some grass clippings from our lawn, which we spread out in a pile in the woods. Later, a board was laid on top of them. In a day or two we lifted the board up, and the surface of the clippings had tunnels of shrews all through it.

Shrews are tiny mammals, ranging from 2 to 4 inches long, excluding tail, and weighing only a fraction of an ounce. They generally have pointed faces, small eyes and ears, and short legs. They are in the family Soricidae, which includes shrews and moles and is in the order Insectivora. There are twenty species in North America, and they include five genera. The shrews with the most widespread distribution are the short-tailed shrew, *Blarina brevicauda*, the least shrew, *Cryptotis parva*, and the masked shrew, *Sorex cinereus*. The descriptions that follow apply to the life of the short-tailed shrew unless stated otherwise.

Getting Around

Most shrews are active throughout the day and night, constantly hunting for prey and eating to fuel their high metabolism. During the day the shrews stay under cover in their tunnels, but at night they may move over the surface of the ground in search of food. In winter it is not unusual to see their tracks on the snow surface. Like mice and voles, shrews are more active on days and nights that are cloudy. One cloudy winter day we spotted a shrew that tunneled up through the snow at our feet, peered around, sniffed the air, and then ran across the snow surface to a tuft of grass, where it then dove down a tiny hole.

Shrews are not inveterate diggers like moles, nor do they prune their grass tunnels like the voles; however, they will readily use the tunnels of these two other animals.

Some shrews, including the short-tailed shrew, are known to produce a musky odor in three scent glands, two on either side near its rear and one on its belly. Some researchers have suggested that this is a defense against predators, for occasionally animals catch shrews but leave them uneaten. This is unlikely, since it has been shown that females, between the period of estrus and giving birth, do not produce the odor. It is more likely that the odor serves to mark the tunnels of the shrews so that they can be individually recognized, thus helping shrews to avoid each other's tunnels and presence.

Shrews often give off high squeaks that are probably a form of communication with other shrews. The short-tailed shrew is also known to help orient itself through high-frequency calls, or *echolocation*, in much the same way that bats do. Echolocation can help it to recognize and explore its dark tunnels, avoid objects, and, when above ground at night, locate cover.

The home range of shrews is not well studied but probably covers an area of ¼ to 1 acre. Shrews are most often found living in woods, fields, or near swamps, and many species swim well. They can be extremely abundant, up to 25 per acre, but usually there are only a few per acre.

The scats of shrews are rarely found, for they are minute and most often left along tunnels or occasionally in a spot near the nest.

Clues:	Tunnels through leaf litter	Common	See page 108
	Tunnels through snow	Common	See page 110

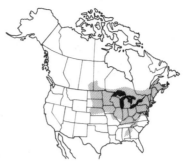

Shrew range map

Food and Feeding Habits

Shrews have teeth that are sharply pointed but lack grinding teeth like our molars. All of our native shrews have a yellowish color on the tips of their teeth.

Some species, such as the short-tailed shrew, produce in the front of their lower jaw saliva that contains poison. When small mammals are bitten by these kinds of shrews, the poison enters their veins and has the effect of lowering their blood pressure, slowing their heartbeat, and inhibiting their respiration. It can even cause death in small mammals such as mice, and it is similar in some ways to the venom of poisonous snakes. The poison can cause severe swelling in humans; thus it is best not to handle live shrews without adequate protection. Undoubtedly the poison helps the shrews kill prey that may be as large as or larger than themselves.

Shrews feed mostly on various animals that they encounter in their runways, such as earthworms, insects, small mice and voles, snails, centipedes, slugs, salamanders, small birds, small snakes, young rabbits, and spiders. They may also eat some vegetable matter, such as moss and seeds, fruits, nuts, and roots. Some of the more aquatic shrews, like the water shrew (*Sorex palustris*), may feed on aquatic insects and their larvae as well as small fish and their eggs.

The short-tailed shrew is known to cache some food in chambers in its burrows or, in the case of partially eaten prey, to cover it with vegetation.

There are no clues to shrew feeding since most of it takes place underground.

Family Life

There is very little known about the lives of shrews, for even though they are common, they are hard to observe because they are tiny and remain underground most of the time. In the case of the short-tailed shrew, breeding begins in January or February and continues until fall. The social relationship between males and females is not well documented. Mating can occur up to twenty times a day for animals in captivity. During mating the male and female become locked together for several minutes; if the female moves during this time she may end up dragging the male backward behind her. Gestation takes about 3 weeks and, within a few days after birth, the female of some species is able to mate again. There are 3 to 10 young per litter and there may be 2 to 3 litters per year.

The nest of the short-tailed shrew is usually placed in a protected spot, such as under a log, in a woodpile, in an old burrow, or under a building. The nests of least shrews have been found under old boards lying out in fields. Shrew nests are about 6 to 8 inches in diameter with a 2- to 4-inch-diameter space inside. They are composed of fine shredded materials from tree leaves, grasses, and wildflowers. Nests for breeding may be larger than those within tunnels, where the animals only rest.

At first the young are totally dependent on the mother. They have no fur, and their eyes and ears are closed. The mother feeds them milk, and by about 2 weeks their ears and eyes are both open and they can move about freely. At about 3 weeks they can leave the nest, and by about 4 weeks they are weaned and on their own.

Baby shrews

Just how sociable shrews are with one another still needs further study, although short-tailed shrews have been reported to huddle together when resting in captivity, possibly for warmth. Least shrews have been reported to build tunnels and nests cooperatively, and

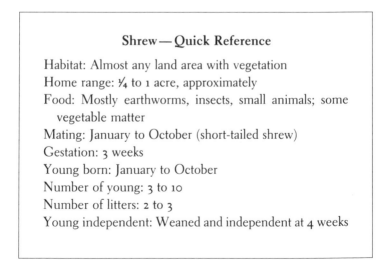

Shrew — Quick Reference

Habitat: Almost any land area with vegetation
Home range: ¼ to 1 acre, approximately
Food: Mostly earthworms, insects, small animals; some vegetable matter
Mating: January to October (short-tailed shrew)
Gestation: 3 weeks
Young born: January to October
Number of young: 3 to 10
Number of litters: 2 to 3
Young independent: Weaned and independent at 4 weeks

sometimes communities have been found — up to 31 animals in a single nest. In the case of the least shrew, it has also been observed that the male may be near the nest when the mother has young in it.

Clues: Nests   Rare   See page 100

Adult mole

EASTERN MOLE /
Scalopus aquaticus

STAR-NOSED MOLE /
Condylura cristata

Two of our most common moles are the eastern mole, which lives in fields, woods, and lawns, and the star-nosed mole, which tends to live near water. Both have a number of adaptations to underground life: fur that can be pushed in any direction so that the mole can go forward or backward in its tunnels; reduced vision; and small external ears, although their hearing can be excellent. Moles' feet are most obviously adapted to underground life, for they are broad, short, and powerful, enabling the animal to tunnel through fairly hard earth.

The star-nosed mole is a strange-looking creature, owing to the ten little projections that radiate off the tip of its nose. These are probably used for sensing the environment and possibly prey. This mole is often found swimming in streams, lakes, and marshes, frequently underwater, and may even catch minnows and aquatic insects. Many observers have even seen these moles swimming under the ice in winter. The tunnels of the star-nosed mole often lead to water and may have entrances underwater.

No doubt you have heard the saying "Don't make a mountain out of a molehill," but have you ever wondered what a molehill actually is? It does exist and indeed is made by moles. Most molehills are no more than a few inches high and about 10 inches in diameter and are composed of loose earth, which the mole has pushed out of its deepest tunnels. They are one of the best clues to a mole's presence.

153

Moles belong to the family Talpidae, which is in the order Insectivora, or insectivores, and includes both moles and shrews. There are seven species of moles in North America, and they represent five different genera. The most widespread mole is the eastern mole, *Scalopus aquaticus*, which lives throughout the East and Midwest. The star-nosed mole, *Condylura cristata*, is also widely distributed, living in the Northeast and the Great Lakes region.

Getting Around

A mole spends almost all of its life in underground tunnels, where it raises young, stays protected, and gathers food. There are basically two types of mole tunnels: those that run just under the surface of the soil and push up a ridge of loose earth, and those that are well beneath the soil. These tunnels are constructed in different ways.

The surface tunnels are made in soft earth or sand. When digging them, the mole turns on its side and uses its uppermost front foot to scrape away soil in front of it and push up the soil above; this makes the ridge in the surface of the earth that we commonly associate with moles. Moles do not push through the soil with their noses, for the tip of the nose is extremely sensitive and pushing would probably be painful. Some surface tunnels are exploratory and used only once, but others may be used repeatedly. Surface tunnels tend to be made in the warmer months, since this is the time when food is most available.

To make deeper tunnels, the mole scrapes in front, first with one foot and then the other, occasionally scraping back the loose earth with its hind feet. After a portion of soil has accumulated behind it, the mole turns around and, twisting its head to one side, puts its foot in front of it and bulldozes the soil out of the tunnel. The soil is pushed out through a hole onto the surface of the earth and becomes mounded above the hole, creating the proverbial molehill. As the mole lengthens the tunnel, it makes new vertical exit holes through which to push out the newer earth more easily. The tunnels can be from 6 to 24 inches below the soil surface. Most molehills appear in spring, when the moles are cleaning out their tunnels once the ground has thawed, and in fall, when the moles move back to their deeper tunnels and have to make repairs.

A mole may have a whole network of tunnels of varying depths to enable it to find food under different conditions. Once a tunnel system has been made, it is continually used by the mole; a tunnel system in an area with lots of food may be used by successive generations of moles. Some tunnel systems have been known to be used for ten years, and in fact there is no reason they could not be used for fifty years or more. In some cases, young moles may come upon abandoned tunnel systems and do not have to make their own.

In general, moles have well-defined home ranges. Those of the eastern mole have been estimated at about 2 acres for males and ½ acre for females. The size of the home range depends greatly on the availability of food in the tunnels; a home range may gradually move as a mole expands its tunnels in one direction and abandons others. There seems to be a great deal of overlap between the home ranges of individuals, though it has been surmised that there is little overlap in the home ranges of female moles.

Moles are believed to remain solitary as adults and avoid contact with other moles. However, there are at least two exceptions. One occurs in spring, when the males start to move around and leave their range in search of females. They may move about for several weeks, even after all the females in an area have mated. The other exception is that occasionally some tunnels are used by several moles; these tunnels are, in a sense, like highways. This communal use suggests that the social system of moles is more complex than we think.

Moles occasionally venture above the snow, but so rarely that there are few good records of their tracks. You will not see mole scats, for they are left in the tunnels underground.

Clues:	Small ridges of earth	Common	See page 94
	Mounds of earth	Common	See page 96
	Holes in ground	Uncommon	See page 84

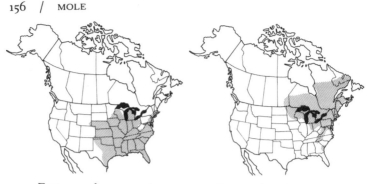

Eastern-mole range map   Star-nosed–mole range map

Food and Feeding Habits

The tunnels of moles are used primarily for collecting food. Once the tunnels are dug, the mole circulates around the network and eats any insects or earthworms that have fallen or ventured in. When existing tunnels do not provide enough food, moles construct more. Occasionally moles travel above ground and capture prey, primarily insects. They have even been known to catch and eat frogs and small mice.

A mole eats quite a bit during a day, the equivalent of approximately one-third its body weight. The bulk of its food is composed of earthworms, at least in habitats where earthworms are prevalent. The larvae of insects are the next most common food. The mole will also kill and eat mice or possibly other moles that it meets in its tunnels, and will feed on any carrion it finds. In a few cases, moles are known to have eaten mushrooms.

Feeding tunnels used in summer tend to be those nearer the surface since worms and insects are more likely to be plentiful there at this time. In cold weather the insects and worms move to lower soil layers, so the moles use deeper tunnels to catch them.

The fact that the star-nosed mole is an accomplished swimmer allows it to take advantage of water insects and their larvae. If a star-nosed mole lives near water, these insects may compose the bulk of its food. The diet of a star-nosed mole that resides most of the time on land will resemble that of the eastern mole.

You won't see any signs of feeding, for the mole eats all of its prey.

Young moles

Family Life

For most of the year moles are primarily solitary. But in spring males tend to move about, often going long distances in search of females. Some of this travel can be above ground. In early spring the male's testes start to increase in size and the female develops an opening into her vagina, which seals over as soon as the young are born. Not much is known about the courtship of moles or periods of estrus in the female. Through most of the year, two moles will fight upon meeting, but during the mating season males and females are more tolerant of each other and may even remain together in the same nest for a time.

Soon after mating, however, the male and female separate and the female raises the young alone. All moles have nests in which to rest or raise young. They are cavities about 8 inches in diameter hollowed out along a tunnel. The pregnant mole comes to the surface to collect dry leaves and grasses and takes them down to line the nest. The nest can also be above ground, under logs, and in piles of leaf litter. One mole may have as many as seven nests in its burrow system. There are actually no outward signs of the nests, for there are no direct entrances to them from the surface.

Gestation lasts about 4 to 6 weeks, and the young are usually born in April and May. The average litter size is 4, though this can range from 3 to 7. There is only 1 litter per year.

Not much is known about the birth and development of moles in North America. The following is a description of the European mole, *Talpa europaea*, which has been more fully studied. At birth the young are hairless and pink. They may not be able to control their body temperature and so are very dependent on their mother and the nest for warmth. When she leaves to feed on her own, their body temperature drops. After about 2½ weeks their fur has grown, and after about 3 weeks the young are almost adult size and their eyes are

---

Mole — Quick Reference

Habitat: Dry or moist loose soil in woods, fields, swamps
Home range: ½ to 2 acres
Food: Small animals, insects, earthworms, mice, etc.
Mating: February to April, approximately
Gestation: 4 to 6 weeks
Young born: March to June
Number of young: 3 to 7
Number of litters: 1
Young independent: 4 to 7 weeks

open for the first time. After 4 weeks they begin to leave the nest but may stay with the mother for another 2 or 3 weeks. After this they go out on their own and migrate over land to find new spots in which to live. This is a time when many of these younger moles are seen, either caught by cats or run over by cars on roads.

Moles are believed to live about 3 years in the wild, but in captivity they have lived up to 5 years.

Clues: Nest   Rare   See page 100

Adult cottontail

EASTERN COTTONTAIL /
Sylvilagus floridanus

IT WAS JUST AFTER an early summer thunderstorm had passed. Our dirt driveway was spotted with puddles, and the meadow grasses on either side were bent over with the weight of the raindrops. We were driving out, and far ahead, at the edge of the driveway, we saw three small brown forms. Mourning doves often feed at this spot, but these did not look like doves. As we drove closer, we could clearly see that they were three baby eastern cottontails. Our proximity did not seem to frighten them, and when we were quite near, we stopped the car and used it as a blind from which to watch.

The little cottontails hopped about with lightning speed, sometimes jumping into the air, other times shaking their heads to get the raindrops off. It started to rain again. Two of the rabbits sat up on their hind legs and looked around alertly; the other jumped and kicked its heels into the air. The rain did not seem to bother them. As we started the car, the cottontails scampered into the grasses. We looked for them and for signs of their mother as we passed by, but they were too quick for us.

When you say "rabbit," one of the first images that comes to mind is Beatrix Potter's Peter Rabbit, wearing a blue coat and eating carrots from Mr. McGregor's garden. Peter's little burrow with furnished rooms makes us think that cottontails live underground. In fact, they do in Europe, where Peter lived. But North American cottontails do not construct burrows; they spend most of their lives above ground. The young are born in a nest-like depression in the ground, adults rest in "forms" on the surface of the ground, and the rest of the time they hop about, nibbling food and eluding predators. Only in severe weather does the cottontail retreat temporarily to better cover, such as a rock crevice, a hollow log, or an old woodchuck burrow, where it remains near the entrance.

It is interesting to compare the cottontail with its relative the snowshoe hare. One important difference between the two is that cottontail young are altricial and the young of hares are precocial. In other words, cottontail young are very dependent on the parent because their eyes are closed, they have little hair, and they cannot hop around. The young of hares are fully furred, can see, and can move about as soon as they are born. One wonders why this difference exists when so many other features of these two animals are nearly identical.

The eastern cottontail, *Sylvilagus floridanus*, is in the family Leporidae (composed of rabbits and hares), and the order Lagomorpha (which includes rabbits, hares, and pikas). There are eight native species of rabbits in North America, and all are in the genus *Sylvilagus*. The eastern cottontail is the most widely distributed. It is 14 to 18 inches long and weighs 2 to 4 pounds. The fur on its upperparts varies from grayish brown to reddish brown mixed with black. Its underparts are whitish, and its fluffy tail is brown above and white below. The nape of its neck is rust-colored, and it may have a white spot on its forehead. The European rabbit, *Oryctolagus cuniculus*, has been introduced into a few areas of North America, but its populations are still small.

Getting Around

Eastern cottontails are most active from sunset until dawn. In summer, they may feed also during the day, since the lush vegetation provides both good cover and abundant food. When eastern cottontails are not active, they are usually nestled into their "form" — a shallow depression 4 to 6 inches wide and 6 to 8 inches long. Forms occur in meadows, hay fields, or thickets, and are usually located next to some extra cover, such as a tuft of grass, a fallen log, or a brush pile. Here the animal is protected from the elements and predators. In bad weather, a cottontail may seek greater protection and go into the entrance of a woodchuck den or some natural cavity.

An eastern cottontail establishes a home range and remains in it throughout the year. Home ranges vary in size from 1 to 14 acres, but usually average about 5, with males generally having larger ranges than females. Several eastern cottontails may live in the same area and have overlapping home ranges, for the animals are not territorial. In winter, the location of the home range may shift slightly to include better cover and additional food.

Throughout their home range, eastern cottontails have well-worn trails. In shrubbery the trails resemble much-used paths 4 to 5 inches wide; in tall grasses they are more like tunnels 5 to 6 inches in diameter. Cottontails also travel along human paths and the edges of roads. When frightened, a cottontail usually dashes to its nearest trail and then follows it. Even when chased, it will try to stay on its trails, for its knowledge of them is an advantage over a predator. When there is snow, the trails are obvious because they are packed down by the animal's repeated use.

Within an eastern cottontail's home range, there is usually a place where the animal dust bathes. This is a small spot about a foot in diameter that has been cleared of vegetation, possibly through the animal's scratching or through repeated wear. The cottontail rolls in this area to help rid itself of external parasites.

There is some evidence that eastern cottontails mark certain spots within their home range by rubbing the sides of their face on twigs. Other species, such as the swamp rabbit, *Sylvilagus aquaticus*, mark more frequently, using scent glands under their chin. The purpose of the marking is not known. The scats of cottontails are not believed to be used for marking. They are deposited throughout the animal's home range, expecially in areas where it feeds.

Clues:

Tracks	Common	See page 18
Trails	Common	See page 106
Holes in the ground	Common	See page 86
Matted vegetation	Uncommon	See page 104
Scraped depression	Uncommon	See page 94
Tunnels through snow	Uncommon	See page 108

Cottontail range map

Food and Feeding Habits

At dusk, cottontails leave their forms and come out to eat. They nibble at any kind of choice vegetation, taking short hopping steps between plants. It has been said that it's easier to list the foods cottontails *don't* eat than those they do. It seems that if a plant is able to grow, a cottontail is able to eat it.

In summer cottontails eat bluegrass, orchard grass, timothy, quack grass, plantain, chickweed, ragweed, alfalfa, clover, dandelions, goldenrod, yarrow, all types of berries and fruits, lettuce, beans, peas, cabbage, and cornstalks. They do not, however, dig up carrots or bulbs.

In winter cottontails eat many of the same grasses as they do in summer, but when these are covered by snow, they turn to woody plants. They eat the smaller twigs, and the bark off the larger branches. Some of their favorite woody plants are sumac, maple, apple, rose, blackberry, and oak. They will dig down through the snow in winter to get at frozen apples. For water, they eat snow in winter and may lick the morning dew off wildflowers and grasses in summer.

Cottontails tend to leave their droppings wherever they have been eating, and this is an excellent sign of their presence. It is extremely common to find rabbit scats under shrubbery, especially in winter when the scats are obvious on the snow. However, cottontails are not as common as the number of their droppings would suggest, for a single animal will void 250 to 500 droppings per day. Like several other common animals that feed on vegetation — beaver, vole, and snowshoe hare — cottontails reingest one type of their droppings. These are usually soft pellets that are voided during the day while the animal is at rest. The cottontail swallows them directly from its anus without chewing. Reingestion, or coprophagy, apparently allows for further digestion of plant material, much like cud chewing in ruminants.

Over the years the saplings from which cottontails eat woody twigs acquire a distinctive shape. Because their new shoots are regularly cut off, the saplings keep producing new branches at the top and look stunted. When rabbits cut off twigs, they do so with a neat 45-degree-angle snip, just as if someone took a knife and made a diagonal cut. This is a distinctive sign of rabbit or hare feeding. Deer, which also eat twigs in winter, rip twigs off. You can also look for evidence of gnawing on the bark of branches. You can distinguish the gnawing of rabbits from that of other animals by the size of their teeth marks.

Clues:	Scats	Common	See page 56
	Twig ends bitten	Common	See page 80
	Bark chewed off	Uncommon	See page 74

Family Life

In the North, the eastern cottontail's breeding season begins in January or February and lasts until September. In the South, eastern cottontails may breed at any time of year.

Young cottontails

Several studies have shown that eastern cottontails have a social organization. Males have a dominance hierarchy in which the most dominant have more frequent aggressive encounters with other males and do the most mating with females. Males are most aggressive to one another when they are trying to make contact with a female in estrus. The most dominant males fend off other males by chasing. Another dominance gesture is scratching and raking at the grass with the forepaws. Actual fights between males are rare. Females are dominant over males, except during estrus. There is some evidence of a dominance hierarchy among females, but in general they do not encounter each other as often as males do and are more tolerant of one another when they do.

The most dominant males have the largest home ranges, for they try to contact as many females as possible. When a male finds a female, he approaches her. If she is aggressive toward him, then he may move on. If she is less aggressive, or he persists in his approach, several types of behavior may occur: He may move toward her, and she in turn may rise up on her hind legs and strike out with her forefeet; he may make a quick dash to her side and spray urine on her, after which she would groom; or he may run right at her, in which case she would jump in the air and urinate on him as he passes under her. Any of these actions can be repeated, and they may occur in any sequence.

When a female is finally receptive to a male, she crouches down and the male approaches her from behind. He mounts her and copulates within a few seconds. Then the two break away. Male and female cottontails mate with many partners. Copulation stimulates ovulation, which occurs about 10 hours after mating.

Before the young are born, the female prepares a nest. These are usually made in open fields but can be found in thickets, orchards, scrubby woods, or near the bases of trees. To make the nest the female digs a hole 6 to 7 inches long, 5 inches wide, and 3 to 4 inches deep, and lines it with grasses and the fur she pulls from her body.

The average period of gestaton is 28 days, but the time can vary by several days on either side. The young are born in or near the nest, and there are usually about 4 or 5 in a litter. At birth the baby cottontails are about 4 inches long, weigh an ounce or less, and are covered by sparse hairs. They are generally quiet as they sleep and snuggle together in the nest. The mother does not stay with them at the nest; instead, she covers them with the soft nesting material and feeds nearby, returning to the nest to feed the young only at night. This behavior has undoubtedly developed to protect the young from being found by predators. When the mother nurses the young, she crouches over the nest and they instinctively reach up to her nipples.

In a little less than a week, the young have fur and their eyes are open. In 10 days they may hop about if disturbed at the nest, and at 2 weeks they can make their first trips from the nest. At first they venture only a short distance and then return to the nest. Gradually they explore farther, and each may make its own little form to stay in. They are weaned at 4 to 5 weeks, and during this time they wander about with the mother or in the company of one another. Eventually they disperse and find their own areas with food and cover. At 5 months they weigh as much as a small adult, about 3 pounds, and at 6 months they can breed.

Amazingly, right after the female has given birth and covered over her young in the nest, she is ready to mate again. A special odor, called a pheromone, is secreted just before the young are born, and it attracts males. A number of males may follow the female around at this time and she may be quite aggressive to them. High-ranking males near her will be aggressive to each other, and the most dominant will mate with her. A female cottontail can have 3 to 4 litters per year, and the average cottontail lives ½ to 2 years in the wild.

Eastern cottontails have three vocalizations: a high squeal given by the female during copulation; a loud high scream of distress; and a grunting noise given by the female when her nest is approached.

Clues: Nest   Uncommon   See page 100

Eastern Cottontail — Quick Reference

Habitat: Brushy areas of woods, fields, suburbs

Home range: 1 to 14 acres, average 5 acres

Food: Lush vegetation, buds, bark

Mating: January to September in North, all year in South

Gestation: 4 weeks

Young born: February to October in North, all year in South

Number of young: 4 to 5

Number of litters: 3 to 4

Young independent: Weaned at 4 to 5 weeks

Adult snowshoe hare

SNOWSHOE HARE /
Lepus americanus

THERE WERE NO TRACKS in the middle of the field, so we moved toward an area thick with shrubs and saplings. As we got closer, we came upon the trail of a deer mouse; it had scampered under cover and then headed out into the open, where it explored several tufts of grass poking through the snow; then it headed back for cover. At the edge of the field was a path leading into the woods. Once we were on the path, there were tracks all through the brush on either side. Some places were even packed-down runways. We knelt down in the snow to get a closer look and sort out some of the individual prints. There, right at our feet, was a large triangular track with four big toes at its broader end. It was clearly the track of a snowshoe hare. In fact, all the tracks were from snowshoe hares, and after looking around we realized why. Throughout the area were lots of sapling birches, willows, and aspens — all favored foods of the hare. We saw where they had nibbled the branches and even left some of their droppings in the snow. It was perfect snowshoe-hare habitat.

The large feet of the snowshoe hare are one of its distinctive features, and they seem to be adapted primarily for travel on snow. In deep snow the hare can support itself on the surface while other animals that are heavier or the same weight but with smaller feet will sink into it. This support helps the hare in two ways. First, it gives the animal an edge over its larger predators, such as the bobcat; and second, with each successive snowfall, the hares can reach a new layer of branches and twigs on which to feed.

The snowshoe hare, *Lepus americanus*, is in the family Leporidae, and the order Lagomorpha, which includes rabbits, hares, and pikas. There are eight species of hare in North America, all in the genus *Lepus*, but the snowshoe hare has the widest distribution. It inhabits areas with heavy snow and can be found throughout Canada and New England and down the mountain ranges of the Rockies and the Alleghenies.

The snowshoe hare is sometimes called the varying hare because the color of its coat changes. In autumn, the snowshoe hare begins to change from its brown summer coat into its winter white. At first it is brown with patches of white, which helps it blend in with the dried vegetation sticking through the shallow snow. By the time winter has fully arrived, its coat is all white except for its nose and ears, which are tipped with black. Unlike the arctic hare, which has pure white fur, just the tips of the snowshoe's fur turn white; the fur is gray underneath. In spring, the hare's coat reverts from white to brown. Molting is caused by the changes in length of day rather than in temperature.

Getting Around

Snowshoe hares are nocturnal, being most active at dusk and before dawn. Occasionally they may be seen moving about during the day, but normally at this time they rest in their "forms." These are slightly hollowed-out areas on the ground within some cover, such as the lower bough of an evergreen; they may be on a knoll, next to a rock, in hollow logs, under fallen trees, or in a clump of shrubs or weeds. When in its form, the animal rests in such a way that it is ready to leap out in case danger approaches, though it tends to rely on its camouflage and will leave the form only as a last resort.

Not much is known about the social structure of snowshoe hares. Outside the breeding season there seems to be no antagonism between hares in a given area, and the home ranges of individuals seem to overlap. Home-range size depends on population density, season, and habitat. In open woods, home ranges tend to be larger than those in areas of dense underbrush. Home-range sizes vary from about 15 to 30 acres. Some people believe that males may have larger home ranges than females. In a single night's wanderings, a snowshoe hare moves over an average of 4 acres.

Within their home range, hares develop a network of well-used trails and runways through the grasses and vegetation. In early winter, these runways take the form of packed paths through the soft snow. The trails are used to get from one feeding or resting place to another. Many other animals use these packed trails; trapping studies have shown that the most frequent users are red squirrels, porcupines, weasels, and ruffed grouse. In late winter, when the snow is more solid, the hares may not use the runways as much. Snowshoe hares prefer to remain in dense cover, so most of the trails are within shrubbery or dense evergreens; only occasionally, when there is no protected route between good sources of food, will they cross open areas. In some areas where hares are abundant, their runways may also be obvious in summer, with the earth and vegetation packed down 1 to 2 inches below ground level.

The snowshoe hare's main defense is to try to sit still and remain unnoticed. If danger is near, the hare alternates hopping 10 to 15 feet with sitting still, moving away all the time. Once discovered by a predator, snowshoes occasionally enter the burrow of another animal but usually depend on their speed and leaping ability to escape. They can run up to 30 miles per hour and leap 12 feet at a bound. When chased, they usually circle around their home range, for their knowledge of its trails is one of their advantages. In the face of danger, hares may thump their hind foot one or several times; they can also make hissing and grunting noises, and a high-pitched scream when they are caught. Among the predators of the hare are the coyote, bobcat, fox, mink, great horned owl, and goshawk.

The winter coat of the snowshoe hare not only camouflages the animal but also conserves up to 25 percent more warmth than its summer coat. The snowshoe hare's entire metabolism slows down in winter, so that the animal requires less oxygen and fewer calories and is better able to survive the cold.

Clues:	Tracks	Common	See page 18
	Scats	Common	See page 56
	Trails and runways	Common	See page 106
	Matted vegetation	Uncommon	See page 104

Snowshoe-hare range map

Food and Feeding Habits

Snowshoe hares tend to be vegetarians, although occasionally they feed on carrion. Their diet changes with the seasons. In summer, when food is abundant, the snowshoe's diet includes all kinds of grasses as well as the flowers and leaves from many wildflowers, among them dandelion and clover. Hares may also occasionally eat ferns.

Once the snow arrives, the hares switch to feeding on the twigs of trees and shrubs and the leaves of evergreens. Some of their favorite winter foods include willow, aspen, birch, alder, pine, spruce, and fir. Small winter twigs are snipped off at a neat 45-degree angle, unlike the clippings of deer, which are roughly torn off. Hares may eat only the bark off larger branches, and they do this by biting sideways along the branch.

In a given area the hares will eat all of the twigs they can reach. Because they can support themselves on snow, they can stand on top of it and reach a whole new set of twigs. Thus, a heavy snowfall can be a great advantage to the hares, since it makes more food available.

Snowshoe hares have two types of droppings: a hard, round pellet and a soft one covered with mucus. The soft pellets are voided during the day, and the hares reingest them by taking them directly from the anus. The pellets are high in protein and B vitamins; by reingesting them, the hare gets additional nutritional value from its food.

Clues:	Twig ends bitten	Common	See page 80
	Bark chewed off	Common	See page 74

Family Life

In the northern states, the breeding season for snowshoe hares starts in March. It begins a little later in Canada and a little earlier in southern states. Its onset may be controlled by the length of the day. The animals are most easily seen during the breeding season, for they seem to move about a great deal at that time.

Outside the breeding season, snowshoe hares in a given area appear to get along with one another and may be seen alone or in groups, but during the breeding season they become more aggressive. Males may fight with other males, causing wounds with their teeth, and males can be seen chasing females several weeks before actual mating occurs.

Snowshoe hares have some unusual pre-mating activities. These include the male approaching the female and sniffing her, and both hares jumping alternatively over each other and, while in midair, urinating on the one below. Both male and female do the jumps and urinating and in no particular order. Sometimes when one hare is in midair, the other runs beneath it. Mating may occur several times over the course of a couple of hours.

Once the female is fertilized, gestation takes from 34 to 40 days. The female can give birth to 1 to 6 young but usually has 3 in her first

Young snowshoe hares

litter and 4 to 5 in subsequent litters. The young are born in dense cover but not in any kind of nest. They are precocial, or independent, at birth: They are fully furred, have their eyes open, and can walk and hop soon after being born. This is one of the main differences between hares and rabbits, for rabbit young are altricial, meaning that their eyes are closed, they have little fur, and they are totally dependent on their mother for warmth and protection.

Snowshoe-hare babies nurse right after they are born. For the first day or two they stay near the mother; afterward they scatter to different locations and stay hidden during most of the day. At this time the mother stays in her own form, which may be located up to 250 yards from the babies. Only once a day do the mother and young come together so that the latter can nurse for 5 to 10 minutes; then the young go into hiding again and the mother feeds or goes back to her form. The young continue to nurse in this way for 25 to 28 days, but by the time they are 2 weeks old they also begin to nibble green vegetation. Young hares reach an adult weight of 2 to 4 pounds in 3 to 5 months, and are sexually mature by the time they are a year old. Most snowshoe hares do not live more than 3 years in the wild.

As soon as the young are born, the female is again in estrus and ready for mating. Because of this, she may have up to 4 litters in a year, although the average is 2 or 3. The last litters are born in July or August. Strangely, litters in the southern part of the range tend to be smaller than those in northern areas. Litter size may also vary in relation to snowfall the previous winter. A large snowfall is usually followed by large litters the next spring, perhaps because the deep snow lifts the hares closer to edible twigs of shrubs and trees and thus makes more food available.

Studies have shown that snowshoe-hare populations fluctuate greatly, from about 0.1 hare per acre to 4 or 5 per acre within an approximate 10-year cycle. There is no definitive explanation for this, though it seems to be in some way connected with predators and the availability of food. As the hare population starts to rise, so do the populations of hare predators, but these have little effect on the rising hare population. Soon the large number of hares depletes the available winter food to such an extent that the hares apparently die of starvation and the population starts to drop. As this happens, predators take a greater toll and further the decline in hares. The population of predators in turn declines due to the scarcity of hares, at which point food sources also recover. With fewer predators and more food, the snowshoe-hare population starts to rise again.

Snowshoe Hare — Quick Reference

Habitat: Brushy areas, woods, fields, swamps
Home range: 15 to 30 acres
Food: Vegetation, buds, bark
Mating: February to July
Gestation: 34 to 40 days
Young born: March to August
Number of young: 1 to 6
Number of litters: 1 to 4
Young independent: Weaned at 3 to 4 weeks

Adult chipmunks

EASTERN CHIPMUNK /
Tamias striatus

W E ONCE HAD A SPECIAL glimpse of chipmunks. We were out
watching bird behavior at a rural nature center. There was a bird
feeder nearby and a split-rail fence leading from the feeder to a patch
of woods. We caught sight of something running across the bottom
rail of the fence; then it stopped and hid in the hole of the first post. It
was going in the direction of the feeder. We stayed still and it moved
again, but it was not alone. It was a mother chipmunk followed by
three baby chipmunks, and each was running with its tail straight up
in the air. Undoubtedly, she was introducing the youngsters to one of
her favorite sources of food.

The eastern chipmunk is certainly one of our woodland's most
charming inhabitants. Scampering busily about as it collects nuts for
its growing hoard, it can be seen at a woodpile, under a bird feeder, or
racing along the top of a stone wall. Fall is its busiest time of year, for
it is collecting a large supply of nuts for winter. Watch a chipmunk,
and you will see that it collects food in its large cheek pouches,
stuffing them until you would think they would burst. It then runs off
to an underground burrow. If you could see into the burrow, you
might well be surprised at the pile of food it has managed to collect.

If you have chipmunks living near you, take some time to watch
them; you may even be able to follow one to its burrow entrance.
They are especially entertaining when there are several living near

each other, for they are constantly involved in chasing their neighbors. By watching closely, perhaps with binoculars, you can come to recognize individuals, for the shape of their tails vary. They can be long, short, tapered, or flat, and some chipmunks may even lose part of their tail in a fight, causing the end hairs to grow in a different pattern.

The eastern chipmunk, *Tamias striatus*, is in the squirrel family Sciuridae, which is in the order Rodentia, or rodents. The Latin name for the eastern chipmunk means striped *(striatus)* storer *(Tamias)*. There are about twenty species of chipmunks in North America. The only one in the East is *Tamias striatus*; the other nineteen are smaller, are all in the genus *Eutamias*, and live in the West.

Eastern chipmunks are reddish brown with one dark stripe down the center of the back and one white stripe in between two black stripes on each side. They are 5 to 6 inches long with a 3- to 4-inch tail, and they weigh 2¼ to 4½ ounces. They run with their tails straight up.

Getting Around

The center of a chipmunk's life is its burrow, and every chipmunk must find or construct one for itself. A burrow offers security, protection from bad weather (be it heat or cold), and most importantly, a place where its valuable hoard of acorns and other nuts can be stored for winter.

It is remarkable that such a small animal is so accomplished an architect. A chipmunk burrow is constructed in such a way that there are no signs of excavation around it. The entrance is a round hole about 1½ to 2 inches in diameter. The chipmunk begins construction by digging a working tunnel. It digs by biting roots with its teeth and scratching earth with its paws and then bulldozing the dirt out with its nose. Excavated earth begins to accumulate at the entrance to the working tunnel, but this doesn't matter, since this will not be the final entrance. After going down about 10 to 30 inches, the chipmunk hollows out a chamber 6 to 8 inches high and about 1 foot in diameter. This will be filled with a nest of chewed-up dried leaves and grasses that the chipmunk carries in from the ground above. The nest is the place where the chipmunk sleeps, gives birth, and hibernates for winter. The chipmunk may store the nuts in this chamber or dig additional storage chambers.

Next, the chipmunk digs outward from the side of the chamber, making the tunnel that will be the real entrance. The entrance is dug from below so there is never any trace of dirt to betray its presence to predators, and the dirt from it is used to plug up the working tunnel. When finished, the chipmunk has a clean entrance that may be as much as 10 to 40 feet from where the animal first started digging.

Some burrows are simple, containing just a single chamber and a few tunnels, but others may be much more complex with several chambers and up to 100 feet of tunnels. Tunnels connecting chambers may be 3 to 4 inches in diameter. Females with young usually live in more complex burrows. Chipmunks frequently spend time elaborating on and fixing up their burrows. They may change the entrance hole often, but only one entrance is used at any one time. Sometimes a chipmunk will seal off the entrance hole from the inside when it goes to sleep for the night and then reopen it in the morning. And before going into its burrow for the winter, it may plug the entrance with soil for added protection from weather and predators.

Chipmunks are active during the day and go to sleep at night in their burrow. They are up at dawn and may begin their day by singing from their favorite perch near the burrow entrance. They spend most of the day, when they are not in the breeding season, alternating periods of foraging and food storing with periods of resting. They have been known to rest in one spot, such as a tree limb, for up to two hours. They are always very alert, and when moving about will stop every few seconds to listen and sniff the air. They return to home base frequently between foraging trips.

Adult chipmunks are solitary, and each lives within its own burrow and moves about over a home range that varies in size from about ½ to 3 acres. Home ranges may expand or shift in fall, when the chipmunk needs to collect food for winter storage, and males may extend their home ranges to contact females during breeding periods. In general, the home ranges of males are larger than those of females. Parts of a home range may overlap with the home ranges of neighboring chipmunks.

Within its home range, a chipmunk has a defended area, or territory. This usually is centered on the entrance of the burrow and extends within a radius of about 45 feet. A chipmunk will defend this space against other chipmunks and will chase off or fight those that enter. Often if one chipmunk is pursuing another, the fleeing chipmunk will turn around and become the pursuer once it enters its own territory.

Chipmunks are not usually seen in the winter because they spend some of the winter hibernating underground. A lot remains to be learned about chipmunk hibernation, and researchers are still trying to unravel its mysteries. One thing is certain — the hibernation habits of the chipmunk are extremely variable. In the North, chipmunks may stay below ground for several months, but in the South they may hibernate for only a few weeks. Even within the same area, chipmunks may have different habits; some may hibernate for a long time, some for a short time, and some may never hibernate at all but remain active throughout the winter. Individual chipmunks may change their habits from winter to winter.

In general, chipmunk hibernation seems to involve a slow transition from a fully active to a fully dormant state. The chipmunk enters hibernation through several cycles of semitorpidity, during which its body temperature and breathing rate decrease in steps alternating with periods of normal activity. When its body temperature has decreased 5 to 7 degrees Celsius and its breathing rate is 20 breaths per minute, the chipmunk has reached full torpidity. It will then increase the length of its torpid state until 3 to 4 days of torpidity alternate with a day of activity, during which the chipmunk is active enough to eat and eliminate. All this time it stays within the burrow.

The best way to find a chipmunk is to hear it. Listen for its "chip" call when you walk through the woods, for a chipmunk often gives a loud warning when it hears you coming. Chipmunks have several other sounds as well, but the high-pitched chip call is probably the one most often heard. People often confuse it with a bird sound. It can be made singly or in a series, as in chipmunk "singing," in which as many as 180 chips per minute can be sounded for as long as a half-hour.

We once were sitting on an old stump near a group of oak trees that had just dropped their acorns. We heard a chipmunk begin chipping, and shortly there were six chipmunks all singing at once. The amazing thing was that they all were chipping on a slightly different pitch, and we wondered if this helped them individually recognize one another.

Another sound a chipmunk makes is a "chuck," which is similar to the chip but lower-pitched. Continuous chucks may indicate a chipmunk is nervous, as for example when a hawk flies overhead. Chucks are also given singly in aggressive interactions between chipmunks. Chipmunks produce several trills consisting of rapidly strung together chips or chucks as well. These may be given when a chipmunk is startled or when it is in an aggressive encounter with another chipmunk.

When chipmunks are close to one another, such as during mating chases or during interactions between a mother and young, they give soft chattering sounds.

Chipmunk range map

Clues: Holes in the ground   Common   See page 84
            Tracks   Uncommon   See page 30
            Scats   Rare   See page 54

Food and Feeding Habits

Chipmunks have a nearly insatiable urge to store food, and this urge is an organizing principle of their lives. Indeed, they spend a good deal of their lives, especially in fall, doing nothing else. The food is stored in their burrows and used to live on through the winter, when they periodically awake from hibernation. This is one reason they are so aggressive to other chipmunks that come near their burrow: They are defending not only their home but also their precious store of food. Pilfering from burrows has been known to occur, and if food is not abundant, it may be more efficient for a thief to enter another chipmunk's burrow and stuff its cheeks than to spend the time looking on its own. To counter pilfering by other chipmunks, burrow owners sometimes bury food in various locations near their burrow. One occupant whose burrow was robbed was seen to immediately go and dig up one of those caches to replace the losses from its burrow.

Chipmunks will often store much more food than they can possibly eat in a year. In an experiment, naturalist John Burroughs once discovered that in 3 days a chipmunk stored 5 quarts of hickory nuts, 2 quarts of chestnuts, and a quantity of shelled corn. All in all, that chipmunk stored a bushel of food. Even when spring comes, a chipmunk will rely on the food it has stored in its hoard until new spring food is available.

A chipmunk goes about the ground foraging, probably relying on smell more than eyesight to help it locate its food. Its cheek pouches are marvelous little shopping bags for carrying food. They are located along the cheek and neck just under the skin. There is an opening to each pouch just between the teeth and lips. One chipmunk was found to have 70 sunflower seeds in its pouches. The chipmunk empties its pouches by squeezing its cheeks with its paws.

Chipmunks eat a variety of foods, but their main diet is composed of seeds, nuts, and fruits. These include acorns, hickory nuts, beech-nuts, partridge berries, blueberries, elderberries, and berries from dogwood, virburnum, and woodbine. They also eat mushrooms. They are excellent climbers and can go high into trees to gather food. Occasionally they dig up bulbs in people's gardens, but on the good side, they also eat beetles, slugs, cutworms, and wireworms. Chipmunks have been known to eat other animals such as frogs, salamanders, and bird's eggs. The chipmunk may venture outside its territory when there is a rich crop of nuts somewhere else.

Many of the signs of chipmunk feeding are similar to those of mice, red squirrels, and gray squirrels, and it is often not possible to distinguish between these animals' signs. Two common signs of the chipmunk are chewing marks on the top of mushrooms and small bits of nut shells or husks on the top of a stump or rock.

Clues:	Chewed nuts or cones	Common	See page 124
	Collections of nuts, seeds, or cones	Uncommon	See page 122
	Gnawed bones	Uncommon	See page 124

Family Life

Chipmunks can have two breeding periods in a year. The first lasts from February through April; the second is in June and July. In certain years chipmunks may not breed in one of these periods. Why this occurs is not fully understood.

Before the spring breeding period, males emerge from hibernation ahead of the females. At this time they may explore female territories. Occasionally a male may try to occupy a female's territory before she emerges and keep other males off it. During courtship the males compete with one another for dominance while chasing in a line after the female. If the female is not yet receptive, she may turn fiercely on a male and bite him.

After a while, the female becomes receptive and mates with one of the males. This may be preceded by some nose touching, licking of

Young chipmunks

each other, and lying about in the same area. When a male approaches a female and gives rapid tail movements, this signals his intention to mate. Mating lasts for 1 to 2 minutes with the male on the back of the female, holding on to her hips. After mating, the two remain together for a while and groom, and then the female chases the male away.

Females that are born in the spring are able to mate in the summer of the same year, when they are 2½ to 3 months old. If they don't breed at this time, they wait until the following spring. Males breed the year following their birth at 8 to 12 months old.

The female is pregnant for 31 days, and near the end of this time she may look noticeably plumper. During her pregnancy she can be seen carrying leaves into her burrow to be used as bedding material in her nest chamber. At birth, the young are tiny, blind, and hairless, and have reddish transparent skin. Spring litters are born in April and May; summer litters are born in July and August. There are usually 4 to 5 in a litter, but there may be as many as 7 or as few as 3.

After she gives birth, the female spends most of her time in the burrow, going outside for brief moments only. The young remain underground as they develop. At 2 weeks they have grown fine fuzzy hair; at 3 weeks they can hear; and at 4 weeks they can see. At this time they also begin to be weaned.

At about 6 weeks they start to venture out of the burrow. They are fully furred and look just like adult chipmunks but are about two-thirds adult size. Their heads are longer and leaner and their tails may be a little thinner. When they first emerge, they stay close to the burrow, and the mother keeps a watchful eye on them. Gradually they travel farther and farther away. This is one of the most social times for them. At first the young interact and play with one another and explore the outside world. Gradually the relationships between siblings become more aggressive, as does that between the young and their mother. Finally, about 1 to 2 weeks after emerging from the burrow, the mother refuses them entrance to the burrow. They are now on their own. Dispersal can be abrupt or gradual, usually occurring over a period of 2 weeks.

Newly dispersed chipmunks must move quickly to find food and a place to stay. If they are lucky, they find a burrow vacant nearby and will move in and settle near their mother's territory. Others leave the area completely.

A curious thing happens at about the time the young disperse. Most of the adults in the area will begin singing — giving continuous "chip-chip-chip" calls from near their burrows. The singing may help advertise the presence of occupied territories. Singing occurs during both the late spring and early fall dispersion.

As the young disperse, they encounter adults who will be aggressive to them and not let them on their territories. The young may become transient until they can either find an abandoned burrow or build one for themselves. Spring-born young have more time to find or build a burrow and stock it. Fall-born young have to hurry to get set up by winter, although a potential advantage to their wanderings is the accidental discovery of a good acorn supply.

The average life span of a chipmunk in the wild is about 2 to 3 years, although a chipmunk in captivity can live as long as 8 years.

Eastern Chipmunk — Quick Reference

Habitat: Brushy areas, stone walls in woods, suburbs
Home range: ½ to 3 acres
Food: Seeds, nuts, fruits
Mating: February to April, June to July
Gestation: 31 days
Young born: April to May and July to August
Number of young: 3 to 7
Number of litters: 1 to 2
Young independent: Weaned at 4 weeks, independent at 8
   weeks

Adult woodchuck

WOODCHUCK /
Marmota monax

ONE MIDSUMMER DAY when walking through an area with wood-chuck burrows, we heard some rustling among the meadow grasses. We stepped carefully over to the spot and there, bounding through the tall grasses like a dog in deep snow, was a baby woodchuck. It was incredibly cute, and we wondered why it was out alone and where its home was. We stood back so as not to scare it and followed the sound of the rustling and the movement of the grasses.

The young woodchuck headed to a nearby woods where there were several burrow systems. It ended up behind a tree and just waited there. We sat down on a log close by and waited, too, until we heard the short, sharp whistle of another woodchuck, followed by its low "churring" sound. It was given several more times. Was this the call of the mother? The young woodchuck made no obvious re-sponse to the sound but after a while did go farther into the woods. We decided not to follow it for fear of keeping it from getting where it needed to go.

True to their name, woodchucks were originally forest dwellers; they lived in the Northeast and westward across Canada. When the land was cleared by humans, the woodchucks left the wooded areas to take advantage of the abundant food in meadows, especially plentiful in summer. They are expert diggers and are said to be able to dig a

5-foot tunnel in a day. They are also good swimmers and can easily climb trees if they need to.

Woodchucks are a member of the squirrel family and a close relative of all the marmots that live in the West. Traditionally, the woodchuck has been considered solitary and aggressively territorial, unlike western relatives, which are known to be colonial. However, recent research has shown that the woodchuck is not territorial, tends to live in loose association with other woodchucks, and may, in fact, have some tendencies toward or vestiges of the colonial habit of other marmots.

The woodchuck is a medium-size, stocky mammal with short legs, short ears, a blunt nose, and a medium-length bushy tail. It is 13 to 24 inches long, not including tail, and weighs 5 to 14 pounds. The color of its coat ranges from yellowish brown to almost black. The woodchuck, *Marmota monax*, is one of five North American species in the genus; others are all called marmots. The woodchuck is the most widely dispersed, living in the eastern and central portions of the United States and throughout most of Canada. The various species of marmots live only in the West or just along the West Coast. All of these animals are in the family Sciuridae, which is in the order Rodentia, or rodents.

Getting Around

Woodchucks are active above ground for only an hour or two each day. In early spring their periods of activity are erratic and can occur day or night, but in summer the woodchuck falls into a regular schedule of being active for an hour in the early morning and another hour or so in the late afternoon. During this time they are either feeding or sunning themselves on a mound of earth in front of their burrow or on a nearby rock. To feed, the animal goes to the nearest spot with foliage. There are usually well-worn trails leading from burrow entrances to feeding spots, and these can easily be seen.

The other main activity of woodchucks is excavation. Burrows are continually altered and reworked, so that several times a week you are likely to see freshly excavated earth on the mounds in front of burrows. This can be a good indication of whether the burrow is in active use.

In spring, woodchucks emerge from hibernation, move from winter burrows to summer burrows, and establish home ranges, which are about 100 to 200 yards in diameter. The home ranges and feeding areas of neighboring woodchucks usually overlap. In these cases, neighboring animals establish which one is dominant through a brief skirmish or fight. From then on, the subordinate woodchuck avoids contact with the dominant one, although it may still share the same area. Woodchucks do not defend territories, but individual entrances may be aggressively defended against intruders.

Burrows are the most conspicuous feature of the woodchuck's life. The traditional description of a woodchuck burrow as having one main entrance with a mound of earth in front of it and several entrances without mounds is simply not accurate. There is much more variety in their construction. The burrows may have from one to eleven entrances, though they average about three, and there may be mounds in front of every entrance, although there are usually a few without mounds. The number of entrances in a burrow can also increase, as in breeding season, or at other times decrease, due to collapsing tunnels.

In fact, rather than thinking of a woodchuck living in a single burrow, it is more accurate to envision it living in a burrow system — a group of burrows that may or may not be connected. Overland trails usually connect most entrances within a burrow system.

A woodchuck usually makes its burrow system near those of other woodchucks, not only because of good soil conditions but also because of attraction to other woodchucks. Thus, in a given area there is usually a cluster of burrow systems and a group of woodchucks living there. At any given time, a woodchuck has one burrow system that it most often uses but does not restrict itself to. It may occasionally use other entrances and burrows nearby or even move to a new burrow system. There is a great deal of flexibility within a burrow system and within a cluster of burrows. However, it is believed that woodchucks rarely move from one burrow cluster to another.

The main requirements for a good burrow system are that it be located on a slope of 30 degrees or more, in a well-drained area, and near areas with lush vegetation and water to drink.

The woodchuck is one of the few animals in North America that goes into a period of deep hibernation. Other animals in this guide may hibernate in a semidormant state, such as the bear, chipmunk, and skunk, but none of these goes into the kind of unyielding torpor that is characteristic of the woodchuck.

In July, woodchucks start to accumulate a layer of fat that will supply them with the necessary sustenance during hibernation. By early fall they have added up to a half-inch of fat all over their bodies. At this time they may shift from their summer burrows, which tend to be out in the open, and move to winter burrows often located in woods or within hedgerows. At first a woodchuck may renovate the burrow and line the main chamber with dry grasses and leaves. When it is ready to hibernate, it enters the chamber and seals it off with earth from the tunnel. During hibernation woodchucks curl up into a ball, their temperature falls to between 38 to 57 degrees Fahrenheit, and their breathing rate slows to about once every 6 minutes. This continues until between late January and March, when they slowly come out of hibernation and become active again.

In northern areas, woodchucks start to enter hibernation in Sep-

Woodchuck range map

tember, and the majority are hibernating by mid-October. In the South, hibernation may start later and last for a very brief period.

Clues:	Holes in the ground	Common	See page 86
	Trails	Common	See page 106
	Tracks	Uncommon	See page 32
	Bark chewed off	Uncommon	See page 76

Food and Feeding Habits

Woodchucks are strictly vegetarians. Their foods include most of the herbaceous plants found in meadows and other open areas. Some of the more common of these are clover, alfalfa, dandelion, chickweed, goldenrod, aster, various grasses, fleabane, daisy, sheep's sorrel, chicory, and many others. They may also eat garden vegetables such as peas, melon, corn, and beans. Woodchucks may nibble the twigs of woody shrubs and small trees, especially brambles, apples, shadbush, and roses. Fruits such as apples may also be eaten.

Woodchucks leave very few signs of their feeding since they are constantly nibbling at all kinds of plants within their range. There is no sign of feeding that will definitely point to woodchuck presence.

Family Life

From late January to March woodchucks begin to wake up from hibernation. Generally, males emerge from their burrows before females and begin to wander about at various times of the day or night, seeking out females with which to mate. It may be that a male can smell the female in her burrow. There is in fact a particular odor in burrow entrances in spring. It is not unpleasant, and to us it smells a little like chicken broth.

Usually each male mates with more than one female. Males do not generally stay with their mates but rather remain solitary, as they do through most of the rest of the year. There are exceptions in which males have remained with their mates, and there are even cases where several woodchucks have hibernated in the same burrow.

Young woodchucks

As the time of birth approaches, the female prepares one of the chambers in her burrow system by lining it with leaves. At the same time she becomes more intolerant of other woodchucks and aggressively keeps them away from her burrow system. Gestation lasts about one month, and the young are born anywhere from late March to mid-May. There is an average of 4 to 6 young in a litter, although there may be as few as 2 or as many as 9.

For the first 4 weeks the young remain in the nest chamber of the burrow, and the mother collects fresh greens for her young as well as feeding them milk. After 4 weeks they may occasionally appear at the mouth of the burrow and play with each other. Not until they are 6 or 7 weeks old do they stray very far from the burrow entrance. The young stay near the mother until about July, when she drives them off. At this time they may occupy abandoned dens in the immediate area. Later in the fall they will move farther away and establish their own home ranges. Rarely do they have to construct new dens, for these are so numerous in most areas that woodchucks can usually renovate an existing one.

Some of the young are able to breed in their first year, but most wait until their second. Woodchucks have only 1 litter per year.

The main sound of the woodchuck is a short, sharp whistle followed by a low churring sound. This is usually given in times of danger or excitement. It is not heard very often.

Woodchuck — Quick Reference

Habitat: Woods, meadows, fields
Home range: ½ to ¾ acre
Food: Grasses, plants
Mating: February to April
Gestation: 4 weeks
Young born: March to May
Number of young: 2 to 9, average 4 to 6
Number of litters: 1
Young independent: 10 to 12 weeks

Adult gray squirrels

GRAY SQUIRREL /
Sciurus carolinensis

W E WERE ONCE TAUGHT a real lesson by a friend from France. He
was visiting us with his family, and we were all sitting around the
breakfast table watching the birds come to our feeder. Suddenly a
gray squirrel showed up. Our friend got up excitedly and in a hushed
voice told us all to remain still. In a few seconds he came back with his
camera and slowly sneaked up to the window. We were amused, and
we kidded him about being the big-game hunter. He was about to
take the picture when the squirrel dashed away. We took it lightly at
first, but after fifteen minutes of his waiting to see the squirrel again
and get it on film, we realized how seriously taken he was by seeing
wild animals so close.

Where he lives in France, they have no squirrels; in fact, they have
no wild mammals that one regularly sees. It made us think twice
about our squirrels. And it made us realize that, as with so many other
things in nature, we tend to dismiss the common things and treasure
the rarities. But in nature, all things are equally wild. The gray
squirrel is no less wild than the deer, the otter, or the fox. It did not
take less time to evolve, it is no less complex, and it is no less
wondrous. It is only our attitudes and complacency that take the
wildness, complexity, and wonder out of the gray squirrel.

It is interesting to look at the history of our native gray-squirrel
populations. When European settlers first arrived, gray squirrels

were extremely numerous and constituted a serious threat to farms and vegetable gardens. In some states there was even a bounty on them. As the settlers cleared the land of trees, the squirrels had fewer places to live, less food from the trees, and fewer places to den. Their population dropped so dramatically that in the early 1900s there was actually some concern that gray squirrels might become extinct. Since then, farming has decreased, the trees are growing back, and the number of squirrels is also increasing. Today it is hard to believe that an animal as populous as the gray squirrel could ever have been in danger of extinction.

The gray squirrel, as is well known to all, is a small animal with gray fur on its back, white fur on its belly, and a large bushy tail. Its body is about 8 to 10 inches long, and its tail is about the same length. It weighs anywhere between 12 ounces to 1½ pounds. Occasionally a gray squirrel is born with black fur, especially in northern areas, and in a few locations there are populations of albino gray squirrels. The gray squirrel, *Sciurus carolinensis*, is the most widely distributed of the five North American members of the genus. The genus is in the family Sciuridae, in the order Rodentia, or rodents.

Getting Around

Gray squirrels are active during the day. Throughout the year their day starts at sunrise and ends a little after sunset. From spring through fall they generally have two peaks of activity each day: in the morning an hour or two after sunrise, and in midafternoon. During the midday hours they are fairly quiet. In winter their day is shorter, and they have one peak of activity at noontime.

Each gray squirrel has a fixed home range in which it lives and of which it requires sources of food, a means of protection, and a place to den. The home range usually consists of several wooded acres and is generally larger for males than for females. It broadly overlaps the home ranges of many other nearby gray squirrels, all of which move about their home ranges freely, for there is no territorial defense.

Defense is limited to the breeding season, when the female may defend her den tree from other squirrels.

The social group for a gray squirrel includes all of the squirrels it comes into contact with; in other words, all squirrels with overlapping home ranges. Within this social group there is usually a strict hierarchy of dominance established through interactions among the squirrels. In general, older squirrels are dominant over younger ones and males are dominant over females. Once the hierarchy has been established, there is very little aggression, for the squirrels recognize their neighbors through sight, smell, and possibly sound, and each knows its place within the hierarchy.

However, young squirrels often attempt to establish home ranges near their birthplace, which can lead to aggressive interactions with resident adult squirrels and a redefining of the local hierarchy. In addition to young local squirrels, there are also young immigrant squirrels who, unable to establish themselves near their birthplace, have moved on. Residents are extremely aggressive to these immigrants and rarely let them settle in the area. The young try to establish home ranges twice a year, in late spring and between midsummer and the middle of autumn. These are the times when you will see squirrels act the most aggressively.

In years when many young are born, there is more movement of young squirrels to new areas. As they move, they are occasionally killed crossing roads. Mammal road kills can be an indication that the animals are dispersing or in a stage of their lives when they roam widely.

Aggressive interaction between squirrels is easily recognized. One form it takes is tooth chatter. The dominant animal chatters its teeth, sometimes audibly, and waves its tail forward and back. Tail waving is a display of general alarm as well. A dominant squirrel may also jump toward another squirrel while both are on the ground, or one squirrel may run at or chase another. The chase can occur either on the ground or spiraling up a tree trunk. Actual fights are rare.

You may have noticed that squirrels tend to use the same branches or routes through the trees. The habitual use of these "highways" enables the squirrels to travel at great speeds from tree to tree. Occasionally you may see a squirrel pause and sniff or even rub the sides of its face on a limb. It is probably smelling or leaving scent marks, perhaps to keep track of other squirrels in the area, especially females who may be in estrus.

Clues:	Tracks	Common	See page 30
	Claw marks on trees	Common	See page 78
	Bark chewed off	Uncommon	See page 76
	Scats	Rare	See page 54

Gray-squirrel range map

Food and Feeding Habits

In August, the large nuts on oaks, hickories, walnuts, and beeches start to mature, and the squirrels immediately take advantage of this. They eat all the nuts they can and store large quantities of them underground. Gray squirrels gather the nuts singly and bury them in the ground, usually somewhere near the source tree. First they dig a hole 3 to 4 inches deep, place the nut inside, and then push it down with their nose; finally they scrape the earth backward over the hole with their front paws. The use of the nose in these actions may in fact be a kind of scent-marking that helps the squirrels locate the nuts later on. They are able to store as many as 25 nuts in a half-hour. The husk of larger nuts is often discarded before the nut is buried.

Nuts are usually collected from all over a squirrel's home range, and possibly are buried at random. Since gray-squirrel home ranges broadly overlap, different squirrels collect and bury nuts in the same area. Who gets which nuts when they dig them up in winter is still not known.

When a squirrel wants a winter meal, it first goes to the general area where many of the nuts were buried and then locates one by smelling either the nut or a scent left on the spot. It then digs down through the snow and earth until it retrieves the nut, often eating it on the spot. Little holes dug to retrieve winter nuts are a common sign of gray-squirrel activity.

Nuts are available only in fall and winter, and during the rest of the year the squirrels find other sources of food. In spring they may eat the expanding buds of many trees, such as oaks and hickories. They may also eat the inner bark from maples, basswoods, and elms. When there is an injury to a maple or birch, the squirrels may lick at the sweet sap that flows from the spot. In late spring, when there is an abundance of young birds and eggs, they may feed on these as they discover them. They also relish the ripened seeds of elm, maple, and basswood.

In summer, squirrels eat the flowers from trees or early fruits such as cherries or mulberries. The fruits may stain the fur around their mouths with their juices. Insects are more readily available in summer, and squirrels may eat beetles or caterpillars they find in the trees. They also occasionally eat insect galls, of which there is an abundance, especially on oaks. In late summer they feed on field corn, biting off the starchy outside portion, discarding it, and then eating the inner kernel. Thus, pieces of outer kernels below a cornstalk are a sign of gray-squirrel feeding. In late summer and fall, squirrels eat some of the many available varieties of mushrooms.

A few other fall foods include apples and their seeds, as well as pine cones. Squirrels eat the seeds within the cones by chewing off the tough outer scales. They usually start at the base of the cone and work their way up in a spiral, following the arrangement of the scales. Gray squirrels can also chew the bark off young conifers and even occasionally girdle them.

Clues:	Shallow digging in the earth	Common	See page 92
	Chewed nuts or cones	Common	See page 122
	Mushrooms eaten	Common	See page 120
	Gnawed bones	Uncommon	See page 124

Family Life

People often assume that the large globular accumulations of leaves and twigs near the tops of trees are bird nests. In fact, they are almost always squirrel nests. Birds build platforms on which to lay eggs, while squirrels build spherical nests inside which they live. At various times of the year you may see squirrels carrying leaves, twigs with leaves, or shredded bark. Following the movements of these squirrels may lead you to their nest. Squirrels never carry such material unless they are building a leaf nest or lining a tree-hole den. Leafy nests are used most in summer, while tree-hole dens are preferred in winter.

One of the most conspicuous activities of gray squirrels is their mating chase. Breeding and mating can occur twice each year, in December to February and again in June to July. One of the first rituals of mating is pre-chase behavior, in which a male squirrel follows a female at a leisurely pace. The female most likely gives off a scent that is left along her trail. As you watch, you may see the male stop to sniff whatever the female has passed over. In fact, he seems to be more interested in her scent than in the female herself. Occasionally he will get close to her and sniff her vaginal area. She merely avoids him in a leisurely way. Gradually the male gives up. This behavior can occur up to 5 days before the female begins the estrous cycle.

Young gray squirrels

When the female is actually in estrus, mating chases begin. They usually occur between 7:00 and 9:00 A.M. Two or more males (and sometimes as many as ten) begin to chase a female among the trees. The female is in the lead, and the males just behind her tend to be the most dominant ones, while the less dominant males are farther back. As in the normal social hierarchy, the oldest males are the most dominant and mate the most often with the females in the area. During this chase, both the males and female produce the repeated "chuck" call that sounds like a stifled sneeze. At times the female will stop and be aggressive to her chasers before running on. At other times the males are aggressive to each other, further determining who among them is the most dominant. Males may go up to a quarter of a mile from their home range to join in a mating chase. They are attracted to the female through hearing her calls and possibly through scents. Females, on the other hand, always mate on their own home range.

The gestation period for gray squirrels is 45 days. Three young per litter is the average, and they are usually born in a tree den that is lined with leaves and softer material. The female aggressively defends this den tree from other squirrels when she has dependent young. At first the baby squirrels are hairless, their ears and eyes are closed, and all they do is keep warm and feed on their mother's milk. At 4 to 5 weeks they are fully furred, their eyes and ears have opened, and they are able to make short trips from the den to explore the outside world; you may see them at this time tentatively climbing about the den entrance. They are weaned by 8 or 9 weeks and are on their own after about 4 months. Male squirrels have no part in raising the young and, in fact, are actively kept away from the den tree by the female.

The young disperse from the mother's home range at the end of

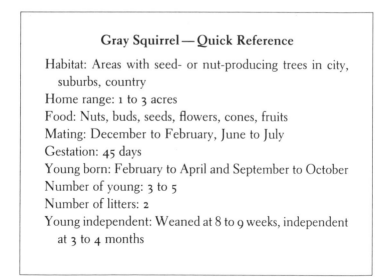

Gray Squirrel — Quick Reference

Habitat: Areas with seed- or nut-producing trees in city, suburbs, country

Home range: 1 to 3 acres

Food: Nuts, buds, seeds, flowers, cones, fruits

Mating: December to February, June to July

Gestation: 45 days

Young born: February to April and September to October

Number of young: 3 to 5

Number of litters: 2

Young independent: Weaned at 8 to 9 weeks, independent at 3 to 4 months each breeding period, in late spring and between late summer and the middle of fall.

| *Clues*: | Leaf nests in trees | Common | See page 102 |
| | Tree holes | Common | See page 118 |

Adult red squirrel

RED SQUIRREL /
Tamiasciurus hudsonicus

OUR STUDY HAS a large picture window that looks out over a small clearing surrounded by woods. We have put up birdhouses on the trees around the clearing, and we throw cracked corn on the ground to attract birds and squirrels. We have also created brush piles and log piles as protected spots for the mice, rabbits, shrews, and voles, and occasionally we transplant some multiflora rose and dogwood shrubs to provide berries; the white pines and red oaks already produce abundant cones and nuts. As a result, a lot of birds and mammals come to the area, and they provide an endless flow of marvelous distractions from our work.

One of our favorite activities is watching red squirrels. This fall we have one red squirrel and at least three gray squirrels living around the clearing. Since gray squirrels are not territorial, but have overlapping ranges, they get along fairly peacefully. But red squirrels *are* territorial, so our red squirrel is continually chattering and chasing as it keeps other red squirrels and the gray squirrels out of its area.

Right now both species are foraging for the bumper crop of white pine cones and acorns that have fallen on the ground. The gray squirrels take one at a time and eat it, whereas our red squirrel only occasionally stops to eat one; the rest it stores in its cache. We love to watch it pick up one of the cones in its mouth, bound across the pine needles, dive into the center of a brush pile, and disappear among the branches. In a few seconds it emerges without the cone, clearly having made a quick trip to its hideout.

The red squirrel is a small mammal, with reddish fur on its back and whitish fur on its belly, a bushy tail, and, in winter, tufts of hairs at the tips of its ears. In summer, there is a black line separating the whitish belly from the reddish back. It is about 7 to 8 inches long, excluding tail, and weighs about 5 to 9 ounces. The red squirrel, *Tamiasciurus hudsonicus,* is in the squirrel family, Sciuridae, which belongs to the order Rodentia, or rodents. There are two species of this genus in North America, the red squirrel and the Douglas squirrel. The red squirrel lives pretty much throughout the North and down the Rockies, while the Douglas squirrel lives only on the West Coast. Both species are often called pine squirrel, boomer, chickaree, or fairydiddle.

Getting Around

Ounce for ounce, the red squirrel seems to be one of the feistiest animals in the woods. When you walk through its territory you will hear it give its alarm call, after which it usually scampers up the nearest tree and rapidly waves its tail. Red squirrels move about from dawn to dusk, and in summer their greatest activity usually occurs in the morning and afternoon. During the midday heat they may rest in underground dens or tree holes to stay cool. In winter, their peak activity occurs in the middle of the day, probably because that is when it is warmest. In very bad weather, such as heavy rainstorms, snowstorms, and extreme cold, red squirrels will stay for a day or two in their nest or den.

Red squirrels lead solitary lives, each squirrel aggressively defending its own territory. They will chase away other intruding squirrels, and may actually attack them with their forepaws and teeth. They may even drive off birds, such as blue jays.

Throughout their territory, red squirrels have certain well-known "highways" through the treetops, which they regularly use. In winter, when there is deep snow they may also dig a network of tunnels through the snow, and in these cases they are less often seen moving about the trees.

Territories average 2 to 5 acres, and their boundaries are sharply defined, such that individual food trees at the edge of two borders are definitely in either one squirrel's territory or another. Squirrels may move off their territories and seek new ones if there is a shortage of food.

Red squirrels make a variety of noises ranging from chattering and squeaking to a bird-like chirping. Studies have shown that red-squirrel vocalizations fall into two categories: those of repeated notes and those of variable notes. Calls of repeated notes are given during territorial advertisement. Calls of variable notes are given during aggressive encounters between squirrels and during moments of alarm. We have noticed that when interacting with gray squirrels, our red squirrel alternates these two calls. The first sounds like a rapid chatter and the second like a variable squeaking.

When red squirrels are not out running about their territories or caching food, they are usually resting in their nest or den. They use tree holes when they are available, and line them with soft material, such as shredded bark or leaves. If a tree hole is not available, they may build a spherical nest that measures 1 to 1½ feet in diameter. The outer shell is made of coarse material, such as leaves, twigs, and bark strips, and the inside is lined with soft materials and has a chamber about 4 by 5 inches. This nest is similar to that of the gray squirrel but usually contains more shredded material and is more compact.

It is a fairly common sight to see red squirrels going about with nesting material in their mouths, and following one is a good way to locate its nest. Nests are often made in the tops of evergreens and usually in trees that are connected to other nearby trees through touching branches. This network provides the squirrel with various routes to and from its nest. A squirrel may make several nests and move about from one to another if danger threatens or if a nest has too many fleas or other parasites.

Red squirrels will also live under fallen logs, in stone walls, in buildings, and in underground tunnels that they dig themselves.

Clues:	Tracks	Common	See page 30
	Nests in trees	Common	See page 102
	Tunnels through snow	Common	See page 108
	Holes in the ground	Common	See page 86
	Holes in trees	Common	See page 118
	Bark scratched or peeled	Common	See page 70
	Scats	Rare	See page 54

Red-squirrel range map

Food and Feeding Habits

In spring, red squirrels eat the buds and flowers of elm, oak, butternut, and a variety of maples; they also feed on the buds of spruce and the male flowers, or "candles," of pines.

In summer, when seeds and fruits begin to mature, the squirrels concentrate on collecting and eating them. They eat the seeds of elms and maples and the green, developing cones of pine, spruce, fir, hemlock, arborvitae, and larch. They are fond of raspberries, mulberries, and blueberries, and may also eat birds' eggs and young.

When fall arrives, the nuts from deciduous trees and the cones from conifers are ripening, and this is the red squirrel's busiest time. Many nuts are eaten, and many more are gathered and stored. The red squirrel usually has a central spot where it caches most of its food, enabling it to protect the food from other squirrels and other animals such as birds and rodents. The cache is usually hidden in a chamber underground, in a stone wall, beneath a brush pile, or in an old burrow. Nuts, such as those of the hickory, may be husked before they are cached; cones are stored intact. Cones are often stored in a damp area since the moisture prevents the cones from opening and loosing their seeds.

During the winter the red squirrel periodically retrieves food from the cache and eats it above ground. It often feeds at the same spot day after day, and this results in a large pile, or midden, of cone scales and nutshells. These are excellent signs of red-squirrel activity. The middens can become very large — 6 feet or more in diameter and several feet high — but often they are quite a bit smaller. Sometimes the squirrel buries other cones or nuts inside the midden.

Not all of the food a squirrel collects in fall is buried in a single large cache. Often small groups of nuts from hickories or other trees are burried under leaf litter or grass.

Throughout spring, summer, and fall, red squirrels also feed on mushrooms. The squirrel has the ingenious habit of taking the mushrooms out of the ground and hanging them up in the twigs or crotches of trees. It leaves them there until they dry, and then it stores them in a tree hole or other safe place until it is ready to eat them.

Clues:	Collections of nuts, seeds, or cones	Common	See page 122
	Chewed nuts or cones	Common	See page 122
	Mushrooms eaten or placed in trees	Common	See page 120
	Twigs on the ground	Common	See page 80
	Gnawed bones	Uncommon	See page 124

Family Life

For most of the year, adult red squirrels live alone on their territories and actively defend them. Amazingly, evidence seems to suggest that

Young red squirrels

the female is receptive for only one day during the breeding period, and it is only on this day that she will let males onto her territory. There can be either one or two breeding periods a year. When there are two, one occurs in February and March and the other in June and July.

A few days before a female comes into estrus, it is believed, she gives off an odor alerting neighboring males that she is coming into heat. On the one day that she is in estrus and receptive, males enter her territory and follow along behind her, seeming to sniff the branches over which she has traveled, possibly to pick up her odor. Generally one male, who is perhaps more dominant than the others, follows within a few feet of the female. Every so often he may stop to chase away or fight off other approaching males. He may continue to follow the female for up to 5 hours or more. At some point the female stops and presents herself to him by lifting her tail up and to one side. The male may groom his genital region, approach her, and then get on her back and mate. Mating may occur several times over the course of a few minutes. The next day, the female is no longer in estrus and will resume her territorial defense, not allowing other squirrels in her area.

After a gestation of 35 days the young are born in the female's nest, which is usually in a tree hole. There can be from 2 to 8 young in a litter, but the average is 4 to 5. In years when there is an abundance of food, there may be larger litters. Young from the first breeding period are born from late March to early May; young from the second breeding period from late July to early September. These are only, however, the peaks of breeding activities; the birth of young has been reported during the intervening time as well.

Baby red squirrels are born without fur and with their eyes closed. At about 10 days they have fine hair, and by 20 days they are well covered with brown hair. After 30 days their eyes open, and they begin to explore the nesting cavity and make short trips to the tree trunk and limbs outside. After about 7 to 8 weeks they are weaned. Before weaning, the mother establishes a territory that excludes the young. She either moves them to a new nest at the very edge of her territory, or she moves to a new territory herself. She weans them by no longer visiting their nest.

They are now on their own, and she will not let them back into her territory. She can be very aggressive to them at this time. They

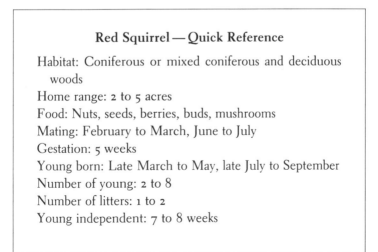

Red Squirrel — Quick Reference

Habitat: Coniferous or mixed coniferous and deciduous woods
Home range: 2 to 5 acres
Food: Nuts, seeds, berries, buds, mushrooms
Mating: February to March, June to July
Gestation: 5 weeks
Young born: Late March to May, late July to September
Number of young: 2 to 8
Number of litters: 1 to 2
Young independent: 7 to 8 weeks

gradually explore the area and find out which objects are food and how to eat them. They also engage in sexual play and mount one another, mirroring the sexual behavior of adults. As they begin to establish their own territories, they invariably encroach on the territories of neighboring adults, but when they do so they give a special short call that seems to appease the aggression of the territorial adult. Through this mechanism they are able to gather food and establish themselves. As they get older they use this call less and defend their own territories. Some young may leave the area altogether. Red squirrels may live 2 years or longer.

Adult beavers

BEAVER / *Castor canadensis*

It was absolutely clear that fall evening as we looked across the still water of the small pond. On the far side was a beautiful reflection of dark pines silhouetted against the sunset. We had been waiting more than an hour for signs of activity around the beaver lodge just 25 feet away. We had visited the lodge several times in the summer, but since we had seen no signs of feeding, we were not sure that it was occupied. It was almost dark now, and still there were no signs of beavers. However, we had not gone unrewarded: Earlier, a muskrat had swum out from near the lodge, and we had watched it feed; we saw a sharp-shinned hawk dive down and kill a blue jay; and all around us mourning doves and robins were flying in to roost in the pines.

Suddenly, off to our right, we saw a head moving silently through the water. It was huge — at least twice the size of a muskrat's head. We knew at once that it was a beaver and that, judging from its size, it was probably an adult.

It swam about in several directions, seeming to inspect the shore and the world outside the lodge to be sure everything was in its place. Then it started to swim directly at us. We stayed as still as we could, barely breathing. It got closer and closer and swam with no hesitancy. We both felt unnerved and wondered what this huge animal might do. About 3 feet from the shore and us, it calmly turned at a right angle and continued on its way as if we had not even been there. Had it seen us or not? There was no indication either way from its behavior.

In a few minutes the animal reappeared with a small branch from a gray birch in its mouth. It went toward the lodge and, when it was about 10 feet in front of the lodge, dove silently underwater, carrying the branch with it. The branch was probably food for the young beavers.

Beavers capture the imagination of many people, not only because of their industriousness but because of their ability to construct huge dams and lodges. Unlike the majority of our other wild mammals, male and female stay together throughout the year and form a lasting bond. Not only this, but young beavers stay with their parents for about a year and a half and even help care for their younger brothers or sisters.

One of the reasons that beavers have such a strong family structure may be the physical demands of building and maintaining the dam and lodge. It would be hard for a single beaver to do all of this work, but easier for a pair, and even easier for a pair with yearlings.

The beaver is in the family Castoridae, which is in the order Rodentia, or rodents. There is only one species of beaver in North America, *Castor canadensis*. When seen in the water, beavers are most often confused with muskrats, but they can be differentiated in two ways. The beaver has a broad, flat tail that does not show behind the animal when it is swimming, whereas the muskrat has a thin tail that is either held out of the water or sways back and forth on the water's surface as the animal swims. Also remember that the beaver is a big animal, 25 to 30 inches long excluding tail and weighing 45 to 60 pounds, while the muskrat is small and weighs only 2 to 4 pounds.

Getting Around

Beavers build larger constructions than any of our other mammals, and their dams are the most conspicuous of these. The dam has the effect of raising the water level and enabling the beaver to get to more food while remaining in the safety of the water. The dammed water may also surround and protect the lodge, although this seems less important since lodges are often built against the shore. The dam measures from 1 or 2 feet to 10 feet high and can be from several to hundreds of yards long.

Beavers will put dam materials over an existing human dam even though they do not add to its efficiency. They will also dam up streams that flow into their main pond. Often other animals use beaver dams as bridges across wet areas, so look for their scats and tracks on top of them.

The stimulus for building dams seems to come from the sound of rushing water; in fact, beavers in captivity have been stimulated to build dams by tape recordings of rushing water. The dam is begun on the upstream side, and the first sticks are stuck into the mud facing in the direction of the current. Although logs, branches, and twigs provide the bulk of the building material, mud, rocks, and vegetation fill in the gaps and make the dam solid. Amazingly, beavers carry mud and rocks in their front paws while walking upright on two feet with partial support from their tail. Dam building takes place in spring, summer, and into the fall. It is especially noticeable in spring because the beavers are repairing winter damage to the dam.

As you walk around the edge of a beaver pond, look for trails about 15 to 20 inches wide that leave the water at right angles from the shoreline. These trails may even be nipped clean of shrubs and sapling trees. They occur in areas where the beaver has been forced to go on land in search of food and/or building materials. They do not usually go farther than 100 yards from water, and at the end of them you will find evidence of feeding and chewing. Most of the time beavers stay in the water, for this is where they are safest. Where the water is shallow, they may even dig channels so they can reach certain areas while remaining in the water.

Beavers are active mostly at night, starting in late afternoon and ending about daybreak. Initially the beavers concentrate on feeding and grooming; later in the night they devote their energy to repairing lodges and dams, and resting and playing. Activities are always centered around the lodge, and the beavers' movements radiate from the lodge to areas used for feeding and gathering building materials.

If you are lucky enough to come upon an active beaver, it may become alarmed and slap its broad, flat tail as it dives underwater. This has the effect of making other beavers, especially those in shallow water or on land, head for deep water. For some reason, tail slapping is done most by female beavers, possibly because an adult female is the dominant member of a colony and the one the other beavers pay the most attention to.

Another sign of beavers is a mound of mud and vegetation a few inches to 2 feet high at water's edge. This is a beaver scent mound. The animals carry mud to the spot and drop it there; then they mark it with castoreum, which is washed out from their castor glands with urine. The scent mounds are most actively built and marked in spring and, to a lesser extent, in fall. There may be as many as 40 to 120 scent mounds within the range of a beaver family. They are distributed fairly evenly throughout a beaver's home range with slightly greater concentrations at the lodge and at feeding areas.

The function of these scent mounds is still unknown. Several theories have been suggested. One is that they are connected with sexual activity since they appear most often in spring. Another is that they mark a family's defended territory, causing other beavers to avoid the area. A third theory is that they mark an area for the family, which gives them a greater sense of security throughout their range.

The size of a beaver's home range depends on the availability of food. In general, a beaver will stay within a few hundred yards of its lodge, but if necessary may swim up to a half-mile away in search of food and building materials. Beavers almost invariably void their scats in the water; in fact, without water, they may have trouble voiding. You are therefore unlikely ever to see their scats.

Clues:	Dam	Common	See page 98
	Trails	Common	See page 106
	Mounds of earth	Uncommon	See page 96
	Tracks	Rare	See page 26

Beaver range map

Food and Feeding Habits

Beavers are strictly vegetarians. During spring and summer they eat the leaves and twigs of trees and shrubs and also the stems and roots of various water plants. In winter, they mostly eat the bark from trees and shrubs. Food is collected in and around the pond, and overland where necessary. In warmer months, the beaver often collects food and then takes it to a favorite spot to eat it.

A common sign of beaver activity is a felled tree. Beavers fell trees for two reasons: first, to feed on the tender bark of the young upper branches, and second, to cut the branches into smaller lengths so they can be used for constructing dams and lodges. Some people think that beavers eat the inner wood of trees, but they do not — they eat only the leaves and bark. The inner wood is chipped away to fell the trees and cut the branches into smaller lengths. Only one beaver at a time tries to a fell a tree, but once it is down, all members of the colony feed or work on it. A 3-inch-diameter tree takes less than 10 minutes to fell, a 5-inch-diameter tree less than 30 minutes.

You may have read that beavers must chew at wood to wear down their incisors. Although it is true that beaver incisors continue to grow throughout their lifetime and so must be worn down, beavers do this through biting their incisors together, a process that both sharpens and wears them.

Beavers are not the master woodsmen they are made out to be. In felling a tree, they start chewing on whatever side is the most accessible. The tree may fall in any direction, even occasionally on top of the beaver, and often gets lodged in among other trees and does not fall at all.

In colder climates where the water freezes, beavers start a large cache of food in the middle of fall. This consists of favorite tree branches secured in the mud underwater and near the lodge entrance. These caches can reach large proportions. In winter the beavers swim underwater, chew off some of the branches, and bring them back to their lodge to feed on. They may also find air spaces under the ice in which to feed.

Their favorite woody plants are aspen, maple, alder, willow, birch, and sweet gum, and in the West they will even eat conifers such as the Douglas fir and pine. Throughout, a very favorite bark is aspen or any other member of the poplar family, such as cottonwood, balsam, poplar, and various willows.

| *Clues*: | Bark chewed off | Common | See page 74 |
| | Branches piled in the water | Common | See page 120 |

Family Life

The beaver is one of our few monogamous wild mammals. In monogamy the male and female stay together through the year and mate only with each other. Beavers are not only monogamous, their family life is also close-knit and long-lived. This is because the young stay with the parents for at least 2 years. Thus, the average beaver family living in one lodge consists of the adult parents, two yearlings born the previous year, and two kits born the current year. In general, they all live together peacefully, and the adult female is the leader and dominant member of the family.

Mating in the North occurs from January through March, and in the South from November through January. Copulation occurs in

Young beavers

the water with the male alongside the female. After 100 to 110 days of gestation, the young are born. The male remains in the lodge even when the female is giving birth. Both may feed on the placenta, or afterbirth, and both care for the young. The yearlings may even be present when the kits are born.

The young are born fully furred and able to walk; they can even go into the water on their first day, but usually wait for a few days. They feed on the mother's milk and are bathed and groomed by both adults. Only one litter is produced per year, and there are usually about 2 to 3 kits per litter. At 10 days the young can dive into the water and at 30 days can leave the lodge with their parents, but they do not usually do this until they are about 2 months old.

As the young beavers are weaned, they begin to feed on leaves brought into the lodge by the adults. Gradually, after a few months, they will begin to feed on bark. The young will be seen outside the lodge in midsummer in the North and early summer in the South. They float higher on the water than the adults, who show only their heads while swimming. Likewise, yearlings show a little more of their bodies than the adults, but less than the kits.

By summer kits weigh about 10 to 15 pounds, yearlings about 15 to 30 pounds, and adults 30 to 55 pounds. Beavers are full-grown at 2½ years old. By fall, all of the beavers in a colony will help build the lodge, repair the dam, and collect food for the cache, but they do not coordinate their actions in any sophisticated way; each one works separately. In general, the females do more building than the males.

In its second summer a young beaver may wander away from the colony, but it usually returns in the fall and spends the winter with the family. In their third spring or summer the young leave for good. Beavers are sexually mature between their second and third year.

Long-distance movement is pretty much limited to the young leaving home, usually in spring or summer. Dispersing beavers may move up to 30 miles from their place of birth. At this time they find a mate, stake out a home range with scent mounds, and then set to work building a dam and a lodge.

A lodge is a mound of large branches and logs, covered with finer branches and vegetation and plastered with mud. It may be along the shore and over a bank den or surrounded by water. Once it is made, the beavers excavate two tunnels through the mud underwater up into the mound and then chew out a chamber inside the mound. The chamber is their living quarters. The very top of the lodge is usually not plastered with mud, to allow for ventilation in the chamber. The outside of the lodge is added to continually over the years in the warmer months, and it can become huge, up to 8 feet high and 40 feet across, but lodges are more commonly about half that size.

A beaver colony may have than one lodge in the territory, but usually the beavers use only one at a time. Sometimes one is used in summer and another in winter.

Clues: Lodge   Common   See page 98

Beaver — Quick Reference

Habitat: Streams and lakes with bordering trees
Home range: Usually within 200 to 300 yards of the lodge
Food: Leaves from plants and bark from trees
Mating: January to March in North, November to January in South
Gestation: 100 to 110 days
Young born: April to July in North, February to April in South
Number of young: 2 to 3
Number of litters: 1
Young independent: Leave lodge at 1 to 2 years

Adult deer mice

DEER MOUSE /
Peromyscus maniculatus

WHITE-FOOTED MOUSE /
Peromyscus leucopus

ONE OF OUR FAVORITE pastimes in fall and winter is to look for the nests of deer mice and white-footed mice. Most of their nests are located in crevices or tree holes and are out of sight. The ones we look for are actually in bird's nests. In fall and winter, certain bird's nests are easy to locate because they were built in deciduous shrubs that have since lost their leaves. This is particularly true of the nests of the song sparrow, catbird, and mockingbird, which are usually located in the shrub borders of fields or country roads. Once you have found a nest, look to see if it still has its cup shape or has been piled high with a dome of extra shredded material. In the latter case, the nest has been renovated by a mouse.

Bird's nests are of course protected by law and must not be removed, but if you are curious, you can gently lift up the material piled on by the mouse and look inside. We once discovered a female with her young inside a nest in late winter. She stood her guard and merely looked defensive, though in another case, three mice ran out of a nest and down the trunk of the shrub so fast that we barely saw them. Inside mice nests you are likely to find scats and maybe bits of nuts that have been eaten.

Mice are in the family Cricetidae, which includes mice, rats, voles, and muskrats and is in the order Rodentia, or rodents. The Cricetidae is the largest family of mammals in North America, having nineteen genera and seventy species. Most of our mammals that are called mice belong to the genus *Peromyscus*. The deer mouse, *Peromyscus maniculatus*, and the white-footed mouse, *Peromyscus leucopus*, are two of the most widespread species. They are similar in appearance, and both have numerous subspecies, making it difficult to distinguish between them. They are 3 to 4 inches long with a 2- to 5-inch tail, and weigh about 1 ounce.

Getting Around

You will see deer mice or white-footed mice mostly at night. They start to become active at sunset, reach a peak of activity an hour or so later, and then are slightly less active until dawn, when they retire to their nests. This schedule changes when there is snow cover or a shortage of readily available food. In the first instance, the animal may be active for short periods throughout the day and night; in the second, the mouse may have to extend its period of activity into the daylight hours to find food.

The social arrangement of deer mice and white-footed mice in the wild is still not well known. In most cases it seems clear that adult mice are solitary except for brief periods around the time of mating, when the male and female may share a nest, and during cold weather in winter, when several to many adults may huddle together in the same nest to withstand the cold. It also seems clear that they live in home ranges that are fixed and fairly small, from $\frac{1}{10}$ to $\frac{1}{3}$ acre in females and from $\frac{1}{10}$ to $\frac{1}{2}$ acre in males. However, some studies have shown the home ranges of deer mice to be as large as $2\frac{1}{2}$ acres. The size of the home range undoubtedly varies with the availability of food.

A recent study of deer-mouse home ranges uncovered some fascinating things. In areas with uniform habitats, such as grasses, the home ranges of males and females were the same size; but in areas with varied habitats, such as shrubby areas mixed with fields, the females had smaller but better-quality home ranges (that is, closer to more food) than males. It also turned out that the females in these areas were larger than males, possibly due to better nutrition. How the female establishes the better home range is not known, but it has obvious advantages during the breeding season. When raising young the female needs two to three times more food than usual to produce milk for her young; she also needs to stay near her young to protect them. With a better-quality habitat, she can stay closer to her young and still get the food she needs.

It is believed that the home ranges of females do not overlap. But the home ranges of males overlap with one another and with the home ranges of females, especially when the female is in estrus. It is not known for certain whether deer mice or white-footed mice are territorial in the wild. In crowded laboratory conditions, male deer mice are fiercely territorial and seem to mark areas with urine. Deer mice have also been observed trailing their bottoms, possibly marking with scent glands. It has also been shown that neighboring mice can recognize each other through scent and that several mice in a larger area establish a hierarchy of dominance. It is most likely that deer mice and white-footed mice are territorial in the vicinity of their nests, and that within the rest of their home range they simply avoid contact with other mice, possibly keeping track of neighbors' movements through a system of marking.

Unlike voles, deer mice and white-footed mice do not create tunnels through the grasses, nor do they dig burrows. However, they will readily use the tunnels and burrows of voles and other small mammals. They move about mostly on the surface of the ground but are also comfortable climbing trees. When on land they gallop, leaving a print much like that of a minute rabbit. They may travel as much as a quarter-mile or more in a given night, as evidenced by their tracks over snow.

The scats of deer mice are small and generally not found except in the nest. This is not because they use only the nest for defecating, but because their scats are small and dispersed over the ground when they are out of the nest. Their scats are the size and shape of vole scats.

Clues: Tracks   Common   See page 30
         Holes in the ground   Common   See page 84
         Tunnels through   Common   See page 110
         snow
         Scats   Uncommon   See page 54

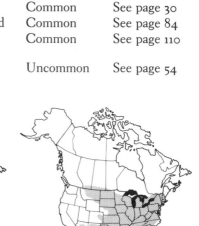

Deer-mouse range map   *White-footed–mouse range map*

Food and Feeding Habits

The feeding habits of the deer mouse and the white-footed mouse are similar. In spring and summer their diet is composed mostly of fruits and seeds. The fruits include berries, such as the raspberry, blackberry, blueberry, viburnum, pokeweed, chokecherry, dogwood, elderberry, shadbush, holly, and Canada mayflower. Seeds include those of the basswood, hemlock, tulip tree, jewelweed, alfalfa, cherry, and rose.

Insects are the next most important food. In fact, they may be the mouse's most common summer food. Some of the more frequently eaten insects include caterpillars, adult and immature beetles, crickets, grasshoppers, and flies.

During fall and winter the bulk of food comprises nuts from shrubs and trees such as oak, hickory, beech, walnut, hazelnut, pine, and spruce, and the seeds of various wildflowers. Insects are also an essential part of the winter diet of mice, who find beetles, flies, and moths — in their adult or larval stages — in the tunnels of other small mammals and among the grasses. Another part of the winter diet is green leaves from the winter rosettes of wildflowers, or the dormant winter shoots of herbaceous plants.

Deer mice and white-footed mice both make caches of food throughout the year. The largest and most important caches are made in fall. Nuts and tree seeds are most often stored in caches. When the mice store the nuts, they often take the outer husk off but leave the nut in the inner shell. They may do this to reduce the chance of storing insects from the husks in the cache, or just to take up less room. There is usually about a pint or quart of material in a cache, but there can be up to 8 quarts of nuts in some cases. We have found evidence of these caches in log piles and knotholes and under rocks.

A study of mouse caches of white pine seeds showed that the caches were in holes 2 to 4 inches underground and contained 20 to 30 seeds all in a little pile 1 to 1½ inches in diameter. About a third of the caches were used before December. Some were visited only once and eaten all at once; others were visited several times, and only a few seeds were removed and eaten each time. Sometimes the caches were dug up and eaten by squirrels.

The rest of the caches were used through the winter and into early spring, at which point some of the seeds had sprouted but were still eaten by the mice. In summer, mice also made caches, but they were located less deeply in the ground and could usually be seen just under the pine needles of the forest floor. These may have been temporary caches that hid the food from competing neighboring mice.

Clues:	Chewed nuts or cones	Common	See page 124
	Mushrooms eaten	Common	See page 120
	Bark chewed off	Common	See page 72
	Collection of nuts, seeds, or cones	Uncommon	See page 122
	Gnawed bones	Uncommon	See page 124

Another sign of feeding we often find is in multiflora rose. In bird's nests in this plant you often find the remains of the rose seeds. And if you look out on the branches, you find the hips chewed off the branches. This is probably the work of the deer mouse, which runs out on the branches, nips off the fruits, and then returns to the nest to eat them. When there is no nest, look under the plant for fruit remains.

Young deer mice

Family Life

Male mice seek out female mice in late winter and spring. The female may be aggressive at first but will then accept the male, and the two may stay in her nest for several days. After mating, the male either leaves or is driven out by the female. Breeding will continue through summer and fall and into winter if it is warm. A female may have up to 4 litters a year.

The female will build her nest when the young are about to be born. The nest is composed of soft shredded materials such as bark, moss, grass leaves, cattail fluff, hair, string, and cloth. It is placed anywhere there is a cavity — under rocks or logs, in small burrows, knotholes of trees even up to 50 feet high, a bird's nest or bird box, or dense shrubbery. In one study it was found that white-footed mice seem to prefer to make their nests above the ground in tree cavities or bird nests. They also seem to prefer the borders between woodlands and open areas where shrubs tend to be abundant. The nest is usually spherical and has one main opening that is closed when the animals are inside. Males also build nests in which to live throughout the year. Nests in winter are usually slightly larger, affording greater protection from the cold.

Deer mice and white-footed mice usually leave their scats in their nest and may even urinate right outside it. Because of this, the nests become foul within several weeks. This may be the reason deer mice and white-footed mice switch nest sites so frequently. They usually do not stay in one nest site for more than a month; however, they may reuse a nest site after being away from it for several weeks.

The young are usually born after a gestation period of about 23 days. There are usually 3 to 5 mice in a litter, and they weigh only a tenth of an ounce when born. The female may gently pull on the young with her teeth as they are being born, to assist in the birthing process. Once they are born she eats the placenta and licks the young clean. They soon begin to nurse. They are tiny and pink and in places almost transparent — you can even see the milk in their stomachs after they have suckled. For the first 2 weeks their eyes and ears remain closed; after that they are open, and the mice become more active and are able to run and jump. The baby mice are weaned after 3 to 4 weeks.

During the first 2 weeks the young may hold onto the teats of the mother so firmly that if she is startled and runs, they remain attached.

This is obviously a survival strategy, for in the event of danger the young mice would not have to be carried one at a time. When the mice are larger, the female does carry them one at a time in her mouth, holding them by the neck with their belly facing toward her.

The female mouse immediately comes into heat 1 to 2 days after giving birth, and if she mates while still nursing young, a delayed implantation of the fertilized egg for 2 to 7 days may occur. This means that while she is raising young, her gestation period will be longer: 25 to 30 days. When she is about to give birth to her second litter, she may leave the first nest and her first litter and give birth in a new nest. The young of the first litter may remain in the old nest for a while and then disperse. In general, the female raises the young alone; however, after the young get older, the male may occasionally be found in or near the nest. Female mice have 2 to 4 litters per year.

Clues:	Nest on the ground	Uncommon	See page 100
	Nest in shrubs or trees	Uncommon	See page 102

Mice — Quick Reference

Habitat: Woods, prairies, meadows, suburbs to country
Home range: $\frac{1}{10}$ to $2\frac{1}{2}$ acres
Food: Fruits, seeds, insects, nuts, cones
Mating: February to October
Gestation: 23 days
Young born: March to November
Number of young: 3 to 5
Number of litters: 2 to 4
Young independent: $3\frac{1}{2}$ to 4 weeks

Adult meadow vole

MEADOW VOLE /
Microtus pennsylvanicus

W E HAD SPENT THE whole morning looking for fox scats, sniffing the air for scent marks, and checking out potential dens. Worn out, we sat down in the middle of a field, feeling warm in the midday sun and comfortable on the dried winter grasses. After being refreshed by a small snack, we began to look around and noticed a tunnel going down among the grasses right between us. It was a sign of vole activity, and it made us wonder how easy it might be to find a vole nest. We decided to explore a little and look for one. There was a mound of grasses nearby and, leaning over to pull them aside, we suddenly found ourselves staring at a little cluster of finer grasses woven into a sphere about 6 inches in diameter. Could it actually be a vole nest? Gently pulling the material apart, we found downy fibers lining a little chamber inside, and our suspicions were confirmed.

Needless to say, we concluded that vole nests were a cinch to find. Wanting to see more, we spent the next 20 minutes pulling apart tufts of grass all across the field, but not even a trace of a nest could be found. Obviously, our first discovery had involved some luck.

The first nest with babies that we discovered was in our garden. We had mulched the paths with newspapers and dried grass clippings a few days before. We went out to weed a bit, and as we walked down a path we heard some squeaking. We traced the sound right to our feet and lifted up the mulching, only to find four pink baby voles, squirming and squealing. We put the top of their nest back on them and went back to get the camera. When we returned, all was quiet. We lifted up the grasses and they were gone, probably because the mother had moved them.

We rarely see voles in the wild, for they tend to stay hidden in their tunnels and run away from you when you walk across a field. One of the most common ways we see the animal, or at least part of it, is in the pellets of hawks or owls. These birds, especially the red-tailed hawk and the great horned owl, may eat two to three voles a day all year round. They eat them whole and then cough up a pellet several inches long that contains the fur and bones of their prey. Within these pellets you can often find, in perfect condition, the complete skulls of voles.

There are at least fifteen species of voles in North America, and most look alike, with only minor external differences. They are stocky, rounded little rodents with brown or gray fur, small eyes, short ears, and tails that vary in length from species to species. They live in various habitats — meadows, tundra, beaches, marshes, woods, prairies, and mountains. Sometimes more than one species occurs within the same habitat.

All voles belong to the family Cricetidae, which is in the order Rodentia, or rodents. The meadow vole, *Microtus pennsylvanicus*, is one of the most widespread species, living throughout Canada and the northern United States. It has reddish or blackish brown fur and is gray beneath, while its tail is dark above and lighter below. It weighs 1 to 2½ ounces and is 3½ to 5 inches long, with its tail adding 1½ to 2½ inches.

Getting Around

A typical day for a meadow vole is divided into many periods of activity, usually feeding followed by rest. These continue throughout the day and night. There may be anywhere from 7 to 16 periods of activity followed by rest, and they can last from 20 minutes up to 4 hours. Voles are generally active throughout the year, although there is some evidence that they are less active when the temperature is below freezing or above 25 degrees Celsius.

The home ranges of male voles tend to shift slightly from day to day, while those of females are more fixed. Home ranges vary with the habitat and population density, but in a typical meadow the home ranges of males are about 200 square yards, while those of females are about 75 square yards. Studies have shown that female voles defend their home ranges from intrusion by other females and are thus territorial. Male home ranges are not defended and overlap with those of females and those of other males.

Meadow voles tend to live in grassy fields and marshes. Within their home ranges they have a network of tunnels winding through grasses and other vegetation. The next time you walk through a field with fairly long grasses, look for a round hole about 1½ inches in diameter among the grass. These holes are most easily seen in fall through early spring, when the grasses are matted down. Pull aside the grass at the hole, and you will see a tunnel underneath. Continue to follow the tunnel by pulling apart the top grasses, and you will be amazed at the extensive network of runways that you uncover. These tunnels are constantly maintained by the voles, which nip the grasses along the bottom and the sides. The tunnels are on the surface of the ground, but occasionally they are underground as well.

As you look through the tunnels you are likely to come across small piles of scats; we often find them at the crossroads of runways. These little piles may be used as scent-markers of some kind. At other times you may find the scats scattered in the tunnels. Meadow voles may also mark their runways with urine.

Within the tunnels you may find a meadow-vole nest. The nests are spherical with a central chamber and are made of fine grass. They are used to rear young, for safety from predators, and as protection from the cold. They may be among the grasses, in burrows just under the ground, or under a tuft of grass, a log, or a rock. The voles may live in them most of the time and go out only during their activity periods.

Clues:

Holes in the ground	Common	See page 84
Tunnels through grass	Common	See page 108
Tunnels through snow	Common	See page 110
Scats	Common	See page 54
Tracks	Common	See page 30

Vole range map

Food and Feeding Habits

Voles feed on grasses and other types of plant matter such as leaves, stems, roots, fruits, seeds, and flowers. In winter they may also feed on bark, particularly from members of the rose family, such as apple, cherry, rose, and cinquefoil. Voles also eat insects, fungi, and carrion. When human crops are available voles will eat root vegetables, leafy vegetables, and hay and grain crops.

Several authors have reported that some species of voles store caches of food during times of abundance, but this has not been substantiated in the case of the meadow vole.

Voles have special adaptations that enable them to eat grass. Because grasses contain tough and abrasive cells that wear down teeth, voles have teeth that continuously grow. To aid the digestion of food, voles practice coprophagy, reingesting their own feces to absorb more of their vitamins and nutrients. These feces are usually softer and lighter in color than the final scats, which are excreted and left alone. Rabbits, hares, and beavers also practice coprophagy. Coprophagy usually occurs during periods of rest that directly follow active periods.

One last note about food habits: Meadow voles are the staple diet of a number of bird and mammal predators. For many owls and hawks, voles often make up as much as 85 percent of their diet, and foxes, coyotes, bobcats, and even wolves also feed on voles. In this sense, voles have become an important link in the food chain between the grasses and the carnivores and birds of prey.

Clues:	Bark chewed off	Common	See page 72
	Gnawed bones	Uncommon	See page 124
	Mushrooms eaten	Common	See page 120

Family Life

Adult meadow voles generally remain as lone individuals throughout the year except during mating. Mating and breeding can occur all year long if the environmental conditions are right. In the South it may be warm enough for the voles to breed continuously. In the North breeding may stop between November and March. But if there is a heavy snow cover, the animals are less exposed and warmer, in which case they may breed right through winter.

When a female is in estrus, she gives off certain scents that attract males from neighboring areas. At this time they may adjust their home ranges to overlap with hers. Mating occurs when the female is finally receptive and chooses a male. She may reject some and fight with them. After a few exploratory contacts, the female pursues the male, smelling his genital area, and then the male pursues the female. Copulation follows, with the male on the back of the female. It lasts

Young voles

only a few seconds and may be repeated several times. Male and female then groom themselves, especially their genitals. After copulation, a mucous plug forms in the vagina of the female, which prohibits further mating for about 2 days. In general, meadow voles are promiscuous.

Before the young are born, the mother builds a nest in a tuft of grass, along a tunnel, or even in a chamber underground. The nest is a round mass of grasses with a hollow chamber inside. The chamber is usually lined with softer fibers, such as finer grasses, milkweed, or cattail dispersal filaments, or perhaps moss. It is about 6 to 8 inches in diameter and usually has an entrance on either side. The mother gives birth in the nest. Other nests used by males and nonbreeding females are similar, except that they tend to be smaller.

The gestation period of a female is 20 to 23 days. She may give birth to from 1 to 9 young, but the average litter is 4 to 5. A female's first or second litter may be slightly smaller. Birthing is usually quick; afterward, the mother eats the placenta. Nursing can begin before the entire litter is born.

At birth the young are pink and hairless, with closed eyes and ears, and weigh about one-twentieth of an ounce. At about 6 days they get hair, and at 9 to 12 days their eyes open. Between the second and third weeks they start to eat some vegetation, are weaned, and begin venturing out on their own. If something disturbs the nest, the young may abandon it, or their mother may carry them to a new spot. While a female is raising young she is very aggressive to intruders and carefully defends her territory. When the young are independent, they disperse.

Meadow-vole populations can increase amazingly quickly. Not only can voles breed all through the year when conditions are right, but females can reproduce when they are only 3 weeks old, just a few days after they are weaned. Populations usually peak every four years or so and then quickly drop within a few months. Why this cycle occurs and what controls it have yet to be fully discovered. The average vole lives only 2 to 3 months, so the female breeds only 2 or 3 times in her life.

Clues: Nest   Common   See page 100

Vole — Quick Reference

Habitat: Meadows with lush grasses, swampy areas, woods
Home range: 75 to 200 square yards
Food: Grasses and seeds
Mating: All year in South; may stop during winter in North
Gestation: 20 to 23 days
Young born: All year in South; may stop during winter in North
Number of young: 4 to 5
Number of litters: 2 to 3
Young independent: 2 to 3 weeks

Adult muskrat

MUSKRAT /
Ondatra zibethicus

Once in midspring we were walking along a dike in a nearby wildlife refuge and heard a rustling among the cattails. We stopped, listened, and slowly moved toward the sound. As we inched ahead, we suddenly saw some small animals through the plant stems. They were three baby muskrats feeding on water plants, feeling about with their paws, grabbing bits of plants, and holding them up to their mouths as they nibbled. Each baby muskrat was no bigger than a softball, and they were extremely cute.

In this same refuge, we like to follow the changes in the placement of various muskrat lodges. Extremely high water in spring seems to destroy many of them, but then in fall we begin to see new smaller lodges that most likely have been built by young muskrats born that year. Farther back in the cattails we know of several huge lodges; they are at least 6 feet high and several years old, obviously withstanding the seasonal flooding. Most of the muskrats from the swamp probably spend the winter here.

Many people mistake muskrats for beavers when they see them swimming on the surface of the water. You can tell them apart using habitat, behavior, and size. Beavers usually inhabit more remote areas than muskrats. Muskrats tend to swim with their thin tail snaking in the water behind them or arched out of the water; you never see a beaver's tail as it swims. Finally, the muskrat is only the size of a football, whereas the beaver is four or more times larger.

The muskrat is a marvelous little animal, for it is found in the country, the wilds, and the city; anywhere there are water and a good stand of cattails there are likely to be muskrats. The muskrat, *Ondatra zibethicus*, is in the family Cricetidae, which includes rats, mice, and voles, and is in the order Rodentia, or rodents. Muskrats are small, stocky animals with glossy coats that are dark on top and lighter on the sides. Their long, thin tails are flattened vertically and are scaly in appearence. A muskrat's body is about a foot long, and the tail adds another 8 to 10 inches; it weighs 2 to 4 pounds.

Getting Around

Like beavers, muskrats have homes they live in throughout the year, and these are a conspicuous clue to the animal's presence. Muskrats can make two types of homes: dens hollowed out in the banks of waterways, and lodges made of vegetation and mud. Bank dens are common in soil that has some clay and not too much rock or sand. Sandy soil is used only if it is held together by lots of roots.

Bank dens in good soil and with a particularly good entrance, such as under a tree root, may be used consecutively for twenty to thirty years by different generations of muskrats. In these cases the dens evolve into an elaborate system of tunnels, chambers, and ventilation holes. The tunnels are frequently as long as 50 yards and can be up to 200 yards long, either paralleling the bank or going directly away from it. The chambers in a bank den are about 8 by 6 inches and lined with shredded plant material that is replaced from time to time. Bank dens are decidedly cooler than the air in warmer months and often are preferred by muskrats in summer.

Lodges are built out in open water. Material for the lodge is collected within a radius of 10 feet from the site. This may clear the immediate area around the lodge and possibly make the water there a little deeper. Vegetation and mud is piled up, and then a chamber and tunnel are dug out from beneath. The chamber is about a foot in diameter. Lodges are often added to in successive seasons.

Lodges are built on platforms, old lodges, mud bars, and tree stumps. They can be as large as 6 feet high and 8 feet in diameter at the base, and may be temporarily used, or added to and used for years. A typical lodge has a central chamber with the floor several inches above water level and two to three entrances underwater. The chambers in a lodge vary in number and placement; there may be one or several, they may be connected or separate, and they may be at different levels. Tunnels from the chamber may exit several feet away from the lodge.

In late summer and fall, lodge and burrow construction increases. Most of these new lodges are simple and small and made by young muskrats born that year. The larger lodges are built by older muskrats and are usually produced through several seasons or years of construction. As it gets colder, the smaller lodges are abandoned and the muskrats gather together in the larger homes. This is particularly true in the North, where it is colder. A single large lodge may have many chambers and up to twelve muskrats staying in it through the winter.

You are most likely to see muskrats at dusk and again in the early morning. They may also be active during the day, especially on cloudy days. They are often seen swimming on the surface of the water, but on windy days they may swim underwater continuously to avoid the waves, coming up to the surface only to get air. Muskrats can stay submerged for up to 15 minutes and then take a short breath and go down again. They spend most of their time in the water.

Occasionally muskrats travel overland to get to feeding spots, especially when there are planted crops such as corn or alfalfa nearby. In these cases you might see trails through the vegetation, about 4 or 5 inches wide. One end of a trail probably leads to the food source and the other to the water.

The home ranges of muskrats vary tremendously, and their size depends on habitat, season, and sex and age of the animal. The average home range in a lake is about 180 feet in diameter; along a stream, the home range will be oblong and may be 300 feet long.

During a typical summer day, a muskrat uses only a small portion of its home range and usually will be found within 40 to 50 feet of its den or lodge.

Whether any part of the home range is defended as a territory depends on the individual muskrat. The most territorial individuals tend to be females who are raising young. Some females can be extremely vicious to other muskrats that come into their area at this time; other females may tolerate other adults even in the same lodge or den. Males are usually more accepting of other muskrats on their home range.

Muskrats in a given area generally recognize and avoid each other. When a new muskrat comes into that area, especially in spring and summer, it is recognized as a stranger and may be attacked. Aggressiveness toward strangers is less pronounced in fall and winter. At this time muskrats are generally more tolerant of each other and may live as groups of adults, all sharing the same den or lodge. Up to twelve muskrats have been found in one lodge. The purpose of these winter aggregations may be to help the animals keep warm, for muskrats can die from exposure in colder climates during winter. They must stay underwater or in their den and also have the added warmth of other muskrats.

Starting in late winter, individuals become less tolerant of each other, and these groups start to break up. The breakup coincides with the coming of warmer weather and also the start of sexual activity. This cycle of aggression and tolerance is especially characteristic of muskrats in the North.

You can easily find the scats of muskrats if you know what to look for and where to look. They are brown, about ½ inch long, and about ⅜ inch in diameter. Look for them on rocks or logs at the edge of the body of water where the muskrat lives. The animals may repeatedly defecate at these spots, and more than one individual may use the same spot.

Muskrats also have musk glands near their anal opening that excrete a strong-smelling yellow substance. It can be smelled by humans several days after being produced. This substance is secreted on places in the muskrat's home range, such as at the base of the lodge, at defecation spots, and on mud bars. Its purpose and function is not known, but it is most likely a form of communication.

There are two times of year when muskrats tend to disperse from their home ranges, and during these periods you are more likely to see road kills because the animals often have to cross roads to get to new areas. The first is in April and May, when the adults are beginning to develop sexually and leave the winter groups. The second period of dispersal is in August and September, and most of those traveling are the young born that spring and summer that are leaving the area of their birth and seeking out new places in which to spend the winter.

Clues:	Bank den	Common	See page 86
	Lodge	Common	See page 98
	Scats	Common	See page 54
	Tracks	Common	See page 24

Muskrat range map

Food and Feeding Habits

While moving quietly in a boat along the vegetated edge of a river or lake, you may see a muskrat feeding. They often are active in the day and will be found chewing off bits of plants and holding the pieces in their front paws while they nibble away. If you move slowly, you can occasionally get quite close to them.

The main foods of muskrats in most of North America are cattails and bulrushes. The parts of these plants that are eaten include the roots, shoots, leaves, stems, and rhizomes. Muskrats also feed on a host of other common water plants — bur reed, arrowhead, water lily, pickerelweed, and others — and on vegetable and fruit crops such as ear corn, apples, carrots, soybeans, clover, and alfalfa. Occasionally in winter some ear corn is stored in the lodge. If there is not much vegetation available during winter, a muskrat may feed on crayfish, mussels, clams, snails, and other small water animals.

The muskrat usually digs up portions of underwater plants and carries them off to a protected spot to eat. These spots may be just a platform of reeds, stems, and leaves, or a small hut, called a feeding station, built in an elevated spot. These are generally used only for a few days and then abandoned. They resemble small lodges and are sometimes placed around a larger lodge.

In northern areas when the water is frozen, muskrats may gnaw a hole 4 or 5 inches in diameter through the ice and push a mound of vegetation up through it. The material lies on top of the ice, and the muskrat uses it for protection when it emerges from the water to feed. It can also be used as a breather hole when the animal is moving about under the ice. These holes are found mostly in the deeper channels of swamps and at the edge of rivers and lakes. They become covered by deep snow and only become visible as the snow melts, collapsing when the ice thaws.

Clues:	Feeding platforms	Common	See page 98
	Feeding shelters	Common	See page 98
	Push-ups	Rare	See page 98

Family Life

Breeding varies according to geographical location. In the South muskrats can breed throughout the year, usually with a peak in spring and fall and a lull in late summer. In the North breeding occurs from late winter through summer and peaks in spring. Very little has been

Young muskrats

observed of the courtship of muskrats, and little is known about the pairing of the male and female.

In general, males and females lead solitary lives. In late winter there is some wandering by individuals of both sexes, and when a female in estrus and a male meet, they may stay together for a while and then mate. Afterward, the two go their own ways. The male may look for another female to mate with, while the female begins to center her activities on a lodge or bank den. She gives birth to the young about 30 days after mating. As soon as the young are born, she comes into estrus and, if possible, will mate within a few days of giving birth. Thus, while caring for her babies, she might be pregnant with her next litter.

There are usually about 4 to 6 baby muskrats in a litter. In the South the litters tend to be smaller but more numerous, whereas in the North the litters are larger and less numerous. Newborn muskrats are almost hairless, and their eyes are closed. They are practically helpless, and when not sucking at their mother's nipples are huddled together to keep warm. When the mother leaves the lodge or bank den to feed, she covers them with the shredded plant material that is on the floor of the chamber, and this helps keep them warm.

After their first week, baby muskrats are covered with coarse, grayish hair. After about 2 weeks, their eyes open and they begin to move about the chamber and are even able to swim and dive into the water surrounding their home. They are weaned after about 3 weeks.

During the first weeks after birth, the mother may carry her young to a new home if there is some danger or disturbance. She carries them in her mouth by the skin on their belly, transporting them one at a time.

After 4 weeks or so, the young are capable of living on their own, and at this time their mother may be ready to give birth to her next

Muskrat — Quick Reference

Habitat: Vegetated edges of swamps, rivers, lakes
Home range: About 100 yards in diameter
Food: Mostly water plants and some crayfish, clams, etc.
Mating: All year in South, late winter through summer in North
Gestation: 30 days
Young born: All year in South, late winter through summer in North
Number of young: 4 to 6
Number of litters: 2 to 3
Young independent: 4 to 5 weeks

litter. She may drive the young away or, if they remain for a while, she will raise her new babies in a separate chamber of the lodge.

A female may have 2 to 3 litters per year. When the young leave their mother, they usually stay within about 100 yards of their original home, moving into old lodges or dens or else remaining within dense cover. After the young are about 4 months old, they may begin constructing a small lodge or a bank den for themselves. These homes can be spotted in late summer and fall. However, in colder climates, they are abandoned when winter comes, and the owners join other muskrats in larger lodges that provide more protection from the cold.

Adult porcupine

PORCUPINE /
Erethizon dorsatum

ONE WINTER DAY, while walking through a nearby woods, we looked inside a hollow log and discovered an enormous pile of what at first looked like brown elbow macaroni. With a more careful examination we realized they were porcupine scats. With the thought that we might be able to find the animal, we looked for trees in which the porcupine might be feeding. We were quite near a group of large hemlocks, a favorite species of porcupines, so we went over to them to look for more signs. As soon as we got under them we knew we were in luck, for there under the largest tree the ground was littered with short sprays of hemlock. Porcupines nip them off the larger branches to eat the needles at their tips and then discard the rest of the branch. Moving back slightly for a better vantage point, we scanned its top for a dark round object. There, nestled next to the trunk, about 40 feet up, was a big, brown bushy ball. The ball unraveled, and from one end, two small, sleepy eyes peered down at us. It was the porcupine.

We always seem to find porcupines sitting quietly up in trees. Unlike a number of other mammals, which always seem to be fleeing in the other direction when they are spotted, the porcupine sits quietly. Even when it is on the ground, it just shuffles along, waddling its heavy body from side to side. The porcupine does not need to rely on speed to escape from predators because it already has an excellent defense in the thousands of quills it carries on its back.

The porcupine is a medium-size animal about 20 inches long, excluding its tail, and weighing from 10 to 28 pounds. Long black and brown guard hairs cover its body and quills are mixed in among them, especially on the rump and tail. The porcupine, *Erethizon dorsatum*, is in the family Erethizontidae, or porcupines, which in turn is in the order Rodentia, or rodents.

Getting Around

Porcupines are active primarily at night. In winter, they climb up into evergreens to eat the bark and green needles; and in summer they wander around fields and orchards where they can find their favorite warm-weather foods.

When not in trees or feeding, porcupines use dens for protection from bad weather and predators. Dens are never very far from feeding areas and can be located in a variety of places — rock crevices, caves, hollow logs, old dens of other animals, abandoned mines, or under houses and barns. In the den there is no bedding material, just the accumlated droppings of the animal. Porcupines may produce from 75 to 200 scats a day, and in well-used dens these can accumulate to form a considerable layer, possibly even crowding the porcupine out. Dens may be used by generation after generation of porcupines. On rare occasions in winter, several porcupines may be found staying in the same den, but in general the animals are solitary.

Porcupines are not territorial. Their movements vary with the season and the availability of food. In winter, they may stay within an area of a few acres if there is a good den and enough food. In summer, their food sources are more varied, and so they may wander more widely, over about 200 acres or more. Other movements of porcupines are irregular and still not well studied. They may travel as much as a mile or more from a summer area to a winter area. They may also go 4 or 5 miles in search of a new home range. Since porcupines are often very widely dispersed, they must move distances to find mates.

Porcupines are most famous for their formidable means of defense, their quills. When a porcupine is threatened, it goes into its defensive posture, lowering its head and shoulders and turning its back toward the threat. It may hide its head in a crevice or climb a tree and back out onto a limb, leaving only its quills exposed. Every quill will be erect, and the tail will thrash back and forth; however, the quills cannot actually be thrown. The porcupine may even "chatter," making a sound usually produced when it is sharpening its teeth.

If a predator is unlucky enough to make contact, it will be stuck with the quills, which easily come out of the porcupine's skin. Quills become embedded in an enemy and actually work their way deeper into its skin, for the tip of each quill is covered with hundreds of minute overlapping barbules that expand when stuck in tissue. Each time the victim's muscle fibers contract, the quill is drawn in deeper. The quills continue to penetrate up to an inch a day and can be fatal if they pierce an important organ. Quills should immediately be removed with pliers. Porcupines remove other porcupines' quills from themselves by grasping them with their incisors and their forefeet.

A porcupine does not have quills all over its body. Quills are most dense on its back and the upper surface of its tail and longest on its upper shoulders. There are no quills on a porcupine's face, its underbelly, or the insides of its legs. Quills are up to 3 inches long, and there can be as many as 30,000 on a single animal. They are controlled by a muscular sheath at the base, which can make them all stand straight out from the porcupine's body when the animal is in danger. Quills that are lost are gradually replaced by new ones, which grow to full size in several months.

Porcupines are preyed upon by great horned owls, coyotes, bobcats, mountain lions, and wolves, but their most formidable enemy is the fisher. It will relentlessly attack a porcupine's face, where there are no quills, until the porcupine is helpless.

Porcupine vision is poor, and the animals see well only at very close range. However, they have an excellent sense of smell and spend a great deal of time investigating their surroundings by sniffing.

Porcupines make a variety of sounds, some of which are often mistaken for those of other kinds of animals. They can make shrill screeches, ascending and descending whines, and low grunts. Females and young make low grunts and whines to each other.

Clues:	Tracks	Common	See page 26
	Scats	Common	See page 56
	Natural cavity (dens)	Uncommon	See page 116
	Claw marks on trees	Uncommon	See page 78

Porcupine range map

Food and Feeding Habits

Porcupines are vegetarians. They eat a large variety of plants, shrubs, and trees. They have 4 large incisors that help them snip off vegetation and chew into bark, and 16 premolars and molars that enable them to grind up their food. The teeth continue to grow throughout a porcupine's life but are kept down by gnawing and self-sharpening as the animal grinds the lower ones against the upper ones.

In the Northeast during winter, the major food of porcupines is the eastern hemlock. In the West, it is western hemlock, Douglas fir, and ponderosa pine. Porcupines also eat other conifers such as white pine, lodgepole pine, piñon pine, firs, spruces, and larches. They eat deciduous trees also — maple, beech, birch, oak, elm, cherry, basswood, and willow. They also eat all kinds of woody shrubs.

In winter, porcupines may remain in the tops of trees for long periods, eating. Sometimes they eat the bark all the way around a tree, thus girdling it and killing the portion above. They also clip foliage and small branches that are in their way as they move around. They will clip oak trees' branches to get at acorns. They may eat the bark off smaller trees at the snow line if the snow is deep. Porcupines have been known to gnaw on other wood objects like old boards, houses, and camp tables. They also are attracted by salt and may chew on any tool that has retained the salt from human sweat, such as the handles of garden tools, axes, and paddles.

In the summer, porcupines shift to feeding on ground vegetation. They eat many kinds of grasses, leaves, dandelions, clover and other wildflowers, farm crops, twigs, flowers, and aquatic vegetation such as pond weeds, water lilies, and arrowhead. They can swim out to water lilies. They also may eat the emerging shoots of skunk cabbage.

Clues:	Bark chewed off	Common	See page 72
	Twigs on the ground	Common	See page 80

Family Life

The breeding season for porcupines occurs between September and early December. At this time males have been seen in vicious fights with other males in which they utter high-pitched screams, get bitten, and receive foreign quills. These fights may be to establish dominance. During the breeding period, males spend a lot of time exploring scents, concentrating on areas where females have urinated such as tree trunks, roots, and rocks. They may also mark these spots by rubbing their own genital area on them. This may be a form of communication that enables males to find females in estrus.

Very few people have observed porcupines mating in the wild. The most thorough study of porcupine courtship has been done in

Young porcupines

the laboratory. How much of this courtship behavior also occurs in the wild is open to question. In the laboratory, males rub their genitals on objects in the cage throughout the year, but this becomes more pronounced during the breeding season. Females do likewise, to a lesser extent. When a male is put in a female's cage, he smells every place the female has urinated. He may then rub up against objects, possibly leaving his own scent. Urine probably conveys certain olfactory information about breeding readiness to porcupines and may stimulate them. When porcupine males are sexually excited, they produce a low- or high-pitched "whining."

Females are in heat for 8 to 12 hours and, if they do not mate at this time, they may come into heat again in another 25 to 35 days. When a male approaches a sexually receptive female, he may rub noses with her and sniff her genital area. Prior to actual mating, the male and the female stand on their two hind legs and again rub noses. At this point the male may spray urine in short spurts over the front of the female. The female may object vocally and run away, but if she is ready to mate, she makes very little effort to move away.

When ready to mate, the female will back up to the male on all four legs, raise her tail, and present her genitals. He will smell her and then rear up on his hind legs and make sexual contact. The underside of the female's tail does not have quills, and the male can lean lightly on this with his belly or paw and does not get stuck with quills. Copulation lasts for several minutes and may be repeated during the next few hours. When the female is no longer receptive, she will reject the male and move away.

The female porcupine is pregnant for 205 to 215 days. Between April and August one baby is born, delightfully referred to as a porcupette. The baby is born in a ground den or shelter and at birth has quills, but these are soft and do not harm the mother. Within several hours after birth the quills have dried and are functional; a baby porcupine can make a defensive posture by turning its head away and striking with its tail. The baby is quite well developed and weighs about 1 pound, has open eyes, and is covered with black hair and quills up to 1 inch long. It will nurse until it is 3½ months old but can eat solid food, such as leaves, from the ninth day onward. Baby porcupines have been observed at play, running about, dodging, erecting quills, and thrashing with their tails. These actions are similar to the ones it will use as an adult to defend itself. A young porcupine remains with its mother throughout the summer and goes out on its own in the fall. Porcupines reach sexual maturity at 15 to 16 months. They may live up to 10 years in the wild.

Porcupine — Quick Reference

Habitat: Woods, often with evergreens
Home range: A few acres in winter to 200 acres in summer
Food: Plants and bark from trees
Mating: September to December
Gestation: 205 to 215 days
Young born: April to August
Number of young: 1
Number of litters: 1
Young independent: Weaned at 3½ months

Adult coyotes

COYOTE /
Canis latrans

ONE SUMMER WE went camping in the Beartooth Mountains in Wyoming. Just as darkness fell and we had settled into our tent, we heard some light rustling nearby. Suddenly we heard a piercing howl and then a little later an answering howl from farther away. It was two coyotes. Their sound was eerie yet beautiful. We had always thought a coyote howl would be a bloodcurdling noise that would make our hair stand on end. But we found the sound not scary at all. We were intrigued. Perhaps they were a mated pair out hunting for their growing pups.

The coyote, *Canis latrans*, is a medium-size, slender member of the order Carnivora and the Canidae, or dog, family. Coyotes have pointed, yellowish ears, a slender, pointed muzzle, and a bushy, rather short tail with a black tip. The tail has a black spot on its top, several inches out from the base, where the tail gland is located. Coyotes vary considerably in color from very pale to very dark, but most are yellowish gray with whitish or buff throats and underparts. They have a dark line running up the front of their lower forelegs. Their coats are coarse and rather heavy, the outer hairs tipped with black, giving the coat a blended or grizzled appearance. Coyotes that live in desert regions tend to be lighter and more yellow than those that live at higher altitudes, which are grayer and blacker. There is no difference in color between the sexes, but males are usually larger than females. Coyotes weigh from 18 to 30 pounds, and an exceptionally heavy male might weigh 48 pounds. They are 23 to 26 inches high at the shoulder and 41 to 52 inches long excluding the tail.

Coyotes may be hard to distinguish from red wolves, gray wolves, and some domestic dogs. What complicates matters even more is the fact that coyotes can interbreed with dogs and wolves and the resulting hybrids may look very much like coyotes. It may be hard to distinguish them on the basis of external features; experts tell them apart by skull characteristics and other measurements.

There is a subspecies of the coyote called the eastern coyote, *Canis latrans var.*, that during the past fifty years has been expanding its range into the northeastern United States and eastern Canada. This subspecies is a result of hybridization between coyotes, wolves, and coyote-wolf types. Eastern coyotes are similar to other coyotes but are somewhat larger (35 to 40 pounds). It is believed that in the 1800s, coyotes were pushed out of the Great Plains by poisoning campaigns against them. They emigrated into Ontario and interbred with the wolves there, *Canis lupus lycaon*. The resulting coyotes then spread throughout New York, New England, and Quebec. Coyotes on the expanding front of their range may sometimes breed with dogs if they cannot find a mate of their own species, resulting in a coyote-dog hybrid called a coydog. But these are not that common and usually do not breed beyond the first generation.

Getting Around

One of the interesting things about coyotes is their variable and flexible social organizations. The basic social unit is the mated pair, but coyotes may live alone or, in certain instances, in packs.

Coyotes live alone when they are sick, disabled, or juveniles dispersing to new areas. Occasionally, lone coyotes are healthy adults, and they are often recruited as new mates or pack members.

When paired, coyotes may live together for quite a long time, sometimes for life. They will hunt together, raise their family together, and even use the same den site year after year.

In certain circumstances, coyotes form packs. These packs have been most studied in Wyoming, in the Grand Teton National Park, and on the National Elk Range. The packs have from 3 to 7 members and consist of a mated pair and their offspring of various ages. They travel, sleep, and eat together. There is a dominance hierarchy within the pack, and the leader is usually a male but it may be a female. They have well-defined territories of about 8 square miles, which they defend from other coyotes by chasing them out. They also mark the boundaries of their territories by depositing urine and feces.

These packs are most frequently seen in winter in areas where there is a concentration of large ungulate carrion available. In places such as the National Elk Range and Grand Teton National Park, deer, moose, and particularly elk concentrate in large numbers, and some die from starvation and other causes. The coyote packs feed on these carcasses in winter. In the summer months when the carrion is less available, coyotes are less frequently seen in packs. They tend to hunt alone and eat mostly mice and ground squirrels.

Not all the Wyoming coyotes live in packs in winter; some are lone individuals and some are mated pairs. These coyotes do not have territories but instead live in home ranges that average 11½ square miles. Coyotes in other areas of the country have home ranges from 5 to 25 square miles.

Coyotes can be active at any time during the day, but they are most active at sunset and in the early morning. They may even have periods of activity during the night.

Through facial expressions, vocal signals, and scent-marking, coyotes communicate with each other. Postures and facial expressions range along a continuum from very submissive to very aggressive. An aggressive coyote will hold its head high with its neck arched and with shoulder and neck hairs erect. Its eyes will be narrowed and its mouth open, exposing canine teeth. A submissive coyote will have its head and body low, ears laid back, tail tucked between its legs, and tongue hanging out. It may paw and lick another's face and may lie down on its side with one hind leg raised and then urinate. When coyotes greet each other, they indicate which one is dominant and which is submissive by the use of such gestures. When they want to play, they signal their intentions by raising their foreleg and making face-licking motions. They may also lower the front end of their body, raise their hindquarters, and wag their tail.

Coyotes have ten or more gradations of vocal sounds, including growls, woofs, barks, howls, and yelps. Woofs and growls are short-distance threat and alarm calls; barks and bark-howls are long-distance threat and alarm calls; whines are used in greetings; lone and group howls are given between separated group members; and a group yip-howl is often done after the group reunites. Group howls and group yip-howls are also given before or after territorial defense.

Coyotes communicate through scent as well. They have two anal glands and a gland on top of their tail. They can impart their scent to their urine or feces or rub scent off on the ground. This scent-marking may identify individuals or groups, and it may also be used to indicate territorial boundaries.

Clues:	Tracks	Uncommon	See page 20
	Scats	Uncommon	See page 64

Coyote range map

Food and Feeding Habits

Coyotes are opportunists and eat a wide variety of food items. They eat many small mammals, including mice, voles, pocket gophers, squirrels, rabbits, and porcupines. They also eat songbirds, poultry, snakes, frogs, lizards, turtles, fish, crayfish, insects, fruit and berries and other plant material, carrion, and garbage. They eat the carcasses of elk and deer that have died of starvation. Sometimes they will kill and eat fawns and adult deer. If they have surplus food, they cache it by burying it in the ground.

When hunting deer, several coyotes may work together, chasing it in relays or ambushing it. When hunting small mammals, they scan the ground and poke into likely places. If they see or hear a mouse, they will stalk it and then pounce on it with their forepaws. They kill their prey by biting into the neck.

Coyotes also sometimes prey on domestic sheep and other livestock, and this has led to expensive extermination campaigns against them. In spite of this harassment, coyote populations have continued to survive and in some cases expand. Failure of the control programs has been due to the fact that the relationship between the coyote's behavioral ecology and its population dynamics is not fully understood. More study is needed in this area.

Family Life

The main social unit of coyotes is the adult pair. Coyotes mate from January to April depending on geographic location. Females come into estrus for only a relatively short time, 4 to 15 days once a year. Males become increasingly interested in a female's urine and feces and may be able to tell how ready she is to breed from her scent. The female will readily accept the male for mating during estrus. Males are sexually ready to mate for only a relatively short time, unlike the male domestic dog, which can breed at any time.

Before copulation, the pair may howl in a duet. The female then presents herself, and the male mounts her, holding onto her hind-

Young coyotes

quarters with his forepaws. Mating is similar to that of domestic dogs. Copulation ends with the pair being "tied" together; that is, the male's penis swells and becomes locked inside the female's vagina for up to 25 minutes. During this time the male has stepped over the female, and they are standing tail to tail facing in opposite directions.

After release, the female may circle the male and lick his face. Copulation may take place repeatedly over the several days during which the female is receptive. When estrus is over, she will reject the advances of the male.

The female is pregnant from 58 to 63 days and usually gives birth to a litter of 5 to 7 young. Larger litters are born in years when there is a more plentiful food supply. Males and females may breed during the season following their birth, but often this depends on the environmental and social conditions in which they live. First-year females are more likely to breed in years with a good food supply. Yearlings that remain with their parents as part of a pack may not breed but instead may help raise their parents' litter.

Coyote pups are born in underground dens. The animals can dig their own dens but usually enlarge the old dens of other mammals such as badgers or woodchucks. The female and pups lie in a hollowed-out area about 3 feet in diameter. There may be more than one entrance to the den and connecting tunnels. Dens are found on slopes, in brushy areas, thickets, gravel pits, strip-mined areas, or woods. On the prairie, they may be on knolls so that the adults can spot danger more easily. Dens can also be under dense clumps of multiflora rose or in hollow logs. Coyote parents may move the pups to another den if there is a disturbance.

The pups are blind and helpless at birth and have woolly, grayish fur. Their eyes open at 8 to 14 days, and at about 3 weeks they venture out of the den for short periods. The female nurses them. Sometimes two females may raise their pups together in the same den. Pups are weaned at 3 to 5 weeks. The young urinate and defecate without help at 2 to 3 weeks, but before this, the adults stimulate them to do so by licking their genitals. Starting at about 3 weeks, the pups begin to eat semisolid food, which has been regurgitated by the mother and father. Occasionally, there also will be helpers, siblings from the previous year that assist in raising the young. At about 6 weeks young coyotes may sleep above ground, except in bad weather.

Coyote pups are more aggressive at an earlier age than wolves or dogs. The pups bite and wrestle with their mother, but she does not initiate interactions with them, and she will not interfere in sibling fights. At 4 to 5 weeks the pups begin serious fighting among themselves, which results in the establishment of a dominance order. Wolves don't do this until they are more than 6 months old. Fighting is gradually replaced by displays that communicate dominance and submission. Following this, there is a decrease in fighting and then an increase in playing.

Coyote pups give clear signals to their littermates when they want to engage in play. These signals include lifting a foreleg and pawing another pup's face while growling and wagging its tail; or the "play-bow," in which the pup lowers the front of its body and forelegs to ground, lifts its hindquarters, and wags its tail. Pups are less likely to enter into play with the most dominant pups, which therefore tend to be more solitary than their littermates and may be the first to disperse.

When the pups are 2 to 3 months old, they may make forays from the den with the adults. At 5 months they may hunt on their own, but

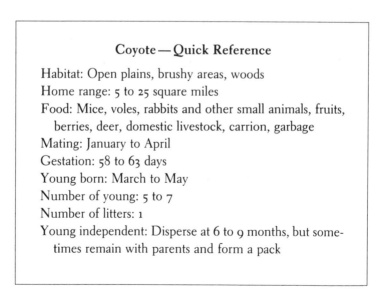

Coyote — Quick Reference

Habitat: Open plains, brushy areas, woods
Home range: 5 to 25 square miles
Food: Mice, voles, rabbits and other small animals, fruits, berries, deer, domestic livestock, carrion, garbage
Mating: January to April
Gestation: 58 to 63 days
Young born: March to May
Number of young: 5 to 7
Number of litters: 1
Young independent: Disperse at 6 to 9 months, but sometimes remain with parents and form a pack

they occasionally rendezvous with the parents. Between 6 and 9 months old, some coyotes disperse. In a Minnesota study, 70 percent of pups dispersed during October and November and traveled an average distance of 30 miles. Not all the pups disperse, and in some cases young coyotes remain with their parents and form a pack in the winter.

Clues: Den   Rare   See page 90

Adult red fox

RED FOX / *Vulpes vulpes*

THE ANIMAL AT THE end of the field moved slowly across the snow, nose to the ground. Expecting it to be a large cat or a small dog, we raised our binoculars and focused. Our eyes moved from the two pointed black ears over the luxurious, thick red coat to the bushy, long tail and stopped at the white tip. Our hearts started pounding — it was a red fox, hunting about 200 yards away, and the time was only 3:30 P.M., so there was plenty of daylight. We were here to count birds as part of the National Audubon Christmas bird count, but this was too good to pass up.

We froze in our tracks near the hedgerow and watched. The fox continued to move toward us. It slowly wandered in an erratic path, nose to the ground, hunting for voles. Interestingly, it kept to the swath of slightly longer grass in the middle of the field, a better vole habitat than the sheared grass at the edge. Suddenly it stopped, pricked its ears forward, and stared at a spot on the ground, listening intently. It stalked forward as if on tiptoe, then froze, one paw out in front. Gathering its body, it leapt high into the air and came down with its forepaws perfectly together as if to pin the vole. After two more quick stabs with its forefeet, it poked its muzzle into the snow and then came up empty-mouthed. It had missed.

It continued forward again and now it was only 50 feet from us — when would it stop? We were flabbergasted! Never had we gotten this close to a fox in daylight without it sensing us. Our binoculars were glued to our eyes and we were barely breathing. Our arms ached because we hadn't moved in 20 minutes.

Then we realized something. An incredibly fortuitous set of circumstances had brought the fox and us this close. We were downwind from the fox, and its eyes were narrowed to slits against the incredible glare of the setting sun reflected off the snow. It probably had neither seen nor smelled us. Suddenly it stopped and stared directly at us. It turned and moved off very quickly in a floating trot with one backward glance toward us before it disappeared into the hedgerow. It had sensed us.

The red fox is an extremely keen animal and one of the few mammalian hunters common enough that we are able to find its signs and trails and thus gain a unique view into its life. The red fox lives closer to us than most people believe, favoring the varied habitats of suburban and rural areas to those of the wilderness. The red fox also leaves behind a great many clues to its presence, and when you learn to read these you may find that the animal passes through your own neighborhood or even backyard. Among the clues to learn are the tracks and the scats. It also helps to know the skunk-like odor of the fox's scent-marking and the appearance of actively used dens.

The red fox is a medium-sized mammal, generally with reddish fur on its back and sides, whitish fur underneath, and black legs and feet. It is the only species of fox with a white-tipped tail. There are other color variations of the red fox: black, which is all black; cross, which has a dark cross of fur across the shoulders; silver, which is really black with white-tipped guard hairs; and intermediate phases. All these varieties of foxes have a white tip to their tail. The red fox is not as large as most people think; it is only 22 to 25 inches long, excluding tail, and weighs only 10 to 15 pounds.

The red fox, *Vulpes vulpes*, is in the family Canidae, or dog family, which is in the order Carnivora, or carnivores. There are four other species of fox in North America, but the red fox has by far the widest distribution. It prefers habitats that combine woods and open areas. The gray fox, *Urocyon cinereoargenteus*, has a gray coat with a black stripe down its black-tipped tail. It is fairly common throughout the United States, but not in Canada. It lives in brushy areas, forests, and chaparral and rimrock country. The kit fox, *Vulpes macrotis*, is the smallest species of fox and has very large ears. It lives in the desert areas of the western United States. The swift fox, *Vulpes velox*, is slightly larger and is found in the Plains states. Also in the family Canidae are the wolf, coyote, and domestic dog.

Getting Around

Foxes are largely nocturnal, becoming active about 2 hours before dark and ending several hours after dawn. A fox spends most of its time looking for food, and how long it remains active on a given night depends on how easily it finds food. In winter, when it may be harder to catch prey, a fox may continue its hunting more into the daylight hours.

During the day, foxes generally sleep out in the open — dens are used only for breeding. In the winter a fox's daytime bedding area is usually located in fields, or on southward-facing slopes, where it can take advantage of the sun's warmth. During thunderstorms or other bad weather, the fox may bed down under evergreens or dense brush. The fox may return to the same area each day to rest but does not usually bed in the exact same spot.

A fox home range consists of a series of pathways between areas of intensive use. Estimates of their home-range size are from 1 to 5 square miles, the size varying with the season, the diversity of the habitat, the abundance of food, and the sex of the animal. In winter, foxes may move farther in search of food; in mixed fields and woods, a range may be smaller due to an abundance of diverse foods; in open farmland, the range may be larger; and when the adults are caring for young they may stay nearer the den.

There is still much to be learned about how foxes define their home ranges and under what conditions they are territorial. One thing that studies show is that the behavior of foxes varies. In some cases foxes are clearly territorial and aggressively defend their boundaries; in other cases they may share an area and have overlapping home ranges. Whether this variety is due to the season, the breeding cycle, habitat, or population density is still unknown.

There is also a great deal of variety in the social organization of foxes. In most cases an adult male and female join together during the breeding season and then may move about more separately during the rest of the year. However, in a dense population of red foxes in England, the animals lived in social groups of up to five adults, composed of one male and several females. In this case one female seemed to be dominant over the others in her group, and each group defended a territory.

A study in Alaska at a feeding station where foxes were offered food scraps found that the foxes that visited the station established a social hierarchy. The most aggressive interactions took place when the top-ranking fox was involved. Usually dominance was settled by ritualized fights in which foxes stood up on their hind legs and pushed each other with their forepaws while snapping their jaws and screaming. The winner was the one who pushed the opponent backward. When members of opposite sex fought, they lay face to face screaming while their noses almost touched.

Foxes scent-mark frequently and in a variety of ways. Scent-marking is most likely one of their main methods of communication and may carry information about the animal's sex and breeding condition and possibly its individual identity. You may be familiar with one of the fox's odors, which is a little like skunk spray but is more pungent and less offensive. It is present in all fox urine. The scent is usually left on prominent objects such as a rock or a tuft of grass, or at the edge of a given habitat. Scats are also often repeatedly left at certain spots along trails, so that several scats of varying ages accumulate. They seem more prominently placed in winter and may play a part in the foxes' communication system.

Foxes have several scent glands. They have one on the top of the tail near the base and two glands on either side of the anus that are under voluntary control. To leave a scent from these glands, a fox may back up to an object and rub up and down on it several times.

In addition to their scent-marking, foxes also communicate vocally. They can bark, yap, howl, and screech. Adult foxes give a "wuk . . . wuk . . . wuk" chortle at the entrance of the den when they bring food for the pups. During the mating season, foxes have been heard to give a variety of barks, howls, and screeches.

| *Clues*: | Tracks | Common | See page 20 |
| | Scats | Common, especially in winter and spring | See page 64 |

Red-fox range map

When following a fox track, be on the lookout for urine marks in the snow or on natural objects. They will smell very strongly, especially when stirred with the end of a stick. Coyote urine does not have such a strong smell, and dog urine is practically odorless to humans in winter.

Humans are generally not aware of smells outside, but if you keep alert for fox scent in winter and early spring, you are likely to come across areas where it is very strong. This is a particularly good clue to a fox when there is no snow on the ground. Follow the strength of the smell, and you can usually find whatever the fox marked.

Food and Feeding Habits

Foxes are opportunists and will not pass up any easily available food source. Their main foods include small mammals, carrion, insects, and fruit. Their most important food is meadow voles, which are eaten throughout the year but probably most often in the fall, winter, and spring. Deep snow can cover the tunnels of voles and make them harder for the fox to catch. In these cases the fox may turn to rabbits, deer mice, and possibly carrion such as dead deer. In summer, foxes eat a great number of insects, including beetles, grasshoppers, and crickets. They also eat a lot of raspberries, blackberries, and blueberries. Because of these changes in diet from season to season, the consistency of fox scats also changes seasonally. After a fox has eaten voles, its scats are composed mostly of hair and bone, and they hold together and last a long time. In summer, after a fox has eaten insects and berries, its scats are crumbly, smaller, and quick to disintegrate. Foxes also eat a wide variety of other small mammals and birds, domestic poultry, bird eggs, turtles, turtle eggs, fruits, nuts, grasses, and grain.

Foxes hunt in several different ways. They may stand motionless, ears erect, looking and listening intently, and then pounce, bringing their forepaws down together and pinning the prey; or they may try to chase it. They may also travel along a trail, making side forays to investigate likely areas for chancing upon prey. Small prey are eaten whole, but the feet and tail of larger prey, such as muskrats, and rabbits, may be left uneaten, as are the wings of larger birds.

Occasionally, foxes cache their food. They excavate a hole with their feet, deposit the food, and cover it by pushing the dirt back with their nose. Sometimes other animals locate and raid these caches. Caches are more common in winter, when food is less abundant and it is more important for the fox to use its kills efficiently.

A fascinating study was done in Canada on the behavior of foxes as they scavenged for food in a national park. It was found that foxes urine-marked places where they had already found and eaten food but where food odor or inedible remains persisted. The next time the foxes hunted over the area, they were still attracted to these spots but could quickly determine that they had already been visited because they were urine-marked. This made their foraging more efficient, for the foxes spent less time at these spots and more time investigating new productive spots.

Clues:	Hornet's nests torn open	Common	See page 124
	Dug-up turtle eggs	Common	See page 124

Young red foxes

Family Life

Starting in December, look for two or more sets of fox tracks moving about together. This is a sign that foxes are joining into pairs or groups and beginning their breeding season. Generally, only one male and one female form the family unit, but there have been cases where one male joins with up to four females. Once paired, the foxes remain together and hunt cooperatively. The breeding season lasts from December until March with a peak in late January. Foxes that live in the South breed earlier than those that live in the North.

At the time that the male and female pair up, they will begin to explore dens within their home range. Foxes can dig their own dens but usually occupy a den from previous years or modify a woodchuck den by enlarging the hole and making a chamber off the underground tunnel for the pups to be born in. Signs of excavation do not necessarily mean that the den is in use. Foxes will excavate several dens in an area and may use any or all of them in the course of the breeding season because they may move their pups. Sometimes the same den is used for generations, and new chambers and entrances are added each year.

Fox dens can be found in fields, woods, on the elevated banks of streams or gullies, culverts, under slash piles, or on rocky ledges. Foxes do not den in areas constantly disturbed by humans. The dens are always in loose soil with good drainage, often on a bank or hill, and usually near fields and water. The average den has several main entrances, which may have mounds of excavated earth in front of them. A fairly typical den we once saw had five entrances and was on a south-facing, sparsely wooded slope where some timber had been cut. The main entrance had a mound of dirt in front of it about 1 foot high and 3 feet wide. There were several lesser entrances, one of them under a fallen log.

Foxes use their dens only for rearing their young and occasionally as places of escape or refuge from severe weather. The den itself is kept free of feces and food leftovers, but this is not true of the entrances. We once saw several scats in and around an entrance to an active den and nearby a large bone with fresh meat on it. There were several worn paths connecting two of the entrances to this den but no large mounds of dirt. It was quite inconspicuous from a distance.

During the breeding season, the female is in estrus for 1 to 6 days, and she will mate frequently during that time. Gestation takes an average of 52 days. She will have 1 litter per year, and the average litter size is 5 pups, but there can be up to 10. Young can be born anytime from March to May, depending on the time of mating. The pups are born with their eyes closed and have only a fine covering of charcoal gray fur. At first the female stays almost constantly with them in the den and nurses them, naps with them, grooms and cleans them, and eats their waste products. The male will bring food to the den for her.

After the pups are 10 to 14 days old, the female will leave the den for short periods to hunt. The male also continues to hunt and bring food for the pups. The adults do not remain in the den any longer, but keep close by when they are not out hunting. If there is a disturbance at the den, it is quite common for the parents to move the young to a new spot.

The role of the male in raising the young is still not clearly understood. Some radio-tracking studies have shown males bringing food to the den and associating with the pups until autumn. Other studies reveal females and young alone and no males participating in their care. It could be that the males are killed during the hunting season. In other studies, it has been shown that there may be several females and one male all at the same den area, and more than one of the females breeding. In these cases it is believed that the females may be related. Why and when these different social arrangements occur in foxes are questions that need more research.

The pups' eyes open when they are 8 to 12 days old. They can walk at 3 weeks, and at 4 to 6 weeks they start to gradually come out of the den. When they are about 25 days old, the pups have vicious fights with one another and establish a dominance hierarchy within a period of about 10 days. The largest pup, whether male or female, is at the top of the hierarchy. This dominance hierarchy determines food allocation; the dominant pups steal food from their more submissive littermates, so that when food is scarce, it is the most dominant pups that will survive.

Gradually the pups begin to leave the den more and more; having established a hierarchy, they also begin to play more with each other.

They explore, play with the remnants of bones and food left by the adults, and begin to hunt nearby by themselves. After the pups are 6 weeks old, the litter may be split up and reared in two separate dens. At 5 weeks the young have sandy brown fur, and by 14 weeks their outer red guard hairs have grown in and their coats resemble the adults'.

When an adult arrives with food, a hungry pup crawls forward on its stomach and reaches up to lick at the corners of the adult's mouth. Interestingly, this juvenile begging behavior is also a submissive gesture made by adult foxes when they meet more dominant foxes. At 10 weeks the pups venture out for short distances without their parents and at 12 weeks explore some of the home range during the day. They are weaned by the time they are 2 to 3 months old and are fully grown at 6 months.

The adults may take the pups on hunting trips and then lead them back to the den. Eventually, the adults stop bringing food so that the young must strike out on their own, although they remain within their parents' home range.

By mid-September to October, the young disperse. Studies of marked foxes indicate that they can wander 5 to 15 miles or more.

Red Fox — Quick Reference

Habitat: Mixed woodland and open country
Home range: 1 to 5 square miles
Food: Small mammals, carrion, insects, fruit
Mating: December to March
Gestation: 52 days
Young born: March to May
Number of young: 5 to 10
Number of litters: 1
Young independent: Disperse at 6 to 9 months

Males generally disperse first and move greater distances. Occasionally a female will remain on her parents' territory and will not breed herself but will help her parents raise their next litter. Young foxes can breed at 10 months and usually breed slightly later in the season than adults.

| *Clues*: | Holes in the ground (den) | Uncommon | See page 90 |

Adult dogs

DOMESTIC DOG / *Canis familiaris*

WE HAVE A GOLDEN retriever named Ego, who considers himself a member of our family, or perhaps it is the other way around — he considers us part of his family. He knows we are not dogs, for we do not smell or act like dogs, yet his behavior toward us is often the same as his behavior toward other dogs. He wags his tail low and licks our hands, or our faces if we bend down; he has a strong urge to associate with us; and he looks forlorn, with drooping ears and lowered head, if he is left behind when we go out. The strength with which he seeks out and solicits our affection is great, persistent, and very different from the attentions of our cat, Pablo, who is very friendly but seems aloof by comparison.

Dogs are very social animals, and much of their behavior is a result of canine genetic makeup. Like their ancestors, who at the present time are believed to be wolves, their inclination is to form packs. To a dog, a human being is a member of his pack and his owner is the pack leader.

Of all our relationships with domesticated animals, perhaps our closest is with the dog. Fossil evidence records a close association between humans and dogs as far back as ten thousand years ago. For thousands of years, we have selected dogs with certain characteristics and controlled their breeding to produce dogs with traits useful to us. Dogs have been bred as companions, as helpers in all forms of hunting and herding, for guarding property, for warfare, to further our knowledge of science, and as guides for the blind.

It is hard to imagine that dogs as seemingly different as Great Danes and Chihuahuas are members of the same species, but it is true. Whether you own a purebred or a mongrel, they are both the same species, *Canis familiaris*. They are in the family Canidae, which includes wolves, foxes, and coyotes and which in turn is in the order Carnivora, or carnivores.

Getting Around

Even though there are so many breeds of dogs, each with its own characteristics and temperament, there is a repertoire of behavioral responses common to all dogs and similar to the behavior of their wild relatives, the fox, coyote, and wolf. It is both enjoyable and useful to know what these actions are and where they originated, for they are used when dogs communicate with other dogs as well as with us.

Much of the behavior we see in our dogs is submissive, since they treat us as though we were their pack leader or a dominant dog. In addition, we keep dogs in a subservient role by continuing to be their food providers, as their parents were when they were puppies. Wild canids, on the other hand, would be on their own by the end of their first year.

When we come home, our dog is almost always peering at us from the end of our long dirt driveway. He stands with his ears alert, tail held high, and an intense look in his eyes; if we were close, we would see him sniffing the air. At a certain point he recognizes our car, probably by its sound rather than by its appearance, and, taking a shortcut through the yard, he races to greet us at the front door. As we get out of the car he comes over, ears back and relaxed, mouth parted almost as if in a smile, ready to nuzzle and lick the first hand offered, tail held low and leading his whole rear end in an energetic wagging. If we don't pet him at first, he nudges our hand and draws it across his head; he may also sit down and raise one paw up at us. One reason it is so easy to teach dogs to hold out their paw, or "shake hands," is that it's an instinctive action.

The backward-directed ears, low tail wagging, tongue licking, nose pushing, and lifting of one forepaw are all signs of active submission. They are indications of an effort to receive affection and social acceptance. In a group of dogs or wolves, these signals are given by the members to the pack leader when they greet the leader.

The roots of this behavior can be seen when parent dogs bring food to their young. The pups nudge and lick the corner of the parent's mouth to stimulate it to regurgitate food. Even earlier in the parent-pup relationship, the pup nuzzles around for the teat of the mother and while nursing lifts one paw up to press on the milk gland if the mother is standing.

You are probably familiar with the behavior of a reprimanded dog: It crouches down with its tail between its legs, flattens its ears, sometimes lies down on its side and raises one rear leg, exposing its genitals, and occasionally, especially if it is a puppy, urinates. When a submissive dog does this to a superior dog, the superior dog often sniffs and investigates the inferior one, particularly in the genital region. These are signs of what has been called passive submission. They express timidity and helplessness and are most pronounced when the superior dog (or owner) has a threatening or severe attitude. These behaviors have a parallel in the passive relationship of the pup to its mother as she sniffs and then licks its anogenital area to clean it.

Dogs also express dominance in fixed ways. When strange dogs meet, they slow down as they near each other, their legs stiff and their bodies raised up, almost as if walking on tiptoe. The hair on the back of their neck (hackles) is raised, and their ears are alert. They may utter low growls, and their lips may be pulled back, baring their canine teeth. One stops and stands absolutely still, tail pointed straight up, wagging rapidly but in a narrow arc. The other slowly approaches the groin of the stationary dog and begins to sniff. Suddenly they both begin to circle each other, each sniffing the other's genital and anal regions. Soon one dog shows signs of submission by lowering its tail and laying back its ears. It may even lie on its back, exposing its genitals to the dominant dog. Then the dogs part.

Encounters like this are not always settled simply. These stereo-typed behaviors are supposed to enable the dogs to avoid an all-out battle and risk of serious injury. If, however, neither dog shows submissive signs, they may begin to fight in earnest. They push and jostle each other, trying to get a hold on the opponent and turn the other over. The growls turn to snarls as they roll over and over, and any part of the body may be bitten.

Male dogs usually fight in disputes over territory. Female dogs usually fight when they are in estrus but not ready for mating, to protect puppies, or to establish dominance over other females. Male dogs are territorial and defend the house or area in which they live. Our dog will let female dogs or young dogs of either sex into our yard, but he will not tolerate other adult male dogs. Dogs differ in their degree of aggressiveness. Some kinds of dogs have been bred to be more aggressive than others. They are often the ones trained to be attack or guard dogs.

Communication between dogs is complex. There are many gra-dations of body postures and facial expressions. Sometimes a dog may simultaneously express contradictory emotions such as fear and ag-gression. It will crouch down in a submissive way and its ears will be back, but its hackles will be raised and its face will show aggression. In addition to body postures, dogs can communicate vocally by barking, whining, growling, and howling. These signals give us information about the dog's emotional state, and they may be used together with body postures to heighten whatever message the dog is conveying.

If you have ever watched your dog outside, or taken it for a walk, you have noticed that it frequently urinates or defecates on particular spots. This is probably a form of scent-marking. One dog's urine or scats do not inhibit another dog's movements; in fact, the other dog usually urinates or defecates over the same spot. Current research suggests that dogs use scent-marking mainly to make the environment familiar to them and to keep track of what other dogs have passed by. When defending their territory, dogs usually bark and chase away intruders, such as other dogs, people, or cars.

Dogs have a much more highly developed sense of smell than humans; through it they obtain much of their information about the world. Besides a well-developed nose, the dog has a second smell organ in the roof of its mouth. The olfactory area of the brain is also much larger in dogs than in humans. When a dog smells the places where other dogs have urinated or defecated, it is gathering information about other dogs in the area. Dogs have anal scent glands that may give an identifying odor to their feces. Their urine may carry their own odor as well. Females in heat, or estrus, have a particular odor to their urine and feces, and they become much more interested in marking and investigating odors at this time. Thus, each dog leaves its own calling card.

Dogs often scrape up the earth after urinating or defecating. This is not to cover up anything, for the scraping is often done to one side, but rather is a visual marking of the site that may also release other odors into the air, making the spot more noticeable. Sometimes dogs will seek out and roll in what we would consider the most foul-smelling stuff. Although it is not known for sure why they do this, it is thought that this novel smell gives them enhanced status when they rejoin their peers.

The sense of hearing is also very well developed in dogs. They can hear much higher frequencies than humans can. You have probably noticed that sometimes your dog suddenly seems to respond to something when you yourself can hear nothing. On the other hand, dogs are visually sensitive to movement but do not perceive form as well as we do. They are color-blind, seeing only shades of dark and light.

Clues:	Tracks	Common	See page 20
	Scats	Common	See page 66

Food and Feeding Habits

Obviously, most dogs are well fed at home and rarely show any of their predatory food-gathering instincts. Dogs retrieve sticks and balls readily because it is probably instinctive for them to chase and retrieve prey. This explains why most dogs are able to play this game with very little training. Dogs that are not able to exercise their prey-catching instincts may take to chasing cars or bikes, or retrieving things that you do not want them to take.

Family Life

Understanding the family life of dogs is complicated for two reasons. First, humans have encouraged the breeding of many kinds of dogs, and each breed varies in its courtship and parenting behavior. Second, most dogs are bred under somewhat artificial circumstances; a female in heat is presented to the male, and the pair is kept together for mating only, after which they are separated. Most puppies are also separated from their mothers 6 to 8 weeks after birth.

Female dogs come into estrus two or more times per year; male dogs may mate at any time of year. Free-ranging male dogs will be attracted to a female in heat because her urine gives off a powerful odor, discernible by male dogs for quite some distance. Some courtship may occur between a female in estrus and a male. They may bound playfully toward each other, run together, nose each other about the head and ears, and wag their tails. The male will gradually spend more time investigating the female's body and then licking her vulva. If the female is not ready to mate, even though she has been playful up to this point, she will resist and be hostile to any further advances.

If she is ready to mate, the female will stand still, present her swollen vulva, and turn her tail to the side while the male mounts. Experienced males orient correctly and mount more quickly than inexperienced males. The male clasps the female around her thighs with his front legs and makes pelvic thrusts as his penis enters her

Puppies

vagina. The posterior portion of the penis swells in the vagina and the muscles of the vagina constrict around it, locking the two dogs together in a "tie." Ejaculation occurs at this time and continues until the end of the tie. While the animals are tied together, the male steps over the back of the female so that the two dogs stand tail to tail, facing away from each other. The tie lasts from 10 to 30 minutes, and when the swelling goes down they separate. The function of the tie is not fully understood, but it may prevent semen from leaking and increase the possibility of fertilization.

Many dogs never have the opportunity to fulfill their sexual urges with a partner of the opposite sex. It is therefore not surprising that dogs sometimes make sexual advances, such as clasping and pelvic thrusting, toward substitute sexual objects including familiar cats or humans, or such inanimate objects as pillows and pieces of furniture. In addition, it is quite normal for puppies to engage in sexual play motions with their littermates.

Female dogs are pregnant for 59 to 63 days. If they have not conceived during estrus, sometimes they experience a pseudopregnancy, in which they display some of the symptoms of pregnancy. A pregnant female will not show much sign of pregnancy for the first 30 to 35 days, for the embryos grow slowly at first. During the remaining 30 days there is a very rapid growth of the fetus, and near birth the female may spend a lot of time resting and sleeping. During pregnancy, the female should be provided with a whelping box in some secluded place to her liking. When the time comes for birth, she will go to her area and lie down. She should be left quietly alone unless an obvious problem arises, for disturbing her could interfere with the birth process or her mothering of the pups.

Anywhere from 1 to 23 puppies may be born, depending on the breed of dog. An average birth takes from 3 to 10 hours. The pups are born encased in individual amniotic sacs, and the mother gently licks and nibbles at each sac until the puppy wiggles out. The mother cuts the umbilical cord, eats the sac and placenta, and licks the puppy dry. The puppy pulls itself forward on its short little legs while its head searches from side to side. Its eyes and ears are both closed. It has a pronounced sense of touch, and as soon as it finds its mother's warm belly, it roots around for a teat and begins to suck noisily. The puppy will instinctively knead the mother's milk gland with its forepaws to stimulate it. The mother at first lies down to nurse the puppies, but as they grow, she may nurse them while sitting or standing up.

The first 2 weeks of a puppy's life are known as the neonatal stage of development, during which it spends most of its time nursing and sleeping. Puppies use their forepaws to propel themselves, crawling not in a straight line but in a small circle, which insures that they never wander far from their source of warmth and food. If a puppy is separated from its mother, it will give sharp cries but will stop if it comes in contact with something warm and soft. The puppies huddle together for warmth because for several weeks their thermoregulatory mechanism is not fully developed. They urinate and defecate only when their mother stimulates them by licking. She then consumes their urine and feces and thus keeps the nest clean. Their eyes open between the twelfth and fifteenth day, but it may take up to 6 weeks for them to see clearly. Hearing is developed between 2 and 3 weeks, and the puppies move their ears in response to noise and recoil from loud noise.

The third week is called the transitional stage of development. This is characterized at first by the puppies investigating their littermates and immediate surroundings. At 3 weeks they also begin to play clumsily with their littermates, biting and tugging on ears, noses, and mouths, and striking out with their paws. Through this the puppy learns how much biting is too much, for a playmate may withdraw in pain or administer a hard bite and squeal. Puppies that are deprived of these experiences with siblings may not learn how to inhibit the strength of their biting when they are older. At the end of the third week they can growl and squeal but not yet bark. Some females will regurgitate food to their puppies, as their wild relatives do. The puppies may stimulate this response by pushing their noses against the corner of the parent's mouth. The mother's milk supply gradually decreases after 5 weeks. The puppies teethe and bite on things while their milk teeth are being replaced by their permanent teeth. Complete weaning ends at 8 to 10 weeks.

The socialization period occurs between 4 and 12 weeks. Puppies learn rapidly during this time, and most of the behavior patterns of adult dogs will begin to be apparent. Puppies, as well as adult dogs, will often signal their intention to play by bowing down their front and wagging their tail. They may bounce forward and then back, and run away as if wanting to be chased. Puppies also do a lot of mock fighting, during which they snap, growl, and assume many of the dominance and submissive postures seen in adult dogs. At times the mock fighting may erupt into real fighting, but it soon turns to ritualized behavior. By 4 months a dominance hierarchy has been established among the pups. Puppies will play with toys, shoes, and towels, and growl and shake them as though they were killing an imaginary prey. Sometimes one puppy will carry a stick in its mouth and the others will follow it, emulating pack-like behavior. It is also very normal for them to display sexual grasping and pelvic thrusts.

This socialization period is a good time to acquire a puppy as a pet. The ideal age is from 6 to 8 weeks, when pups are adaptable and are eager to learn and form relationships; at this age they will take readily to humans. Puppies that have been isolated from human contact and are acquired after 12 weeks do not always make good pets. They are harder to train and may never form a close attachment to humans.

The juvenile period lasts from weaning until puberty, during which the dog continues to develop, grow, and gain strength. The kind of environment it is in will continue to affect its adult personality. If it is treated with affection and attention to its needs, it will develop into a healthy adult dog. Some say that the dog does not reach emotional maturity until it is 1½ years old. Dogs reach sexual maturity at about 7 to 10 months, but this differs from breed to breed.

Domestic Dog — Quick Reference

Habitat: Fields, woods, human habitations
Home range: Varies widely
Food: Small animals, pet food
Mating: Females in estrus 1 or more times a year; males may mate any time of year
Gestation: 59 to 63 days
Young born: Variable; depends on species
Number of young: 1 to 23
Number of litters: Variable
Young independent: Weaned 8 to 10 weeks, reach sexual maturity from 7 to 10 months, but this differs from breed to breed

---

Adult black bear

BLACK BEAR /
Ursus americanus

ONE MORNING ON a remote northern lake, as our canoe drifted silently around a point of land, cutting through the glassy surface of the water, we heard a movement among the highbush blueberries on shore. As we turned to look, we got a glimpse of a large black object disappearing among the shrubbery. We sat still in the canoe and waited for the animal to reappear. There was some more rustling among the brush, and suddenly a huge black bear raised its head, licking its mouth, probably to get the last sweetness out of the blueberries it was eating. At first it was unaware of us, but after quickly scanning the lake it fixed its gaze in our direction. It seemed to pause briefly, trying to figure out exactly what we were. Within seconds it knew, and with amazing grace it bounded back through the brush and into the evergreen woods.

Most views of black bears in the wild are equally brief, for these animals can be very shy. Only when they regularly feed at dumps in urban areas or at trash cans in campsites do the animals get used to the presence of humans and stay in view longer.

Contrary to our usual image of bears being ravenous meat eaters, the black bear's main foods are fruits, nuts, and insects. It is extraordinary that such a large animal can satisfy its hunger on a diet of this kind and even build up a fat layer that it can live on through its winter hibernation.

The various sizes and colors of bears that can be found in North America would seem to indicate a bewildering number of species. In fact, there are only three: black bears, grizzly bears, and polar bears. Polar bears are all white and live only on the northernmost edge of the continent. Grizzly bears are brown to black, have a hump on their shoulders, and live in the extreme Northwest. Black bears have the widest distribution, living throughout Canada, down the East Coast and West Coast of the United States, and in the Rocky Mountains. Despite their name, they can be black, brown, cinnamon, and even occasionally grayish. The brown bear, or Alaskan brown bear, that lives in the Northwest and is our largest bear, is now thought to be a subspecies of the grizzly.

Bears are in the family Ursidae, which is in the order Carnivora. The black bear, *Ursus americanus*, can vary in size, weighing from 200 to nearly 600 pounds.

Getting Around

Black bears are generally solitary animals, avoiding or seemingly ignoring each other's presence. The only social units formed are the mother and her cubs during their first year, and the adult male and female when they are paired for a month or so in the summer. Several unrelated bears may be drawn to a food source, such as a dump, but they will avoid each other. Generally the larger bears are most dominant and feed first in these situations, while the smaller bears may have to wait their turn.

Bears stay within a home range for most of the year, leaving it in the fall only if they are forced to find better sources of food. The size of their home range varies considerably from 5 to 15 miles in diameter. In general, home ranges of males are three or more times larger than those of females.

Within their home range there is no particular place to which the bears continually return. Rather, they are nomadic and wander throughout their home range. They usually move on well-worn paths that they have created or paths used by a variety of animals. They may also use human paths. Trails may be used by several bears, for their home ranges often overlap. A home range must include water, for bears drink often and may even wallow in muddy shallows, possibly in an attempt to keep insects off. Also within the home range is the winter den, where the bear hibernates.

There are three things that you may see along bear trails: tracks, scats, and what have been called mark trees. Mark trees are created when a bear stands on its hind legs in front of a tree and reaches up to scratch and bite the bark. It also may rub its head and back against the tree, leaving fur and scent. These trees are used by both males and females, and any one tree may be used by more than one bear. The function of tree-marking is not known, but since it mostly occurs in midsummer when the bears are courting, it may be a form of communication between the sexes. Rubbing against trees may also be used to help get rid of excess hair during molting, which occurs all through summer.

Black bears move about during the day and are most active during dawn and dusk. In summer, feeding may keep them equally active throughout the day. When bears rely on humans for food, their schedule changes. If they are getting handouts they are most active at midday, and if they are feeding at dumps or trash cans they become active at night. Temperature also affects their rate of activity; if it is below freezing or above 90 degrees Fahrenheit, bears are less likely to move about.

At various times during the day or night a bear may bed down, usually in a slightly hollowed-out area within dense brush. A typical bedding area may be about 36 to 30 inches and about a foot deep. Young bears generally rest during the day in trees.

Clues:	Scats	Uncommon	See page 66
	Tracks	Uncommon	See page 28
	Claw marks on trees	Rare	See page 78

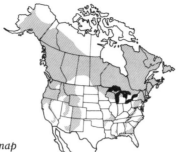

Black-bear range map

Food and Feeding Habits

Food usually determines where black bears are, for they need to eat a tremendous amount, especially in fall, when they have to build up the fat reserves necessary to get them through the winter and early spring. Unlike the grizzly bear and polar bear, black bears tend to be vegetarians. In spring they eat primarily grasses and emerging plants; in summer they eat mostly tree and shrub fruits and berries; and in fall they consume berries, larger fruits, and nuts such as acorns and beechnuts.

Throughout spring, summer, and fall, bears eat insects, especially the colonial species like ants — licking them off their paws as they disturb the nest — or wasps and honeybees, eating both the larvae and the adults, and, in the case of the bees, the stored honey. They also eat grasshoppers in late summer and beetles, either adults or grubs, that they find in rotted logs.

Black bears eat some meat as well. They may catch small mice or voles accidentally uncovered in their search for other food, or they may feed on carrion. They are generally not fish eaters simply because they are not good at catching fish, unlike the grizzly bear, which is an excellent fisherman.

As bears look for food they may turn over rocks or logs, rip open rotten logs or stumps, and pull down apple limbs to get the fruit. In the Northwest they are also known to strip the bark off evergreen trees and eat the inner bark. When bears eat, they often get bits of refuse mixed in with their food, such as sticks or leaves. These bits of material show up in their scats.

Black bears have rapidly adapted to feeding on human refuse, and there are numerous reports of bears at dumps, garbage cans, or near campsites looking for food. These bears can become a nuisance, but it is really our own habits that are creating the nuisance; the bears are just collecting food wherever they find it.

There are many signs of bear feeding, though none is absolutely conclusive; they must be used in conjunction with other clues. Large rocks turned over are a good sign of bears, since most other animals are not strong enough to do this. However, raccoons may turn over smaller stones.

Clues:	Bark scraped off trees	Uncommon	See page 72
	Fruit-tree limbs broken	Uncommon	See page 82
	Rotted logs broken apart	Uncommon	See page 82
	Hornet's nests torn apart	Uncommon	See page 124

Family Life

Through most of the year adult males and females avoid each other. In June a male may begin to follow a female of its choice, and the two move about, feeding and resting together for almost a month. During this time other males may challenge the paired male's right to the female. Most mating occurs in late June and early July. Soon after mating, the male and female go their separate ways, for the female raises the young on her own.

The egg of the female is fertilized at the time of mating, but it does not start to develop until about November. Beforehand it remains in a state of arrested development; this is called delayed implantation. Actual implantation starts in November, and from then on gestation lasts only about 6 to 8 weeks, which seems like a very short time for

Young bears

such a large animal. The result is that the cubs are born very small, weighing only 6 to 10 ounces and measuring about 8 inches long.

The young are born in January and February, when the mother is still semidormant in her den. It is not known how aware she is of the birth itself, but she must cut the umbilical cord and clean the cubs by licking. The young crawl up to the mother's teats, feed on milk, and stay warm in her fur. Their eyes are closed, and they have practically no hair. The female's first litter will consist of only one cub, but she usually has twins with each successive litter. There are occasionally 3 cubs and rarely 4 in a litter.

The baby bears remain in the protection of the den and the warmth of their dormant mother for another month or two, sleeping and suckling. After a few weeks, they have a coat of fine fur, and after about 40 days their eyes open. Anywhere from late March to early May they emerge with their mother from the winter den, and at this point the cubs weigh about 5 pounds. If before this time the mother has been disturbed — by a human presence, for example — she may rouse herself and move the cubs to a new den.

Mother and cubs stay together through the summer and fall, and by fall the young weigh about 55 pounds. In early winter, the mother seeks out a suitable den, and she and her young den together. Thus, in this year the female does not re-mate and does not have a new litter. The next spring, the yearlings and mother emerge from hibernation and, as the female gets ready to join up with a male for mating, the young are forced out on their own, either by the mother or by the male that decides to join her. A female black bear, therefore, has young only every other year. After the yearlings have left their mother they may separate and go on alone, or they may stay together for another year. Bears reach sexual maturity in 3½ years. Sexually mature male black bears stay alone through the year, except for the few weeks in midsummer when they pair up with females for mating.

Almost all black bears in the wild spend 2 to 4 months in winter dens, except in the South, where a few bears may remain active. Prior to this, in the fall, they eat a great deal and build up a thick layer of fat. They enter the dens anytime between October and January depending on the latitude; in the North bears may enter dens a little earlier. Generally, adult females are the first to enter dens, then the yearlings, then males.

Dens are usually located in the bear's spring and summer home range. The bear may have moved from this home range in fall to search for better food, but when ready to den it returns. In the few weeks just before denning, bears are less active and eat less. This may be to adjust their digestive tract to the dormant period. Also at this time a plug of material forms in their lower colon; the bear does not defecate during the entire denning period.

The den must provide some shelter from weather and some cover from predators, and it must be well drained so as not to collect water. Dens that provide a lot of cover can be among boulders; in rock crevices; under logs, upturned stumps, fallen limbs, or buildings; or in holes that the bears excavate. Dens can also be right out in the open, such as under conifers or even in the middle of deciduous underbrush.

When a black bear enters its den and becomes dormant, its temperature drops about 8 degrees Celsius, its heart rate drops from 50 to 15 beats per minute, and its metabolism is reduced by about 50 percent. Bears do not go into deep hibernation from which they cannot be roused, like the woodchuck. On the contrary, bears can be roused quite easily. Even if left undisturbed, they may get up, leave their den for an hour or two, and then return. Obviously the mother bear must also be awake enough to take basic care of her cubs. During hibernation, bears shed their footpads and also lose aboout 20 percent of their weight.

Black bears emerge from hibernation from March through May. Adult males are the first to emerge, followed by the females with young. At first they are sluggish and do not eat too much except a few grasses and a little bark. They discharge their fecal plug, and their digestive system slowly returns to normal. At first they continue to lose weight; in fact, weight loss occurs at a much faster rate now that they are mobile again. This is a hard time for them since fruits, insects, and plants are not at their most abundant. But luckily the bears still have enough fat reserves to get them through the spring. Bears live about 12 to 15 years in the wild.

Clues:	Natural cavities	Rare	See page 112
	Holes in ground	Rare	See page 92

Black Bear — Quick Reference

Habitat: Forests, wooded mountains
Home range: 20 to 175 square miles
Food: Berries, insects, garbage, carrion, small mammals
Mating: June to July
Gestation: 7 to 8 months
Young born: January to February
Number of young: 1 to 4, usually 2
Number of litters: 1 every 2 years
Young independent: 18 months

Adult raccoon and young

RACCOON /
Procyon lotor

I REMEMBER CLIMBING up a white pine when I was younger, to get a view of a nearby meadow. I got about two-thirds of the way up and stopped to look out. After a few moments, I decided to climb higher, and as I looked up for the next branch, there staring me in the face was a huge raccoon. At the time I didn't know that raccoons climbed trees, and I was both scared and amazed. I slowly backed down the trunk, alternately looking down for footholds and up for the animal's reactions. In fact, all it did was climb a little higher and nestle next to the trunk on a whorl of branches.

We now know that raccoons spend the day resting or sunning in protected spots such as trees, and several times a year we come across these spots and get a glimpse of the animals. Before raccoons climb trees they often leave scats at the base of the tree. Sometimes finding the scats this way will lead you to the animal up among the branches; at other times the scats may be old and just a clue to a previously used bedding site. Tree holes or rock crevices also can be used as resting spots, and whenever we find one we try to check it for a raccoon. We look for raccoon hairs around the entrance to the hole or along the trunk leading up to it, or we take a thin stick and gently place it in the hole to see if we can feel the animal inside.

The raccoon is a medium-size mammal with a black, mask-like pattern on its face and a long bushy tail alternately ringed with dark and light stripes. The animals range from about 25 to 35 inches long without tail and from 15 to 40 pounds. The raccoon, *Procyon lotor*, is one of three North American species in the family Procyonidae, which in turn is in the order Carnivora, or carnivores. The other two members, which live strictly in the Southwest, are the ringtail, *Bassariscus astutus*, and the coati, *Nasua nasua*.

Getting Around

Raccoons are active at night. How much of the night depends on the availability of food, the season, the sex of the animal, and the weather. It has been found that raccoons are less active on nights with full moons, and that raccoons near the sea may adjust their schedule to low tide to be able to feed on animals in the mud flats. During winter in northern areas, raccoons may remain sleeping in dens for days and weeks at a time and not venture out at all.

Raccoons have fairly fixed home ranges within which they use smaller portions for several days at a time. Their home ranges vary tremendously in size — from about 10 acres to several square miles — with most of the variation probably due to the availability of food. When traveling from one spot to another, they tend to use certain fixed routes, which over time become narrow worn trails through woods and underbrush.

Adult raccoons are generally solitary except during mating, when male and female remain together for several days. The home ranges of neighboring individuals may overlap broadly, and there is no part of the home range that is defended as a territory. Neighboring raccoons generally avoid each other, but occasionally they meet when competing over a common source of food, such as a trash can or dump. During these confrontations they will posture and possibly fight. Through these interactions the raccoons in a given area probably develop a dominance hierarchy, which reduces fighting in future meetings.

Raccoon scats may be left repeatedly at certain spots within the animal's home range, such as along trails or in prominent spots such as on a rock, a bluff, a fallen log; scats can even be found up in trees where the raccoons have bedded for the day. These piles of scats may be the result of more than one raccoon and may function as scent posts that help individuals know which other raccoons have been in the area. Raccoons may also leave scent marks by rubbing their anal scent glands along logs, rocks, and other prominent objects.

During the day, when raccoons are inactive, they either rest in protected spots, such as dens, or in more open areas where they can bask in the sun. The dens may be in tree holes, under tree roots, or in woodchuck burrows; the more exposed sites can be in the crotches of tree branches, on hummocks in marshes, on a muskrat home, or on a squirrel nest. In urban areas, raccoons may sleep for the day in drains or culverts, under porches, and even inside chimneys. After foraging at night the animal goes to this bedding spot, settles down, and sleeps there through the daylight hours. In New England the animals often choose large white pines for bedding spots, and they often leave their scats at the base of the tree.

A bedding area is rarely used on successive days; rather, the animals tend to move to a new spot each day. A bedding area may be as close to the old one as a hundred yards or as far away as half a mile.

Clues:	Tracks	Common	See page 24
	Scats	Common	See page 62
	Claw marks on trees	Uncommon	See page 78

Raccoon range map

Food and Feeding Habits

When it comes to eating, raccoons will eat just about anything they can get their paws on. In general, the raccoon takes advantage of whatever food is seasonally available.

In late spring and early summer, the bulk of its food is composed of animals such as crayfish, earthworms, slugs, frogs, turtles and their eggs, snails, oysters, small clams, salamanders, and insects. If the raccoon is near a body of water where crayfish live, these will be the most prominent item in its diet. Other foods occasionally eaten at this time include birds nesting in tree holes, young rabbits or young muskrats, fiddler crabs if the animal is near the shore, wasp and bee nests, and chickens and their eggs.

In late summer and fall the raccoon feeds more often on vegetable matter. All kinds of berries are eaten, and most kinds of crops or garden vegetables. Raccoons' favorite crop is corn when it is just ripe. Perhaps you have waited for your own corn plot to mature, only to find many ears ransacked by raccoons the day before you were going to pick them. Their favorite wild food at this time is acorns, which they continue to eat through winter.

In southern areas during winter, the raccoon will continue to feed on acorns and small mammals. In northern areas, the animals usually stop eating and stay in their dens.

Most raccoons in the North start to accumulate a layer of body fat in summer, and by fall they may be twice their spring weight. This layer sustains them throughout the winter. Late winter and early spring can be a time of shortage for raccoons, for there is very little plant food available, and the small animals they usually prey on may still be dormant and inaccessible.

Urban raccoons feed primarily on garbage. They seem to have mastered the trick of opening the various lids, latches, and clasps of our garbage containers, sometimes gnawing their way in.

There is a lot of controversy about whether raccoons wash their food before they eat it or just dip it in water for some other purpose. Most of the reports of washing come from studies of captive raccoons. One thing is clear: This action is certainly not washing, for after an initial dipping the food is eaten whether it is clean or dirty. Nonetheless, water seems to bear some relation to raccoon feeding in the wild. Raccoons collect much of their food in water by feeling around among the rocks and mud. They also may pick up an object on land, take it to water, and dunk it before eating it. At other times they may find food on land and eat it without dunking it, but in these cases they still seem to manipulate it in their hands before eating it. In any case, food is chewed thoroughly, possibly because the animals have a narrow gullet.

Although the raccoon is a common mammal and has a varied diet, there are few distinctive signs of feeding because it eats many of the same foods as opossums and skunks. One report states that when raccoons eat crayfish, they tend to discard the head and/or claws in shallow water. Like opossums and skunks, they may dig up turtle eggs from the ground and scatter the shells, and in fall they may rip apart wasp and hornet's nests.

Clues:	Hornet's nests torn open	Uncommon	See page 124
	Dug-up turtle eggs	Uncommon	See page 124

Family Life

In midwinter the female comes into estrus. In the South this occurs in December, and in the North it occurs in January and February. During this time the male wanders and may even leave his usual home range. He may travel as far as 8 miles in a single night, going from den to den as he searches for females. When he locates a den with a female who is in estrus, he enters the den and mates with her. He may stay with her for a day or so but then leaves in search of other females. The female may return to her winter sleep when the male leaves. She is receptive for about 3 to 6 days. If she does not become pregnant at that time, she may have another estrus period 2 to 4 months later.

Young raccoons

About a month after mating, a pregnant female becomes very active and wanders about her home range, feeding and looking for an appropriate breeding den. Breeding dens differ from winter dens in that they are usually in trees and have smaller, more protected openings. Sometimes a winter den has the right characteristics, and the female continues to use it in spring. A tree has to be about fifty to seventy-five years old to be large enough to house a raccoon and to have had a cavity rot out in it. The den can be from 10 to 60 feet high and can have an entrance as small as 5 by 3 inches, but it is usually more like 6 by 4 inches. Inside the tree, the cavity may go down 6 to 10 feet below the entrance and is usually about 8 to 13 inches in diameter. The raccoon may scratch or chew the inside wood or entrance to modify the den's dimensions, and it may create a wood-chip lining. In urban areas raccoons sometimes use a chimney for a den, and you end up hearing the sounds of the young through the flue of the fireplace. You may also find scats on the roof or around trees that they climb to get into the roof.

After a female chooses a breeding-den site, her nightly trips get shorter and shorter. Finally, one night she stays in the den and gives birth. Gestation lasts about 63 days. In the South births occur in February; in the North the months are March and April. There are usually 3 to 5 babies in a litter, but there can be as many as 7. At birth the young are slightly furred, only 4 inches long, and about 2 ounces.

The mother stays with her young for the first day or two. Thereafter she leaves for only an hour or two at night to feed but doesn't stray more than a few hundred feet from the den. For the first month, in fact, she rarely goes more than half a mile from the den to feed.

After 2 weeks the young raccoons' "masks" and tail rings are beginning to show. At 3 to 4 weeks their eyes open and after 5 weeks the mother goes out most of the night to feed. The young huddle together in the den and make sounds that at first resemble the twittering of birds; later, growling and "churring" sounds are made. At about this same age the young may climb to the den entrance and begin to look out. Sometimes they fall from the den, but even a fall of 20 feet does not seem to hurt them, and the mother retrieves them.

At about 6 to 9 weeks the mother may move the young to a den in or near the ground. They stay in this den until they are about 10 weeks old. Weaning now begins, and the young start to eat more and more solid food with their new teeth. After 10 weeks or so, the young leave the den with their mother while she forages nearby, and soon after that they all go out for the whole night and bed together in new bedding areas.

After the sixteenth week, the young are weaned, and they no longer stay right behind their mother while foraging. They begin to be more independent and roam on their own for up to several nights at a time, after which they may join their mother for several nights. However, they do stay within the mother's range. In early fall they may roam more widely. In the South the young disperse in fall; in the North the female and young may come together and spend the winter denning near each other, with the young dispersing in the spring. In general, young males venture farther than young females, traveling between 10 and 150 miles from their birthplace.

Clues:	Natural cavities	Common	See page 116
	Holes in the ground	Common	See page 88

Raccoon — Quick Reference

Habitat: Woods near streams in country, suburbs, city

Home range: 10 acres to several square miles

Food: Crayfish, insects, frogs, berries, fruits, vegetables, garbage

Mating: December to February

Gestation: 9 weeks

Young born: February to April

Number of young: 3 to 7

Number of litters: 1

Young independent: Weaned at 10 to 16 weeks, independent 4 to 6 months

Adult fisher

FISHER / *Martes pennanti*

THERE ARE PROBABLY more misconceptions about the fisher than about any other common mammal. Most of them are due to the animal's secretive nature and to the fact that it is rarely observed in the wild. In fact, even researchers have trouble locating fishers for firsthand observation, and thus most of the information available comes from tracking them. Tracking can be very informative, but it can only be done over long distances when there is snow. Thus, most of our knowledge about fishers concerns their winter habits.

Some of the fisher's common names, fisher cat and polecat, reflect the misconception that fishers are strange wild hybrids of weasels and domestic or wild cats. This in turn stems from the myth that weasels and cats interbreed, as well as from the physical similarities between fishers and cats. Both have long tails and are approximately the same weight and length, but the fisher has shorter legs and a longer body and is therefore proportioned more like its true relatives, the weasel, mink, and otter. Fishers look all black from a distance, but close up the fur around the face and shoulders is noticeably lighter.

Some tales suggest that fishers eat only porcupines, killing them by flipping them over on their back and attacking their belly. Others affirm that the quills of porcupines have no effect on the fisher because they cannot penetrate its fur. As with all hearsay, these tales contain a kernel of truth, as will be shown later, and a good deal of embellishment.

The fisher, *Martes pennanti*, is in the family Mustelidae, commonly called the weasel family, though it also includes the skunk, otter, and mink, among others. This family is in the order Carnivora, or carnivores. There is only one species of fisher, but it shares the genus in North America with the marten, *Martes americana*. Fishers are 20 to 25 inches long excluding tail and weigh 6 to 12 pounds. Although fishers are primarily northern, their range is slowly spreading south.

Getting Around

Fishers can be active at any time of the day or night, and daily activity patterns seem to vary greatly with individuals. Like most other members of the weasel family, such as the skunk, weasel, marten, and wolverine, the fisher is a solitary animal that avoids contact with other fishers except for the day or two when mating occurs. Avoidance of other fishers, and possibly some territoriality, may be accomplished through scent-marking with feces, urine, or anal glands, but this is still only conjecture, since fisher scent-marking behavior has not yet been studied in depth.

The average home range of females is 5 to 6 square miles, and that of males is 7 to 8 square miles. A fisher knows its home range well and moves about it in a roughly circular fashion, sleeping in different den sites as it travels. Circulating about its home range means that it will repeatedly pass over certain spots every few days, depending on how large its range is and how much it moves. An average distance traveled in a 24-hour period is 3 to 6 miles. Females in summer move less than males because they have young with them. The home ranges of members of the same sex rarely overlap. But male home ranges may overlap with those of several females, and this obviously facilitates sexual encounters during the mating season.

Fishers seem to avoid areas where there is little or no overhead cover, such as fields and open land, even though some of their food—voles, for example—is more accessible out in the open. Thus, fishers are always found in forested areas, and of these areas they prefer those with the densest canopies, such as evergreen forests. There is some evidence that they may hunt in grown-over fields in summer, when the young trees and shrubs provide cover, but they avoid them in winter, when the leaves are gone.

Clues:	Tracks	Common	See page 22
	Scats	Rare	See page 60

Fisher range map

Food and Feeding Habits

There is some truth to the stories about fishers eating porcupines. In fact, they are one of the few animals that successfully prey on the porcupine. They do get stuck by its quills just like any other animal, but they do not flip the porcupine over or circle around it to confuse it during the kill. Rather, they use their speed and long muzzle to attack the porcupine's face. The porcupine's defense is to turn its back and tail—and thus the majority of its quills—toward its attacker, but the fisher moves swiftly to stay in front of it. After many strikes by the fisher over half an hour or more, the porcupine is finally killed. The fisher then flips the porcupine over and starts eating from the belly, where there are no quills. Only if the porcupine is able to lodge its head into a protected crevice or hole, or sit facing outward on a branch, is it safe from the fisher's attacks.

Some wildlife biologists believe that the fisher can be used to control porcupine populations, especially where they are damaging forests. Therefore, in some states, fishers are being reintroduced in the hopes of reducing the number of porcupines. The tactic *seems* to be successful, but there is no conclusive evidence one way or the other.

Although fishers will feed on porcupines when they are available, their staple is the snowshoe hare. In fact, their most common foods, in order of importance, are snowshoe hares, porcupines, squirrels, mice and voles, and birds. Fishers will also feed on carrion when it is available, such as a dead deer or moose, often denning near the carrion and feeding on it for several days until there is none left.

The fisher hunts in two ways. When hunting porcupines, it tends to head straight for a known porcupine den and go after the animal. When hunting other prey, it moves through the woods until it comes to an area with prey, and then it explores all the spots where prey may be hiding, such as under logs, rocks, or evergreen boughs. When the prey is flushed out, the fisher catches it after a short chase and kills it with a bite at the base of the neck.

There are few distinctive signs of fisher feeding. If a porcupine has been killed and partially eaten, and the main focus of attack seems to have been the animal's face, then this is likely to have been a fisher kill. Other prey that the fisher might kill — such as rabbits, hares, squirrels, and mice — would be completely consumed, so there would be very little evidence. Since fishers may remain near a dead deer or dead moose for several days feeding on the carrion, you may see their tracks in the snow nearby.

Family Life

Female fishers are sexually mature in their second year. They come into estrus in March and April, and it is believed that males locate them through scent. The male may follow the female for a day or so before mating with her; actual mating can last up to several hours.

Young fishers

Fishers are probably promiscuous, with males continuing to search for other females after they have mated with one.

After mating, the fertilized egg of the female remains in a dormant stage until about January or February, when it becomes implanted in the uterine wall and resumes development. Thus, fishers have 10 to 11 months of delayed implantation. From this point, gestation takes 30 days.

Before the female fisher gives birth, she seeks out a suitable den. Fishers have two types of dens: temporary dens used for cover and sleeping, and breeding dens used for raising young. The temporary dens are used for several days at most and are located in protected places like a hollow log, brush pile, burrow, or even a tunnel dug to connect with a larger tunnel in the deep snow. The breeding dens that have been discovered have been mostly in the hollow portions of trees, 20 to 30 feet up. In some cases there have been signs of prey remains and scats at the base of the den trees, and in other cases there has been no sign at all.

The young are born in the den in March and April, and within 10 days the female has mated again. Thus, she is pregnant for all but 10 days of every year. At first the female spends almost all of her time with the young, leaving the den for only 2 to 3 hours per day. As the young begin to demand more food, she has to spend more time away from the den hunting. The male does not help raise the young. The young are born with their eyes closed, but after 7 weeks they are open. At 10 weeks the young are weaned, and by 12 weeks they begin to climb around the den. The young probably stay with their mother for the rest of the summer and may disperse in fall.

As we mentioned, there have been very few firsthand observations of fishers, and much more investigation needs to be done to understand even these basics of the fisher's life.

Clues: Natural cavities (den)   Rare   See page 114

Fisher — Quick Reference

Habitat: Mixed forests in wilderness

Home range: 5 to 8 square miles

Food: Other small to medium-size animals

Mating: March to April

Gestation: 11 months (10 months' delayed implantation)

Young born: March to April

Number of young: 1 to 4

Number of litters: 1

Young independent: Weaned at 10 weeks, independent in several months

Adult weasel

LONG-TAILED WEASEL /
Mustela frenata

LEAST WEASEL /
Mustela nivalis

ERMINE / *Mustela erminea*

WE WILL NEVER forget a time in summer when we were sitting out in a grassy meadow watching birds. We heard a sound in the grass, looked up, and saw a long-tailed weasel bounding through the tall grass right toward us — maybe it had not seen us because we were so still. It continued to approach to within a few feet of us and then, suddenly recognizing the danger, sped off toward the safety of a nearby blackberry patch.

People are often confused about the various species of weasels. They know there is something called a weasel that is reddish brown, and something called an ermine that is white. What they usually do not know is that these animals can be one and the same. There are actually three species of weasels in North America: the long-tailed weasel, the ermine (previously called the short-tailed weasel), and the least weasel. In summer, they all have reddish brown fur on their backs and whitish fur on their bellies, and in the northern part of their range they all turn white in winter.

All three weasels have similar body proportions and habits. The main difference among them is their size. The long-tailed weasel is the largest, measuring 11 to 22 inches long excluding tail and weighing 7 to 12 ounces. It has brown feet in summer, while the other two species have white feet all year round. In winter, in the northern part of its range, the long-tailed weasel is completely white except for its black-tipped tail; in southern areas it remains brown. The ermine is slightly smaller, being about 7 to 13 inches long excluding tail and weighing about 2 to 7 ounces. It, too, turns white in winter in northern areas and has a black-tipped tail. Thus, in winter these two can be difficult to distinguish. The least weasel is the smallest, 6½ to 8 inches long excluding tail and weighing 1½ to 6½ ounces. Throughout its range this weasel turns white in winter. It can be distinguished from the others by its tail, which never develops a black tip, summer or winter. There is also pronounced sexual dimorphism within each species, with the males about one-third longer and about twice as heavy as the females.

The long-tailed weasel, *Mustela frenata*, the ermine, *Mustela erminea*, and the least weasel, *Mustela nivalis*, are in the family Mustelidae, which also includes the fisher, mink, otter, and skunk. This family is in the order Carnivora, or carnivores. The information below applies generally to all three weasels, unless otherwise stated.

Getting Around

Unlike most other predatory animals, weasels are active day and night; they seem to alternate between periods of activity and periods of rest throughout a 24-hour cycle. In fact, available evidence seems to suggest that they are better suited to hunting during daylight, especially at twilight.

Some of the most beautiful tracks to see in the snow are those of the weasels, small pairs of prints spaced about a foot or more apart. They are delicate and exciting, for they seem to express the energy and activity of the animal as it hunts for prey. We usually find them in trails at the edges of fields in among the underbrush or along marshes and swamps.

Weasels are solitary animals, and adult males and females make contact only during the breeding season. They have fixed home ranges, except during the breeding season, when the male may wander more widely to find females. The home range for least weasels varies from about 2 to 35 acres. Home ranges for male ermine can be 16 to 35 acres and for females 5 to 25 acres. In the case of the long-tailed weasel, the home range is about 35 acres. Generally, the home ranges of females are about one-third the size of those of males. The great variance in home-range sizes is probably a reflection of prey density; home ranges can be two to three times larger when there is a food shortage.

The home ranges of weasels of the same sex do not usually overlap; however, in general the home ranges of males overlap with those of females. Within a weasel's home range there is usually a smaller area that is a defended territory. Males will generally avoid going into the territory of a female who lives within his home range, except during the breeding season. Through most of the year males are dominant over females, but when the females bear young, they are at least as dominant as the males.

Movement within the home range varies with the season and the sex of the animal. Females often have a central den, and their trails radiate outward from it. Males tend to circulate around their territory, visiting one hunting spot after another, or they may patrol the boundaries of their territory, especially those sections that are adjacent to another male's territory. Some researchers have found that long-tailed weasels and ermine make regular circuits around their territories about every ten days, repeatedly going over the same route. One study found that male long-tailed weasels traveled about 230 yards per night and females 115 yards per night.

Weasel scats are usually found along trails on top of rocks. There may be more than one scat at a certain spot, each a different age, showing that the animal has repeatedly passed by. Scats may also be left in a small pile a short distance from the entrance to a den. Piles of scats may be a form of scent-marking. Weasels can also scent-mark by dragging their anal scent glands across objects, and the urine of the female during estrus advertises her presence and reproductive state. Weasels react in a startled manner when they encounter the scent of another weasel.

Clues: Tracks   Common   See page 22

Scats	Uncommon	See page 60
Tunnels through the snow	Uncommon	See page 108

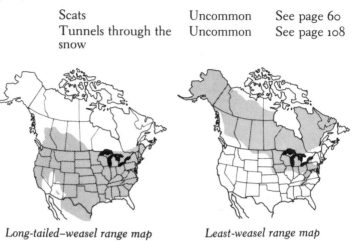

Long-tailed–weasel range map   *Least-weasel range map*

Ermine range map

Food and Feeding Habits

Weasels are often thought of as bloodthirsty predators that kill for the pleasure of killing, but nothing could be further from the truth. They are merely very efficient predators, well adapted for killing other small mammals. They also have a very high metabolism, which needs to be constantly sustained.

Weasels hunt by moving about the areas where their prey live, frequently checking out the burrows and tunnels of small rodents, and wandering about within the brush and hedgerows at the edges of fields. Their small, thin bodies enable them to squeeze into the tunnels of other small rodents; the least weasel can even enter and go through tunnels that are only an inch in diameter. When there is deep snow, weasels may tunnel underneath it in search of food.

It is thought that weasels hunt by scent, but there is good evidence that they also are dependent on sight and sound. When they catch animal prey, they bite it at the base of its neck and wrap their body around it as best they can. The bite usually kills the prey instantly. Prey, once killed, is eaten a little at a time over several hours; any surfeit is usually cached in a burrow nearby. Sometimes the weasel may eat only the most nutritious parts — the viscera, muscles, and brain — and leave the rest. If a nest is discovered, the weasel will kill all the animals present, cache them, and return to eat them gradually.

The most common prey is the vole, followed by mice, cottontails, rats, and shrews. Other food items include fish, amphibians, bird eggs, birds, insects, and some vegetation.

The sexual dimorphism that exists in each species of weasel seems to lead to a difference in the prey chosen by males and females. This could be advantageous because it lessens the competition between males and females whose ranges overlap. Usually female weasels prey on the smaller rodents and are often able to go right into their tunnels, whereas males tend to feed on slightly larger animals. Studies also show that a male and female living in the same general area hunt in different places.

There are very few distinctive signs of weasel feeding. One clue is that the weasel is a small predator. Unlike a larger predator, which would eat all of its prey at one time, the weasel may eat only a small portion and cache the rest.

Family Life

Although the weasel is fairly common, it is secretive and rarely seen. As a result, very little is known about its social and family life.

Both the long-tailed weasel and ermine breed only once a year, in

Young weasels

June, July, or August. In the case of the female ermine, spontaneous ovulation occurs in June and recurs in July and August unless the female mates. Ovulation is believed to be induced in the long-tailed weasel, occurring possibly up to 3 days after mating.

Male weasels probably mate with females on their home range, but if there are no females, they may roam farther to find one. During mating, the male bites the fur on the back of the female's neck and then mounts her. In the case of long-tailed weasels, copulation may last from 2 to 3 hours; if the male and female remain together, they may mate several more times in the following few days. After weasels have mated, male and female go their separate ways. The male plays no part in raising the young.

Even though the female long-tailed weasel and female ermine mate in mid- to late summer, they do not actually give birth until April or May of the following year. The female is pregnant for 205 to 335 days, but owing to delayed implantation, the fertilized egg remains relatively static for about 8 months. The actual development of the young takes only 25 to 27 days. During the time that the female is pregnant, she may expand her territory, become aggressive, and be at least as dominant as the male.

The den where female weasels give birth is a burrow or hollow lined with grass, leaves, fur, or feathers. It can be the burrow of a small rodent, such as a chipmunk or squirrel, or it may be a natural cavity — for example, the space under a rock wall, a fallen log, tree roots, a building, or a pile of debris. In one study, three least-weasel nests were found in eastern-mole tunnels. The nests were in cavities only 4 inches in diameter, contained grasses and some corn silk and husks, and were located 6 inches below the ground surface. In fact, the tunnels themselves may have been made originally by mice. There may be several tunnels leading to a den.

There are usually 6 to 7 babies in a litter of long-tailed weasels or ermine, and there can be as many as 9. The young are born blind and helpless, with only a fine covering of whitish hairs. Their eyes open after a month or so. The mother first feeds them milk and then gradually brings them prey. They may accompany her later on hunting trips and learn some hunting skills. They are believed to be independent of their parents in about 3 to 4 months. The young females are mature by their first summer, after they are 3 to 4 months old, while the males do not become sexually mature until their second year.

Long-tailed weasel females do not come into heat again until at least 2 months after young are born. Ermine females may come into heat during lactation.

The least weasel has an entirely different breeding pattern. Both the male and female become sexually mature at 3 to 4 months and may breed up to three times a year. However, most young are born in midwinter or spring. There is no delayed implantation in the least weasel, and gestation takes about 35 days. A litter contains from 3 to 6 young.

Not much is known about the average weasel life span. Least weasels are believed to live only a year or so, and long-tailed weasels may live from 3 to 5 years.

Clues:	Construction in the ground (nest)	Rare	See page 102
	Natural cavities (nest)	Rare	See page 116

Weasel — Quick Reference

Habitat: Brushy woods, meadows in country

Home range: 2 to 35 acres

Food: Small rodents, rabbits, shrews

The following refer to long-tailed weasel and ermine. For least weasel, see text.

Mating: June to August

Gestation: 7 to 11 months

Young born: April to May

Number of young: 6 to 9

Number of litters: 1

Young independent: 3 to 4 months

Adult mink

MINK /
Mustela vison

FROM A DISTANCE, something looked strange about the rock in the middle of the river. As we drifted closer in our canoe, we realized that an animal was lying on top of it. We were in a suburban area, and although we wanted to believe that it was a mink or otter, we couldn't quite convince ourselves that either would live this close to humans. Drifting still closer, we saw that indeed it was a mink, stretched out on the rock and staring at us. We stopped the canoe, thinking the animal would soon be scared, but strangely it did not move. After a while we decided to move closer. We were within 30 feet, then 20 feet, then 10 feet, and still it did not move. Finally, at about 5 feet away, the mink gave a sharp bark and dove under the rock. It made us realize that the reason we do not see certain animals in our area is not because they prefer more remote wilderness, but just because they are mostly nocturnal and secretive.

Seeing mink tracks is much easier than seeing the animal itself. To find the tracks, walk along the edge of a stream or river a few days after a good snow. Last winter we were walking along a swamp in a nearby state park and were delighted to find the mink's neat pairs of prints skirting the water edge. After following them for about a quarter of a mile we found many more sets of prints. We couldn't tell whether the prints indicated more animals or just an area more heavily used by the same animal. As we began to sort out the various trails, we noticed that several of them headed to a point on the bank where there was a fallen log with a 3- to 4-inch-diameter hole beneath it. By looking closely at individual prints we could see that the tracks went into and out of the hole. It was most likely a mink den, but whether is was used for just a day or for several days was unclear. After a new snowfall we came back to the spot, but there were no tracks, so we assumed the mink must have moved on.

Say the word "mink" and most people's first thoughts are coats, for mink coats have always been considered one of the ultimate signs of luxury. At first, wild mink were trapped, but since the time of the Civil War, mink have also been raised on farms. Because of this, the area of the mink's life that has been studied most is its reproductive cycle, for this area of knowledge is critical to mink farmers. It is often the case that economics determine the course of scientific inquiry.

The mink is a small mammal with a long body and short legs. Its fur varies from brown to black, and it has a white spot under its chin. It is from 19 to 20 inches long, excluding its tail, and weighs from 1½ to 3½ pounds. The males are larger than the females.

The mink, *Mustela vison*, is in the family Mustelidae, or weasel family, which in turn is in the order Carnivora, or carnivores. There is only one species of mink in North America, and it lives throughout the continent, except in the Southwest. But in the same genus, *Mustela*, are all of the weasels and the black-footed ferret.

Getting Around

When you are near water, especially streams, lakes, rivers, and marshes, think mink, for these are the areas where mink live and hunt. Look for their tracks in winter in the snow, right beside the edge of the ice where a pond or stream has frozen over. In warmer months look for their tracks in the mud. Mink can also be found in canals and ditches, and in the South you can find them in coastal marshes and cypress-tupelo swamps.

Mink are active throughout the year, mainly at night, although they can occasionally be seen during the day. They spend a great deal of their time hunting for small mammals and fish. Mink are excellent swimmers, and swim with the head just above water and the rest of the body submerged. They can dive underwater to a depth of 18 feet to pursue their prey. When they are on land, they most commonly move by bounding, in which their forefeet move forward together and their rear feet land exactly in the tracks made by their forefeet. Their springy back arches with each bound. Like otters, mink may also slide down snow-covered slopes on their bellies.

Mink are solitary animals except during the breeding season, when the male and female get together for mating. They live on home ranges whose size varies depending on the sex of the mink, the season, and the availability of prey and den sites. Males' home ranges vary from 2 to 3 square miles, and females' from ½ to 1½ square miles. Larger areas may be used by dispersing juveniles, males during the breeding season, and by any mink when food is scarce. A radio-tracking study of mink in Idaho found that they were not territorial; that is, they did not actively defend any portion of their home range from other mink.

Mink stay in dens when they are not traveling around or hunting. They may use a den for several days and then move to another one, or use the same den for a much longer period of time. Dens can be located in a variety of places, such as under a log, in an abandoned beaver home, in a tree cavity, or along a stream bank. They can dig their own den if they need to. Sometimes they take over a muskrat home or bank den and kill the inhabitants. There may be two to five entrances to a bank den, and they can be found along the edge of the water, often under tree roots. The entrances lead to a tunnel 4 to 6 inches in diameter that extends up to 8 feet or more and is 1 to 3 feet under the ground.

Mink deposit their feces in piles near the den site. They have anal scent glands from which a strong-smelling musky liquid is discharged when the mink is disturbed or excited, such as when it is fighting or caught in a trap. Since the scent is especially strong during the breeding season, it may help males and females locate each other. Their urine also has a distinctly musky odor.

Clues: Tracks — Uncommon — See page 22
Dens — Rare — See page 114
Scats — Rare — See page 60

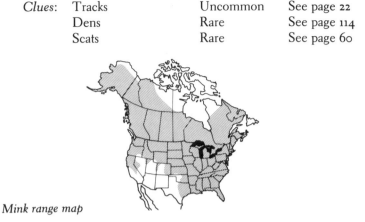

Mink range map

Food and Feeding Habits

Mink are carnivores and will eat whatever prey they can find. Their diet is extremely varied. On land they catch mice, voles, rabbits, moles, bats, songbirds, waterfowl, poultry, lizards, and earthworms. In the water they catch all kinds of fish, including pike, perch, sunfish, trout, and catfish, in addition to frogs, turtles, snakes, crayfish, and muskrats. They are fierce hunters and can attack and kill animals larger than themselves. They can follow prey by scent since their sense of smell is better developed than sight or hearing, and they kill prey by biting it in the back of the neck. They often cache their food and may drag it a distance to their den, where they may store it or eat it. The den may contain scraps or even a carcass.

Mink are well known for feeding on muskrats, for both animals are often living in the same area. In careful studies of predation, it was shown that the majority of the muskrats that were eaten were diseased, victims of drought, or were driven out by other muskrats.

Digestion is very rapid in the mink. Food may pass through the digestive system in an hour, including the hard, indigestible parts, such as bones or scales, which then show up in the next scats.

Mink are preyed upon by foxes, bobcats, lynx, wolves, alligators, owls, and humans. They defend themselves with their sharp teeth and claws, and their strong-smelling musk.

There are very few identifiable signs of mink feeding. But any signs of feeding on animals near the water, such as remains of fish, crayfish, or muskrats, may be a clue to the mink's presence.

Young mink

Family Life

During the breeding season, male mink roam widely in search of females. Females are in estrus once a year for approximately a 3-week period occurring between late February and late April.

Courtship for mink may consist of furious fighting. If a female is receptive, she will eventually copulate, but not without a struggle. Successful copulation depends on the male securing the right hold on the female's neck. The male is larger and uses this to his advantage as he struggles to get a firm hold. If the female arches her back and resists, the male will try to straighten it out with his hind feet. After the female's back is straightened out and her tail cocked to one side, copulation takes place.

Copulation may be short, but it is generally prolonged, lasting up to 3 hours. During prolonged copulation, periods of pelvic thrusting are followed by periods of rest. At no time does the male release his grip on the female's neck, for to do so signals that copulation is over. After copulation, the male and female groom themselves and rest. They may stay close to each other for a short while, then each goes its own way.

When a female mates with a male, the act of copulation causes her to ovulate within 33 to 72 hours. After this first mating, she may have one or more additional periods of receptivity during which she will mate. When she is finished mating altogether, a female mink may have several sets of eggs, each fertilized by a different male. Thus, the young in her litter may have different fathers.

After the eggs are fertilized, there is a delay of variable duration — 12 to 43 days — before they are implanted in the uterine wall. Once the ova are implanted, gestation takes 28 to 32 days. Thus, the total pregnancy of a female mink may last from 40 to 75 days.

Mink — Quick Reference

Habitat: Lakes, rivers, large ponds, streams
Home range: ½ to 3 square miles
Food: Small mammals, fish, birds
Mating: February to April
Gestation: 40 to 75 days
Young born: May to June
Number of young: 1 to 8
Number of litters: 1
Young independent: 2 to 4 months

The young are born in May or June in an enlarged area of the den that is lined with grasses and fur. A litter can contain from 1 to 8 babies, but usually only 4. At birth the young are 1 to 2 inches long and weigh about an ounce, and their backs are covered with a few downy white hairs. Later they develop thick dark fur. Their eyes open at about 3 weeks, and at that time they begin to consume some solid food that the female has brought to them. By 5 weeks they are weaned, and after several more weeks they leave the den.

At this point they are extremely playful and will cavort with one another and engage in mock battles, snarling and hissing. They float and bob in the streams and follow their mother about on her hunting trips. By 8 weeks they are capable of capturing some prey on their own. They remain with the female until the end of the summer and then disperse to find their own place to live. The longest distances traveled by mink are covered by the juveniles as they disperse. One was followed for 28 miles as it moved from its birthplace. At 10 months mink are sexually mature.

Adult skunk

STRIPED SKUNK /
Mephitis mephitis

Most of our experiences with skunks have occurred in the city rather than the country. At one time we lived in an area dense with houses. The only greenery around was the little patch of grass behind the house and the weeds and trees grown up between our property and the one behind us. One spring night, after we had just driven home and were getting out of the car, we smelled a strong odor. Our noses told us it was a skunk, but we couldn't believe a skunk could live where there was so little greenery and so many people. We tried to tell in which direction the odor was strongest, and then we walked that way. It didn't take long to confirm our suspicions, for there up ahead, crossing the road under a street lamp, was a large, striped skunk. We watched it waddle across the sidewalk and disappear in the narrow passageway between two houses.

We now live more in the country but still see signs of skunks most often around the house. In early summer we discovered 2-inch-diameter holes in our lawn, signs of a skunk digging for beetle larvae. The same skunk had left a small scat at the corner of the house. We also had a skunk that regularly visited our doorstep throughout the autumn to feed on leftover bits of cat food. We usually watched from behind the glass panel next to the door, but one night we carefully opened the door and discovered Pablo, our big orange house cat, calmly watching the skunk finish the remains of his cat chow. Fortunately, the skunk was unperturbed by any of us, and after finishing its meal, slowly ambled away.

The striped skunk is a medium-size black animal with a thin white stripe on the forehead and a broad white stripe that splits in two as it goes toward the tail. The striped skunk is about 15 inches long, excluding its tail, and weighs 6 to 14 pounds. There are four main species of skunks in North America: the spotted skunk, the striped skunk, the hooded skunk, and the hog-nosed skunk. Taxonomists disagree as to whether the spotted skunk and the hog-nosed skunk are two distinct species. Of all our skunks, the striped skunk, *Mephitis mephitis*, is the most widely distributed, living all across the United States and southern Canada. Skunks are in the family Mustelidae, which in turn is in the order Carnivora. Other members of the mustelid family include the weasel, mink, fisher, and otter.

Getting Around

Skunks generally become active at dusk and spend the night wandering about in search of food and inspecting any burrows they may find. They cover about a mile or two of trail on any given night. Before dawn they retire to a protected spot and rest throughout the daylight hours.

In the warmer months, skunks' daytime resting spots are usually above ground, such as among the grasses of a hay field, on a hummock in a swamp, or in a protected area of brush. They may also be found in culverts or under buildings. As the weather gets colder, skunks take an increasing interest in underground burrows, often spending the day in them.

Skunks can excavate their own burrows, but generally do so only if no others are available. Usually, they use old woodchuck burrows or crevices under buildings. Inside the burrow they create a hollow chamber and line it with shredded leaves and grasses gathered from the immediate area around the den entrance. They usually scrape up the material with their front feet, pulling it toward the den. Once in the den entrance, they continue to pull it in bit by bit. On especially cold nights they may plug the entrance of the den with grasses and leaves. Occasionally they may leave their scats near the den entrance.

After the first few days of below-freezing weather, skunks stay in their burrows and sleep. This sleep is not a deep hibernation like that of the woodchuck, but just a slight slowing-down of the skunk's basic metabolism. If there is a sudden thaw, the skunks may resume aboveground activity for a day or two.

Skunks are generally solitary, but in winter it is common for several skunks to den together. An interesting feature of this communal denning is the ratio of males to females. Generally there is never more than one male in a den, but there may be from one to ten females with him. Why this occurs is not yet understood. It is known that the male is promiscuous in his mating habits, and some have suggested that he is protecting these females from other males who might want to mate with them in spring.

Occasionally skunks may be found in burrows that at the same time contain woodchucks, opossums, or rabbits, but they are usually in separate sections of the burrow and do not disturb each other.

How long skunks sleep varies with geographical location, sex, and age. In the South, they may retire for only a few days, whereas in the North they may sleep for several months. Female and juvenile skunks are believed to den the longest. Adult male skunks seem to be the most irregular in their denning patterns.

Aboveground activity of skunks resumes in late winter and spring, and its start is probably influenced by several factors, such as temperature, snow cover, available food, and the male skunk's sexual drive.

Not much is known about the home ranges of skunks. The animals will travel long distances of several miles in a night, but this is never in a straight line, with the result that the animal rarely roams over an area larger than about ½ square mile. Although adult animals are usually solitary from spring until fall, their home ranges may overlap. Scent-marking by skunks has not been studied, and whether certain dens are defended as part of a territory is also not known.

The skunk is best noted for its potent defense of spraying ill-smelling liquid at its enemies. This fluid is a yellow oily musk that chemically is a sulfur-alcohol compound called butylmercaptan. It comes from two oval scent glands located on either side of the skunk's anus. When about to spray, the skunk bends its body in a **U** shape with both head and anus facing opponent. Powerful sphincter muscles contract, and one or both glands discharge the musk in a fine mist or a stream. The musk is sprayed out in an arc and can reach up to 15 feet.

However, spraying is usually a last resort for a skunk. Before this, it may do several other things to rid itself of a possible predator. The first is to run away. If this is not possible, it may stamp its stiffened front legs and shuffle backward. It may also hiss and growl. If none of this works, then it will lift its tail and bend its rear around toward the disturbance and spray. This amazing defense deters most would-be predators, and the black and white stripes may advertise the warning. Given this weapon, skunks walk around rather fearlessly and usually have rather docile natures.

To remove skunk odor, wash clothes in detergent and household ammonia. We once rid our dog of skunk odor by washing him in tomato juice and then soap. The most effective chemical for removing skunk odor is the water-soluble form of neutroleum-alpha, available from hospital supply houses. Spray in eyes won't cause permanent damage but will sting intensely for a while.

Clues:	Tracks	Common	See page 22
	Scats	Common	See page 60
	Holes in the ground	Common	See page 92
	Natural cavities	Common	See page 116

Skunk range map

Food and Feeding Habits

Skunks are omnivores and take advantage of seasonally abundant foods. In spring, the main item on their menu is often voles, which skunks will catch among the meadow grasses. In late spring and early summer they may feed a great deal on the white grubs of june beetles often found in lawns and grassy areas. If you find small holes about 1 to 2 inches deep in your lawn, they are probably due to skunks going after these beetle larvae. In midsummer, skunks eat all kinds of insects but especially grasshoppers and crickets, beetles, moth larvae such as cutworms, as well as the eggs of birds and turtles. Midsummer is also berry time, and skunks eat strawberries, blueberries, and, a little later on, raspberries and blackberries.

In fall, skunks turn to apples, grapes, and Virginia creeper berries. Voles again become important in fall and early winter, but skunks will also prey upon deer mice, shrews, and even rabbits. Crickets and grasshoppers reach their largest size in fall, and at this time they are the most common insects eaten by skunks. A few green plants, such as the leaves of clover, are also consumed.

Skunks are opportunists, and this has enabled them to move comfortably into suburban and city areas, where they feed on garbage, insects, plants, mice, and other available foods.

Areas of tall grasses all torn apart along with some digging may indicate that skunks have been hunting for voles.

Clues:	Torn-up grasses	Common	See page 104
	Shallow digging in the earth	Common	See page 92
	Dug-up turtle eggs	Common	See page 124
	Hornet's nest torn open	Common	See page 124

Young skunks

Family Life

Skunks begin their mating season in February or March. At this time, male skunks become very active and start wandering about in search of females in dens. They will travel longer distances than usual at this time, up to 5 miles in a single night, and on their route they will explore all potential dens. Their explorations may bring them into contact with other male skunks, and fighting can occur.

Skunks are promiscuous in their mating habits, and after a male has mated with one female, he will search out others. When a male finds a receptive female, either in or outside a den, the two will mate. The male grabs the female at the back of her neck with his teeth, gets onto her back, and then copulates. Copulation lasts about a minute, during which neither animal makes any sound. If a female does not become pregnant during her first estrous cycle, she may come into a second estrous cycle 4 weeks later. Female skunks that have already mated will fight with other males that try to mate with them.

Female skunks are pregnant for 62 to 66 days. Then they give birth in their den, and the average litter is 5 to 7 kits. The older and larger females give birth to larger litters than first-time mothers. The babies are born blind, wrinkled, and toothless. They have only the faintest bit of hair, although their future black-and-white pattern is already evident on their skin. The mother has 6 pairs of nipples and nurses the babies by sprawling over them; later on she will lie down to nurse. At about 3 weeks the kits' eyes open, and they are able to spray scent from their glands. They grow rapidly and soon are fully furred. By 2 months the young are weaned and are following their mother on her hunting trips. The young will have become independent by fall and will have dispersed to make their own lives. Skunks live from about 2 to 4 years in the wild.

Most of what is known about skunk-breeding behavior comes from observations of captive skunks. There is a real need to study skunks in the wild in more depth to get a true picture of this common mammal.

Striped Skunk — Quick Reference

Habitat: Deserts, grassy plains, woodlands, suburbs, cities

Home range: ½ square mile

Food: Voles, mice, beetle grubs, insects, eggs of birds and turtles, berries, garbage

Mating: February to March

Gestation: 62 to 66 days

Young born: April to June

Number of young: 2 to 10, average 5 to 7

Number of litters: 1

Young independent: Weaned at 2 months, independent by fall

Adult otter

RIVER OTTER /
Lutra canadensis

IT WAS ONE OF THE first good tracking snows of the season, about six inches of powder, and for the last two days it had been neither melted by sun nor blown by winds. A tracker's dream, the tracks had accumulated on the surface over a period of two days and, more importantly, two nights, the time when most mammals venture out.

We locked the car in the nature area's parking lot, put on our snowshoes, and headed out with a journal to draw and record the tracks that we found. Going right across the parking lot was a trough through the snow. We quickly assumed it had been made by a child's toboggan, but as soon as we realized that it went directly into some very dense underbrush, we knew this did not make sense. There was no more than a foot or so of clearance above the trough, and, in any case, who would sled into the underbrush? We went over to have a closer look and saw that tracks began where the trough ended. We had never seen anything like this. We worked our way through the underbrush to study the prints. Each had 5 toes with claws at the tips, as do the prints of members of the weasel family. But they were huge. Then it dawned on us. The trough was the slide and these were the tracks. It was an otter.

We were surprised because the nature area was located in a town, only 20 miles from a huge city center. We had previously thought that we would have to be in the real wilderness before we ever saw otter tracks. We quickly got out our journal and recorded our findings. We decided to follow the otter's trail in the hopes of spotting the animal. We had visions of finding an otter slide and seeing the animals gliding into the water, as we all have seen in nature films.

After about a quarter of a mile on level ground, we suddenly came upon an incline with a slide going from the top to the bottom. Here was the slide we had always heard about. But as we approached, there was one problem; we began to realize that if this slide belonged to the animal we were tracking, then it must have slid *up*hill, not *down*hill. The animal had indeed taken several short slides to get up it. Once at the top, it had continued running. We had learned something: An otter's sliding is not just for "fun" but is also an important means of traveling overland for this large and heavy animal.

Otters are almost always near water since this is where they feed and where they enjoy the greatest mobility. They are most common at the ends of rivers and streams, where the water flows more slowly and the greater concentrations of nutrients support a larger number of smaller animals for the otter to feed on. When areas are densely settled by humans, or the water becomes polluted, the otter leaves. Until the 1700s, otters could be found in most of the major rivers of North America. Soon after this date they became scarce in the Midwest, Southwest, and those mid-Atlantic states not bordering on the coast.

The river otter is a fairly large animal, 3 to more than 4 feet long, not including its tail, and weighing about 10 to 30 pounds. It is important to remember this, for many people mistake the mink — which is only half this size — for the otter. The otter has very dark brown fur with a slightly lighter-colored belly; the throat of the otter is whitish.

The river otter, *Lutra canadensis*, belongs to the weasel family, Mustelidae, which is in the order Carnivora. It is the only inland otter species in North America. However, there is also a sea otter, *Enhydra lutris*, which is found in the Pacific Ocean along the West Coast.

Getting Around

Otters are active from dawn to midmorning and then again in the evening. Either is a good time to go out looking for them. The animals are fairly nearsighted, so if you see them, but stay still and downwind, they may not notice you.

The home ranges of otters vary according to habitat, season, and sex. The home ranges of females vary from 12 square miles when they have newborn young to 30 square miles when the young are becoming mature. Male otters' home ranges are usually about 60 square miles.

A male's home range does not overlap with the home ranges of other males; it is distinct and possibly even defended. But a male's home range will overlap with the home ranges of one or more females. Occasionally the male will associate with these females, spending the greatest amount of time with them during their period of estrus. Females with young occupy the best feeding locations within a given area, and their home ranges do not overlap with those of other females.

Adult males, and females with young seem to have the most stable home ranges and habits. Other males and females, perhaps young adults, may move around more, have temporary associations, and live between or at the edges of the home ranges of more established otters.

Some trappers and observers have reported that otters regularly travel around their home ranges and can be counted on to pass a certain spot in their range every several days like clockwork. This is sometimes true of male otters in winter, when they may continually pass along a route that brings them to the same spot every 3 or 4 days. But this is an oversimplification. Many things may divert them from an established pattern, such as the presence of other otters, a female in heat, the abundance of food elsewhere, or frozen water. This regularity is thus probably the exception rather than the rule.

An otter is very aware of certain key spots in its home range and pays close attention to them. These spots include common borders with an otter of the same sex, the places at which streams flow into lakes and there is abundant food, and areas with suitable dens. At these locations there tend to be more signs of otter activity, including "rolling places" and "scent mounds."

Rolling places are spots at the edge of a lake or stream where the animals climb out of the water and roll vigorously on the ground, possibly to dry off and possibly to mark the spot in some way. Scent mounds are prominent spots such as a rock, fallen log, mound of earth, or tuft of grass where the animal leaves its scats. These are used repeatedly. Urine or scent is also left at these spots. When these spots occur along a common border between two male home ranges, there may be as many as 30 to 40 scent mounds in the space of a half-mile. They are most often placed at the inflow and outflow of streams or ditches from lakes. All otters in an area use the scent mounds and regularly visit them to smell them and leave their mark.

Otters may also make trails along the edge of a lake or stream, leading from one cove to another across a peninsula, for example, or alongside a stretch of rough rapids in a stream. They are about 6 to 7 inches wide and may lead to rolling places or dens.

Otters like to slide and will slide down a mud bank as well as on snow, although snow is preferred. They may regularly use one spot. However, these sliding areas are not as common as popular literature and films suggest.

The average distance traveled by an otter on a single winter night is about 2½ miles for females with young and about 9 miles for males.

Clues:	Tracks	Uncommon	See page 22
	Scats	Uncommon	See page 62
	Mounds of earth	Uncommon	See page 96
	Matted vegetation	Uncommon	See page 104

Otter range map

Food and Feeding Habits

Otters feed mostly on other aquatic animals, such as fish, frogs, crayfish, snakes, and turtles. They do most of their hunting along the shallow edges of lakes, at the outflow of lakes, or where streams flow into lakes. They swim under the water and, when they see prey, chase after it, often staying beneath it, possibly to follow its movements against the light from the water's surface. They may also hunt by nuzzling about in lake or river bottoms, perhaps using their sensitive whiskers to find food. While hunting, they come up to the surface every 30 seconds or so for air and then immediately submerge themselves again.

Otters catch their prey with their teeth. If the prey is less than 4 inches long, they may eat it while holding their head out of water. If the prey is larger than 4 inches, they tend to take it ashore and eat it there. Fish, frogs, and snakes are eaten head first, possibly because this kills the prey and makes eating the rest easier.

The choice of prey depends not only on what is available but also on the relative vulnerability of the prey itself. For example, the fish that otters feed on are usually the smaller and slower species, such as mud minnows, sticklebacks, and suckers. These fish constitute 35 to 60 percent of their food. Game fish such as bass and trout compose about 15 to 25 percent of their food. The average size of prey fish is 4 to 6 inches long. The rest of the otter's diet consists of crayfish, snakes, turtles, mammals, and various invertebrates. Occasionally they will eat berries in late summer. In northern climates during winter, otters tend to leave frozen lakes and move to streams where there is some open water so that they can feed more easily.

Otters chew their food very thoroughly and leave very little behind. Because they chew so well, the remains of prey in their scats are few, except for fish scales, which are not digested. In fact, there are very few signs of otter feeding, for they tend to eat all of the prey they catch. It has been suggested that with larger fish, otters may bite the head off first, and that this or other parts of the fish may be left. They may also leave the claws of crayfish.

Family Life

Male and female otters are only loosely associated with each other through the year, except during the time of mating. The female comes into heat from about December to April. For any given female, estrus lasts only 6 weeks with peaks of receptivity occurring about every 6 days. During estrus, the female probably releases a scent at prominent points within her range, such as at rolling places, at scent posts, or near the den. One or more males may follow a female in heat, and there may be fights or shows of aggression between these males as they vie for dominance.

During mating, which often occurs in the water, the male holds onto the scruff of the female's neck with his teeth; the female may give a loud caterwaul. Mating lasts 15 to 25 minutes, and a pair may mate several times over the course of a couple of days.

Although a female has mated, her pups will not be born until the following winter. This is due to delayed implantation, in which the egg cell is fertilized but does not continue its development until being implanted in the wall of the uterus, 9 or 10 months later. In some cases, it is believed, the female comes into heat right after giving birth and mates again at this time. There is also evidence that

Young otters

some female otters give birth only every other year; if so, a female could mate at any time during the breeding season.

Before the cubs are born, the female prepares a den. Otter dens can be any natural cavity, for they do not excavate their own. They may use a muskrat or beaver home, or any other hole in a bank; they may also use hollow logs or upturned stumps. The den is usually lined with fine shredded plant material, and although it is usually near water, otter dens have been found in woodchuck burrows up to half a mile from the nearest body of water.

Once implantation takes place, gestation lasts only about 7 weeks. The young cubs are born in the den, and there are 2 to 4 per litter. At first they have no teeth and their eyes are closed, but they are fully furred — an advantage when they are born in below-freezing weather. Delivery takes several hours, and afterward the female curls around the newborns to keep them warm. The young can be born at any time between November and April, but most births take place from February to April.

Very young otters are never seen because the first 2 to 3 months of their lives are spent inside the den. After 5 weeks they open their eyes and begin to play with each other and with their mother. After 10 to 12 weeks they start to venture outside the den. They are also given their first solid food at this time, and a few weeks later they are weaned. Their first experiences in the water in no way suggest their future talent as swimmers, for they seem head-heavy, and learning to keep their heads above the water requires practice. The father will not be permitted near the young until they are about 6 months old.

The male may associate with the female and with her young on his range after they are 6 months old, but only on a casual basis and for

---

River Otter — Quick Reference

Habitat: Rivers and large lakes in country and wilderness
Home range: 12 to 60 square miles
Food: Small aquatic animals, especially fish
Mating: December to April
Gestation: 9 to 10 months (all but 7 weeks are delayed implantation)
Young born: November to April
Number of young: 2 to 4
Number of litters: 1
Young independent: Weaned at 3 to 4 months

short moments. The young remain with their mother through summer, fall, and possibly winter, depending on whether the female is pregnant with another litter. The young probably leave the mother in mid- to late winter and disperse.

Young otters are sexually mature when they are 2 years old, but even so, males do not seem to mate successfully until they are about 6 or 7 years old. Otters are known to live up to 14 years in the wild.

Clues: Den   Rare   See page 114

Adult bobcat

BOBCAT / *Felis rufus*

W E WERE OUT tracking on a rocky hillside. It was a cloudy, moist day in late winter, and the snow cover was becoming patchy and granular from the warmer air. Although it was not good snow for tracking, we continued to zigzag through the woods, skirting large clumps of mountain laurel and pausing to gaze down from rock outcroppings. Below us we could see a small field, the kind usually full of voles, and it was surrounded by lots of shrubs among which we had seen rabbit scats and the signs of their feeding.

We were about to move on when we spotted a faint trail on the snow surface. Since there were no clear prints, identification was difficult, so we began to follow the trail. The snow surface was so stiff that the animal had barely left an impression. It was unlikely to be a deer, for its hooves and weight would have left more of a mark. The size of the stride and straddle narrowed it down to either a dog, fox, coyote, or bobcat. Still, we needed a clear print to be sure.

The tracks approached a rock outcropping, and it was here that we found what we needed. When leaping on to the rocks, the animal had pushed off from deeper snow, leaving a print that was round, four-toed, without claws, and about 2 inches in diameter. It was a bobcat.

We wondered what it had been doing. Had it gone to the rocks to look at the field below? Was it going to hunt for voles or rabbits among the grasses and shrubs? Did it have a den nearby among the rocks of the hillside? These questions would have to be answered at another time, for soon the trail became too faint to follow.

The bobcat is amazingly widespread, living in southern Canada and throughout the United States, with the exception of Alaska and the southern Great Lakes states. In the Northeast, look for its signs wherever there are rock ledges, for this is where it prefers to den. In the South it is often found hunting among the swamps. In the West, look for signs in areas of rimrock and in chaparral, although in the North it often keeps to conifer swamps, especially in winter.

Even though it is widespread and fairly abundant, the bobcat is rarely seen. This is because it is primarily nocturnal, does not come near human habitations, and is only a little larger than a big house cat. This last point is important, for it helps you realize that the bobcat could be present more often than we think yet still remain inconspicuous. Also, very few people are familiar enough with its signs to be able to identify them. Through more knowledge of the signs, we hope, more information can be gathered about the lives of these secretive but beautiful and fascinating cats.

The bobcat, *Felis rufus*, is in the family Felidae, or cats, which is in the order Carnivora, or carnivores. Other wild cats in North America, such as the mountain lion, *Felis concolor*, the lynx, *Felis lynx*, and the ocelot, *Felis pardalis*, are also in the genus *Felis*. Even the house cat belongs to this genus.

Getting Around

Bobcats are most active from late afternoon to midnight and then again during the hours leading up to dawn. The home ranges of bobcats can vary tremendously, depending on food availability, season, weather, population, and sex. They can be as small as ½ square mile and as large as 20 square miles. An average home range might be about 12 square miles.

Female bobcats usually have a favorite site — a rocky ledge, for example — that becomes the center of their range. They come and go from this site regularly and tend to use the area around it intensively. A female bobcat averages about 2 miles of traveling per day. The ranges of females are not believed to overlap, and because of this, female bobcats rarely come into contact with one another; they may also carefully avoid each other by communicating through scats and urine-marking.

Male bobcats have larger ranges than females and roam more widely. They travel an average of 3 or 4 miles per day and move about throughout their range, rather than using one area intensively. The ranges of males do not generally overlap, but they may overlap with those of several females.

Bobcats mark trails and possibly ranges by means of urine, scats, scrapes, and perhaps scratching posts. Most members of the cat family have the habit of burying their scats by scraping material over them; you may have seen your house cat do this. Scats are usually left along the side of trails on slightly elevated spots. One researcher found one scat for every 3½ miles of trail that he followed. Thus, scats are not often found. Bobcats cover their scats about half the time. They are often left uncovered in the frequently used and more central parts of the bobcat's range and covered at the fringes of the range. Uncovered scats are also common near dens.

Urine markings are more common than scats but are seen only in the snow. Urine may be eliminated on the ground in a scrape as the bobcat squats down, or it may be sprayed higher up on objects. You may have seen your house cats do this as well. The bobcat has two anal glands, which are also used to leave scents on scrapes, feces, and other spots.

Clues:	Tracks	Uncommon	See page 18
	Bark scratched	Rare	See page 70
	Scraped depressions	Rare	See page 94
	Scats	Rare	See page 64

Bobcat range map

Food and Feeding Habits

Bobcats eat almost no vegetable matter but feed on a variety of insects, birds, mammals, and other animals. In order of importance, their diet most commonly consists of rabbits, snowshoe hares (in the North), rats, deer, squirrels, mice, and voles.

The bobcat primarily uses sight and sound to find its prey. After ambushing or stalking its prey, the cat pounces and kills with its claws and teeth. Since rabbits are the bobcat's most common food, the animal spends a great deal of time in rabbit habitats, such as the brushy thickets along streams, overgrown fields, or meadow edges.

Bobcats occasionally kill deer. Thus, a killed deer may be a sign that bobcats are in the area. In fact, a deer kill is the main sign of bobcat feeding, for the more common, smaller animals in the bobcat's diet tend to be almost totally eaten, with few remains left behind.

When trying to determine whether a deer has been killed by a bobcat, look for puncture wounds in its neck; bobcats kill deer by jumping onto their backs and biting them at the base of the skull or in the neck. A deer may even run a short distance with the bobcat on its back until it is weakened or killed by the cat.

The bobcat usually starts eating the deer in the hindquarters or forequarters. After feeding, the bobcat may drag the prey to cover, under brush or low evergreen boughs, or it may rake leaf litter and debris over the remains by reaching out and scratching materials toward the prey. Look for these scratch marks in the ground around the prey; if they are 1 or 1½ feet long, there is a good chance they are signs of the bobcat. If the scratched marks are 2 to 3 feet long, then it may well be that the predator was a mountain lion, for this animal kills and covers deer in the same way but has a much longer reach. When bobcats kill deer, they may stalk them in the deer's bedding areas or wait for them along deer trails and pounce on them.

Young bobcats

Family Life

Adult bobcats lead solitary lives most of the year, except for a brief period in midwinter. At this time the female comes into estrus, and one or more male bobcats become attracted to her — possibly through a scent she gives off—and begin to follow her. The male mates with the female while holding onto her neck fur with his mouth. The two may stay together for a while, hunting and possibly feeding together. After this, the male leaves the female, possibly to mate with other females, and both adults resume their solitary lives. Most mating occurs in January and February. The female raises the young on her own.

While the female is pregnant, she may remain in a smaller area of her home range, where she seeks out a suitable natural cavity—a spot under a log or a natural crevice among rocky ledges — in which to raise her young. She may use this den as the center of her activity and stay protected in it during rain and snow; she may also use it for sleeping. Gestation is 50 to 60 days, so most bobcat kittens are born between March and May; however, female bobcats can remain in estrus up until August, so it is possible for kittens to be born as late as October.

There are 2 or 3 kittens per litter, and as soon as they are born they begin to suckle milk from their mother. She in turn licks their fur to clean it and also to stimulate activity. For the first few days the kittens'

Bobcat — Quick Reference

Habitat: Woods, fields, swamps, chaparral, wild areas
Home range: ½ to 20 square miles
Food: Rabbits, hares, mice, squirrels, occasionally deer
Mating: January to February
Gestation: 50 to 60 days
Young born: Primarily March to May
Number of young: 2 to 3
Number of litters: 1
Young independent: Weaned at 8 weeks; independent at 4
    to 5 months

eyes are closed, and the mother remains with them constantly, feeding them milk and keeping them warm. Then the mother leaves them for short periods to hunt for herself. After about 4 weeks in the den, the kittens begin tentatively to venture forth and peer out the den entrance for their first view of the outside world. At this time, the mother bobcat starts supplementing their milk with meat.

After 8 weeks they are weaned and wander about outside the den, playing and exploring the world around them. They probably follow the mother about as she hunts for another month or so, and then in fall or winter they go out on their own and begin to establish their solitary adult habits. When they reach their second year, they are sexually mature.

Direct observation of bobcats has been very limited, and there is still a great deal to be learned.

Clues: Den   Rare   See page 114

Adult cat

HOUSE CAT / *Felis catus*

W<small>E HAVE A LARGE</small>, orange tabby cat named Pablo. He loves people and comes over to be petted whenever anyone is near; he also follows us when we take walks in the woods. He is a lap cat and purrs loudly and endlessly when petted, unfortunately also drooling and occasionally kneading with his paws. We love him a great deal and enjoy watching all of his behavior as well as his marvelous ability to find the sunniest and warmest spot in the house, where he falls into a delicious sleep.

However, every once in a while Pablo comes back to the house, his fur ruffled and looking as if he has been in a fight. We know that there are other cats in the area, and occasionally neighbors have mentioned a very aggressive tabby cat in their area. Could this be our loving, sleepy Pablo? We are not sure, but it does point out the dual nature of a domestic cat's existence. Pablo lives in two worlds. One is in our house, where he is the center of attention, playful and friendly to people; the other is outside, where he is a tomcat among other tomcats. Other reminders to us of Pablo's other world are his expert prey-catching abilities. Just when it looks as if he is getting fat and lazy, we spot him hunting in the field and see his lightning speed and relative ease in acquiring his own food. Also, even though neutered, he still exhibits territorial behavior by spraying on objects around the property.

In the wild, most species of cats are solitary animals. The house cat is no exception. Cats avoid each other's presence, and if they spot another cat, will wait patiently until it leaves before they move on. Cats do not bound up to greet each other as dogs do, but are much more likely to gaze at one another from a distance and then walk away.

You may wonder why, if cats are such solitary creatures, they enjoy the company of humans and can even share a house with other cats. The answer seems to be that the relationship between cat and owner is an extension of the relationship between kitten and mother. The kitten phase is the only social and gregarious time in a cat's life, and as dominant owners we perpetuate that phase of the cat's behavior. At the same time, however, adult behavior is demanded of the cat in its relationships with other cats.

Our domestic house cat, *Felis catus*, is a descendant of the European wild cat, *Felis sylvestris*. All cats belong to the family Felidae, which is in the order Carnivora.

Getting Around

Sometimes when we are lying on the floor playing a board game with the kids, our cat walks over, comes right up to my face, and almost touches my nose with his. This is, in fact, the usual way that cats greet each other. When two cats meet, the first thing they do is come together nose to nose and sniff. If all goes well, each cat will then smell the other's neck, flank, and, finally, anal opening. However, the first cat to proceed after the nose sniff is considered the more aggressive, and the other cat may respond by pulling back. The aggressive cat may attempt an anal check, in which case the other cat may strike at it with a paw or, after a while, just stand still and let it sniff.

At some point you have probably seen your cat go up to a tree, reach up with its front paws, and pull down, scratching at the bark. This may help the cat to clean or exercise its claws, but if done in front of another cat, it may be meant to intimidate. Cats usually have a favorite tree or other object — hopefully not your couch — where they do most of their scratching.

If for some reason you are forced to scold your cat verbally, you may notice an interesting behavior. It will walk a short distance from you, sit down quietly, and stare away from you. Your cat is treating you as it would another dominant cat. In interactions between two cats a direct stare is considered aggressive behavior. In these situations the subordinate cat will sit and stare everywhere but at the other cat.

Each cat has a home range, a given area in which it moves about. Within this home range it generally has a central area, such as your house and yard, that is well known and within which it has a special spot or room for resting, as well as other spots for sitting, watching, sunbathing, and post-scratching. Radiating from this core are trails that lead to outlying areas used for hunting, courting, and possibly fighting with other cats. The gaps between trails are generally not used.

Neighboring cats may have overlapping home ranges and even common trails, but even in these cases the cats rarely come into contact with one another, for cats generally are very reclusive. In fact, they will pointedly avoid one another, and if there is a chance that their paths will cross, one will wait for the other to pass. This can even occur between two cats in the same house, one waiting at the entrance to a room while the other goes by. Who waits probably has less to do with dominance than with who happens to get there first.

The home range of a cat is generally not defended against other cats, but during the breeding season male cats become much more defensive, and their home range becomes a territory or defended area. They will mark their area frequently by backing up to conspicuous objects, their erect tail quivering, and spraying urine mixed with scent from anal scent glands onto the chosen object. They have a sexual periodicity, independent of being near a female in heat, which causes them to scent-mark more at certain times than at others. The presence of a female in heat also stimulates this. Unlike dogs, however, they will not spray over another cat's mark.

Almost all cats have the habit of coming up to their owner or another friendly person, rubbing their cheek against that person's leg, then passing by and rubbing the tip of their tail across the same part of the leg. We tend to interpret this as affection, but it is also the case that the cat's chin and tail contain scent glands, and this is one way it leaves its scent on objects. Another scent gland located on the cat's head is often used to mark other cats with which it is friendly. Thus two cats that meet and are friendly may briefly rub foreheads.

An interesting exception to the usual solitariness of cats occurs outside of the breeding season. Cats from an area may gather together in the early night at neutral locations, sit near one another, and actually groom each other. Then they return to their respective home ranges. No one knows the function of these gatherings.

In an area where many cats live, a relative hierarchy exists among the members of the community. One cat may be dominant most of the time. But dominance over other cats in fights may not extend to dominance over food. We used to have two cats: One was dominant over the other when they fought, but the other one always got first choice when food was put out.

Male cats may fight over territorial rights at certain times. These fights can involve biting and scratching, but before this occurs the cats will signal visually to each other. These visual displays involve complex facial expressions and body postures. When a cat is displaying extreme aggression, its body is high on its legs, its back straight, the hairs on the middle of the back raised, and the base of its tail angled straight out and then down. The facial expression for aggression would include narrowed pupils and erect ears turned outward so that the backs of the ears face the front.

Display of extreme defensiveness would include dilated pupils and ears flattened to the side. The cat's body is pressed close to the ground, its head is pulled in, and the hairs all over its body stand up. A defensive cat may roll over on its side and strike out with a front paw, or roll onto its back so that it can strike out with all four paws. A house cat may even adopt this defensive posture when a stranger tries to pet it. There are many gradations between the aggressive and defensive displays. In fact, when cats are frightened, they may display both aggression and defense. The typical picture of the Halloween cat with its back arched, tail raised, ears erect, and eyes dilated is believed to be an example of this.

You will not see cat scats, for they are usually buried. The cat scrapes out a small depression, defecates in it, and then pulls debris over the scats with its paw. Urine is also generally covered in the same way except when a male is scent-marking.

Clues:	Tracks	Common	See page 18
	Scratching posts	Uncommon	See page 70
	Scats	Uncommon	See page 60

Food and Feeding Habits

Have you ever seen your cat suddenly become slightly wide-eyed, crouch down, twitch the tip of its tail, and then leap across the floor, beating the air with its front paws? Or seen it sit at a window for long intervals and stare at birds outside, its tail twitching all the while, then turn back to the room and jump on a ball or shoe, batting it with its paws?

These are all expressions of feline prey-catching instincts. Pouncing on thin air is believed to be a kind of overflow of the prey-catching drive. When a cat has been watching unattainable prey, it may redirect its instincts and attack something else. In either case, if the cat finds you staring at it, it will probably stop. For some reason, cats don't like to be watched at these times.

Much of our play with cats involves stimulating their prey-catching instincts. Scratching a cushion or rustling paper will start a cat off. A cat will respond to a small object moved quickly back and forth by crouching low and possibly twitching the tip of the tail. It may pounce on the object and, if it is furry, like real prey, it may even bite it.

Cats are excellent hunters of birds and small mammals. They can climb, leap, or watch quietly for long periods. They usually detect prey through sound or sight, noticing a movement in the grass or leaves or hearing a high-pitched squeal or bird sound. A cat will immediately turn its head toward this sound or sight and trot nearer the spot with its belly close to the ground. Then it adopts a watching posture: hunched over, the tail is out behind the body, its tip twitching, and the hind paws begin to tread up and down. Suddenly it rushes out and, with a few bounds, catches the prey in its claws, and bites it in the back of the neck, possibly severing its spinal cord.

Once the prey is caught and stops moving, the cat usually puts it down. Typically, the cat grooms a little and sniffs the immediate area, then picks up the prey, walks a little farther, and puts it down again. Because of this habit of repeatedly walking short distances and dropping its kill, the prey sometimes has a chance to escape. It may be still while it is held in the cat's jaws, but it scampers away as soon as it is released. Finally, the prey is carried to a private place and eaten. If it is a large bird, the feathers are first pulled out; if it is a mammal, only the longer fur is removed, and then the prey is eaten in large bites.

Watching our cat eat a vole is amazing, for he seems to finish it in about 30 seconds. He follows a pattern of eating typical of all house cats. Hunching over the prey, he starts either at the vole's head, eating it, or at the neck, leaving the head. After a few bites, he removes the vole's digestive system. This may be eaten or sniffed, licked, and then left, though usually only the stomach and cecum are left. Our cat then turns his head to the side to cut up the prey with his back teeth and then swallows large portions whole, without chewing.

Your cat may have brought dead mice, voles, or birds back to your doorstep and then eaten them there. This is a throwback to the instinctive behavior of mother cats, who bring prey back to their young when raising them. You also may have noticed that your cat gives a special call when returning with prey; this is the same sound that alerts kittens to their mother's return with food. Male cats will also bring prey back to their owner.

When a mother brings food to her kittens, they come to her with their tails raised in the air. Again, you will notice that this same behavior occurs in your adult pet cats when you come to feed them.

At this same time they may rub their cheeks against your leg, possibly marking you with their scent.

Family Life

Cats are solitary animals through most of the year, avoiding other cats by staying on their own home range. Breeding seasons generally occur twice each year, usually from late January to early March and from early May to late June. During each breeding season the female will be in heat several times if she has not already mated. Her estrous period is 2 to 3 weeks long, and during that time she is receptive to the male for 4 to 6 days. Ovulation is stimulated by mating with the male and occurs 30 hours after mating.

Kittens

A female cat in estrus follows typical behavior patterns. She rubs the side of her head, then the back of her head and her back on the floor, all the while giving low calls. A male locates a female in heat through scent, and when he is near her, he may rub his cheek against objects. He also sniffs the area around her and may mark by spraying urine. He may also circle her as she crouches down, lifts up her hindquarters, and treads with her feet. When both are ready, the male grips her neck with his mouth, then mounts her and copulates. After copulation the female pushes the male away, and both groom themselves, licking their paws and genitals. The female may also roll on the ground again and rub up against objects. Cats may mate several times in succession. Cats separate after mating, for there is no bond between a pair of cats, and the male takes no part in raising the young.

It is interesting to note the behavior of cats in response to sniffing the plant catnip, *Nepeta cataria*. Male and female cats that have sniffed catnip roll around on the ground in the same way that a female in estrus does. It is believed that something in the odor of catnip approximates the scent of cats in estrus, thus stimulating sexual behavior.

Gestation in cats lasts 63 to 65 days. Most kittens result from the earlier breeding period, and so are born from mid-March to mid-May. A day or two before giving birth, the mother cat seeks out a dark protected spot and spends an increasing amount of time there. This is where she will give birth and raise the young. Delivery of the kittens can last from 2 to 4 hours, and each kitten is followed by the placenta. The female eats the placenta and chews off the umbilical cord.

For the first few weeks, all the kittens do is either sleep or feed on the mother's milk. The mother must lick the anus of the young kittens to stimulate them to defecate since they cannot do this on their own for the first 2 weeks. When she is not feeding her young, she leaves them snuggled together and goes off to eat by herself. After 2½ weeks, the kittens begin to move about unsteadily on their own and may wander a little. By 5 weeks they start to be weaned from the mother's milk and may eat some solid food. Weaning is usually complete by 8 weeks, and at this time the young begin to follow the mother on her hunting forays, learning the necessary hunting skills by the time they are 2 or 3 months old.

When kittens nurse, they purr. Purring is believed to have been adapted to nursing, for it can be done with the mouth closed and even while eating. It is thought to communicate the well-being of the kittens to the nursing mother. The mother may purr as well. Clearly, purring also is one of the major experiences we have with our house cats, every time we scratch their head or stroke their back. Some experts theorize that this physical contact and reassurance of being petted by its owner brings out the purring reaction, almost as if the cat were still a kitten with its mother.

Kneading with the front paws and drooling are also common to house cats. Again, this is believed to be part of the original nursing behavior, kneading to help stimulate the mother's flow of milk and salivating to digest it.

Cats also purr in other circumstances. When a young cat approaches an adult to play, it purrs; and when a dominant cat approaches a subordinate cat and wants to play, it also purrs. In these situations, it seems as if purring may be a reassurance of friendliness.

House Cat — Quick Reference

Habitat: Fields, woods, human habitations
Home range: Varies widely
Food: Small rodents, birds, pet food
Mating: Mostly January to March but can occur later
Gestation: 63 to 65 days
Young born: Mostly March to May but may be later
Number of young: 1 to 8
Number of litters: 1
Young independent: Weaned at 8 weeks, independent at 2
   to 3 months

Adult deer

WHITE-TAILED DEER /
Odocoileus virginianus

IT WAS JUST BEFORE sundown when we spotted our first deer from
the dirt road. We stopped the car, picked up our binoculars, and
watched. There were five deer, and we assumed that it was a "doe
group" — an adult female with her yearlings and fawns. Soon the
largest deer noticed the car and held its head up straight and still, its
ears out to the sides like antennae, listening for any hint of sound.
The deer moved toward us in a very stiff-legged manner. Then it
stamped one of its hooves several times and moved forward again. At
that time we heard it snort as it expelled a burst of air from its nostrils.
Finally it turned, flagged the bushy white underside of its tail into the
air, and bounded effortlessly off into the shrubbery, followed instantly by the others, also with their tails raised. The stamping,
snorting, and tail flagging were all displays of increasing alarm in the
deer. Only if we had startled them would they have bounded off
without display.

After driving farther down the road, we decided to get out and walk
up to a field on top of a hill. It was getting close to dusk, and our
human vision was failing. Off to one side we saw a cottontail and
joined it in a frozen staring contest. For a second we turned to listen
to a rustle behind us. It was nothing, but when we looked back the
rabbit was gone. Then up ahead of us we could dimly pick out what
we hoped we might find. There was a doe with a very young,

still-spotted fawn. It must have been born late in the year. Through our binoculars we could see the fawn bounding about and making mad dashes through the meadow grasses while its mother fed peacefully nearby.

Off to the right of them, not more than 50 yards away, we saw something whitish move among the grass. As we edged closer, we were thrilled to see that it was a young great horned owl that had just dived down after prey. It flew back into a tree, where it joined two other young owls. We wondered what the deer thought of the owls. Had they seen them before? Undisturbed, the doe continued to feed and the fawn continued to romp. For a moment the owls and the deer seemed like parts of the peaceable kingdom, two spectacular examples of nature both going about their lives in the low light. Soon it was too dark for us to see, and we turned to go home. We felt privileged to have had this glimpse of nature at its most beautiful.

White-tailed deer are one of our largest native mammals. They are 3 to 3½ feet high at the shoulder and weigh from 50 to 400 pounds. Their long, thin legs give them great speed and jumping ability, which enable them to bound off through dense tangles of brush. They are best suited for quick getaways, for when chased over longer distances by domestic dogs, for example, they soon tire and are often killed. Another feature of deer that seems to have evolved as a protection against predators is its digestive system. At dusk and dawn, deer eat large quantities of vegetation, gathering and chewing them very quickly so that they can go back to cover as soon as possible. They then regurgitate their food into their mouths a little bit at a time and rechew it. This is known as chewing their cuds. Such behavior minimizes the deer's exposure to predators.

The white-tailed deer, *Odocoileus virginianus*, is in the family Cervidae, or deer family, which is in the order Artiodactyla, comprising all those hoofed animals with an even number of toes. There are two main species of deer in North America, the white-tailed deer and the mule deer, *Odocoileus hemionus*. Within the species of mule deer is a subspecies called the black-tailed deer. These deer live only in the West, whereas white-tailed deer live all across North America, being absent only in the Southwest, northern Canada, and Alaska.

Getting Around

Adult bucks and does remain in separate groups through most of the year. The buck groups contain two to five deer; doe groups contain two to nine deer and are composed of does, their yearlings, and their fawns. A typical doe group contains one doe, one yearling, and two fawns. Larger groups of deer may be seen together at various times; these are not stable groups, however, but have probably gathered temporarily in response to a good feeding site. When the animals stop using the site, these larger groups break up.

If you spot a group of deer, watch them for a while and look closely for interactions between the deer. In any group there are dominant members and subordinate members. A dominant member is usually more aggressive and asserts itself through a variety of gestures, or displays. The mildest display is called ear-drop and involves the deer lowering its ears so that they lie flat against its neck. A slightly more aggressive display is called the hard look; here the deer lowers its head, puts back its ears, and stares at the offending deer. Slightly more aggression is expressed through "sidling," where the deer moves sideways toward its opponent. If none of these actions makes an opponent move, then the dominant deer may "strike," that is, pick up a front foot and attempt to bring it down on the other's back. Finally, both deer may rise up on their hind legs and strike at each other with their front feet; this has been called flailing. These last two displays rarely involve actual contact. In fact, the purpose of displays seems to be to solve conflicts without real fighting.

In fall, when bucks have full-grown antlers, they may also be particularly aggressive to each other as they compete for access to an area or a particular doe. They also use the ear-drop, hard look, and sidling, but instead of striking or flailing they resort to two other displays: "antler threat," in which they lower their heads and point their antlers at an opponent, and "antler rush," where they actually crash horns with another buck. Although antler rush is frequently shown on nature films, it rarely occurs in the wild. Instead, bucks tend to settle disputes through the less dangerous displays of ear-drop, hard look, sidling, and antler threat.

The daily routine of a deer is to become active at dusk, feed for a short while, and then retire to protected bedding areas to rest and chew its cud. Before dawn, the deer again becomes active, feeds, and retires to safe areas to rest and chew its cud for the remainder of the day.

Bedding areas are secluded spots where deer can remain safe while inactive. At night they may use areas of heavy brush for cover, or dense evergreens for protection from the wind. During the day they may bed in areas, such as high ridges, that can give them some respite from insects and allow them to see approaching predators. A south-ward-facing slope will provide added warmth in winter.

Deer often use the same trails from feeding places to bedding spots, and over the months these become worn down. You can often see these trails as paths cleared through low vegetation. They may be used for years if the food sources and bedding areas remain good. In northern areas in winter, the combination of extreme cold and deep snow may result in several small groups of deer gathering in an area of dense evergreens, which provides protection from the winds, a shallower layer of snow to walk through underneath, and green browse to feed on. These areas become a network of trails through the snow that the deer all use because the trails become packed and provide easier and safer walking. The trails may also lead from bedding sites to feeding sites and back. This network of trails is called a deer yard. When there is less snow and the temperature rises slightly, these temporarily large groups of deer will break up into their normal smaller groups.

White-tailed deer usually remain in a fairly fixed home range of about 2 to 3 square miles and often have very fixed patterns of movement through this area for weeks at a time. Deer are very reluctant to leave their home range when chased, for while they know all the routes within it, once outside it they may get trapped in gullies or dense vegetation. They may shift to other areas within their home range due to seasonal changes in food availability or to the onset of cold weather. Does tend to keep to their home ranges, whereas bucks stay in one area from late winter to summer but roam more widely in fall and early winter, when they are looking for does with which to mate.

Bucks may define territories in the rutting season through the use of rubs and scrapes. But how or even if this is really the case is still not known.

Clues:	Tracks	Common	See page 16
	Scats	Common	See page 56
	Trails	Common	See page 106
	Matted vegetation	Uncommon	See page 104

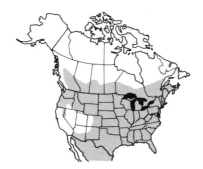

Deer range map

Food and Feeding Habits

White-tailed deer are vegetarians. During summer they feed on the leaves of grasses and on wildflowers, shrubs, vines, and trees. Some of the many plants they may eat include wild cherry, wild roses, catbriers, sweet fern, maple, and corn when it is ripe. In fall deer take advantage of the abundance of such fruits and nuts as apples, persimmons, and acorns.

Winter is the hardest time for deer, especially in the North, for the green leaves of deciduous trees are gone, grasses have died back or been covered with snow, and few large fruits or nuts are still available. At this time of year, deer feed mainly on the twigs and bark of woody plants. Some of their favorites are maple, oak, sumac, dogwood, aspen, and willow. They also feed on evergreens such as yew, white cedar, hemlock, pine, arborvitae, and fir. Which of these plants they feed on depends on the abundance and relative nutritional merits of the plants. It has been shown that deer instinctively choose or seek out the most nutritional species. In spring, deer continue to eat winter browse until new greenery has grown or been uncovered by melting snow.

For an explanation of deer digestion — their four stomachs and their cud chewing — see "Moose," Food and Feeding Habits.

Clues:	Twig ends bitten	Common	See page 80
	Bark chewed off	Common	See page 74

Family Life

Adult bucks and adult does generally lead separate lives throughout the year, except for a brief time in fall when does are in estrus and bucks mate with them. For the rest of the year bucks tend to live in small groups with other bucks, and does tend to live in small groups with other does, their yearlings, and fawns.

A conspicuous feature of the breeding cycle is the buck's growth of antlers. The antlers are shed and grown anew each year. Bucks start growing antlers in about April to May. Nourishment for them comes from a velvety covering of skin and blood vessels. There is no way to tell the age of the buck through the size of its antlers or the number of prongs, for their development is largely controlled by the quality and quantity of food that the buck has been able to find. Of two bucks the same age, one in a good environment may have large antlers, while one in a poor environment may have just small stubs.

By about August or September the antlers are fully grown, and the

Young deer

velvet covering starts to die back and peel off. The buck aids this peeling by rubbing its antlers against trees and shrubs. Rubbing occurs mostly in September, and by the end of that month most of the velvet is off. These early rubs, which may wound a tree or expose a little of the inner bark, are more frequent but less conspicuous than the later rubs, which expose about 10 inches of inner bark. This suggests that the September rubs may function primarily to scrape the velvet off the antlers, while the October rubs may function more as visual markings. These rubs may also serve as scent marks, for bucks develop enlarged scent glands on their foreheads in fall, which they rub against the tree when scraping it.

It has also been discovered that bucks favor certain sizes and species of trees. One study showed that the rub trees tended to be about 1 inch in diameter and 6 feet tall. It was also discovered that the deer favored rubbing against certain species of trees, such as pine, cherry, red cedar, and sumac. All of these have aromatic bark, and

perhaps this gives added scent to the mark. Other preferred characteristics of rub trees include few lower branches and generally
smooth bark. Each tree is used only once; rub trees tend to be
clustered in a given area.

Another activity that bucks, and occasionally does, resort to at this
time is scraping. The animal paws at the earth, creating a visible
depression 1 to 2½ feet in diameter. It may be rectangular or slightly
more circular. After making the scrape, the deer may defecate or
urinate in it. Scrapes are usually made in open areas clear of underbrush, often beneath an overhanging limb that the deer already has
rubbed its head against or licked. Scrapes tend to be clustered in a
given area. The majority of scrapes are made by males, and most are
made during the peak of the mating period. They may function to
help females in estrus and males locate each other for mating.

In August and September, when bucks' antlers are full-grown and
their necks enlarged, the buck groups break up and each male goes
out on its own. By October, the does begin to come into estrus; and
each is receptive for about 24 hours. If a doe does not mate in this
time, she will come into estrus again in another 28 days. Males follow
females around during this time of year, mainly by scent. More than
one male may follow a female, but usually the dominant male is
nearest to her. Once a male and female have mated, the male moves
on to look for another female, while the female returns to her maternal group. Matings may occur from October through January, but in
the North they mostly occur in November. A doe remains with her
female group at this time, moving slightly away only briefly during
mating.

Gestation takes about 200 days, so most fawns are born in June.
When the doe is about to give birth, she leaves the other deer in the
doe group and goes off alone. Her first birth is usually a single fawn;
in successive years she usually gives birth to twins and occasionally
triplets.

For the first month of their lives, the fawns remain hidden among
vegetation and rarely move more than 30 feet from their birthplace.
Their greatest protection at this time is their ability to lie still and

remain unseen by predators. The mother usually feeds nearby and then returns at intervals so that the fawns can nurse.

After the first month the fawns travel with their mother, and they may move together to areas where there is abundant food, good cover, and possibly relief from insects. These areas are often at the edge of a stream or lake, allowing the deer to eat water plants and go into the water. In August and September the doe and fawn are likely to rejoin the doe group.

By spring the new fawns are yearlings. During summer, when their mother is raising new fawns, the yearlings go off and feed on their own but remain in the vicinity of their mother. In fall they will rejoin their mother and spend another winter with her. The following spring they will leave her — the males will join buck groups and the females will become a part of a doe group.

Deer molt twice a year. The summer coat is reddish and short-haired and acquired during the spring molt in May and June. The winter coat, acquired in September and October, is longer, with grayish hairs that are actually hollow and can easily be broken by pulling at either end. This coat provides greater insulation for the deer in the cold. The fawns molt slightly later than the adults in the

---

White-tailed Deer — Quick Reference

Habitat: Mixed woods, fields, and brushy areas
Home range: 2 to 3 square miles
Food: Leaves of plants, bark from shrubs and trees
Mating: October to January, mostly in November in North
Gestation: 200 days
Young born: May to July, mostly June
Number of young: 1 to 2
Number of litters: 1
Young independent: About 1 year

fall, and during this molt they lose their spotted coat. This occurs in October, November, and December, when the fawns are 4 to 6 months old.

Although deer may be common in an area, their antlers are rarely found. One of the reasons for this is that many members of the rodent family — such as mice, voles, and squirrels — will gnaw at and eat the antlers to get their nutrients. Deer shed their antlers each year at some time in late winter after all mating is finished, usually in January and February. Around April they begin to grow a new set.

Clues:	Scraped depressions	Common in fall	See page 94
	Bark scraped off	Common in fall	See page 70

Adult moose

MOOSE / *Alces alces*

ONE BEAUTIFUL MIDSUMMER day, we were hiking in the Rocky Mountains. We had just waded through thousands of flowers in an alpine meadow and were now scrambling down a rocky slope, headed toward a cool stream that ran through the valley below. We were so busy picking our way through the glacial till that we did not have a chance to look up until we reached a large flat rock by the edge of the stream. There, about 100 yards in front of us on the other side of the stream, was a cow moose and her small calf. They had been watching us all the time and did not seem particularly alarmed.

Instead of approaching closer, we decided to watch them from where we were, for we knew that cow moose can be quite protective of their calves. The baby moose lay down for a while in a small thicket and was hidden from view. The mother stayed close to the calf as she alternated short periods of browsing on grasses with long bouts of chewing. After a while the calf got up, and they both moved into the shadow under some spruces, possibly for relief from the midday heat. We cooled off by numbing our toes in the icy stream before continuing on our way. As we looked back, it was hard to make out the moose, for their large forms melted into the dark shadows of the trees. And we might have overlooked them if we had just come upon the scene. We felt lucky to have shared some of their day.

Most people probably underestimate the size of moose. A large bull moose can weigh as much as 1,400 pounds, nearly three times the weight of a large black bear. At the shoulder the moose is already taller than most of us, 6½ to 7½ feet tall. The moose's great size has made it better adapted to its environment, allowing it to browse higher on trees and wade out into deeper water to feed on aquatic plants. The long legs of the moose enable it to walk through deeper snow and not get trapped as easily in deep drifts.

The moose, *Alces alces*, belongs to the family Cervidae (as does the deer), which is in the order Artiodactyla, or hoofed mammals with an even number of toes. The moose is the largest member of the family, and there is only one species in North America. Its coat color ranges from tan to practically black, and it has a long flap of skin hanging down under its chin called a dewlap. The moose lives primarily in Canada, Alaska, the Rocky Mountains, the states that surround the Great Lakes, and New England.

Getting Around

Moose can be active at any time of the day or night. In general, they alternate a few hours of feeding with a few hours of resting. In areas with substantial human activity, they may be more secretive during the day, feeding in more open places only between dusk and dawn.

The social organization of moose is seasonal. In September adult moose begin to gather in areas where mating will take place. Bulls and cows will be seen together for 1 to 2 weeks at a time as they court and mate; calves remain with their mother throughout this time. Other bulls or cows may be seen alone, looking for mates, or challenging others of their own sex for access to mates. (Young moose of both sexes will not participate in mating activites but instead stay in small groups away from the mating areas.)

In November and December, as the mating season comes to an end, up to twenty moose may form groups. These groups include bulls, cows with their calves, and young moose.

In spring, these large groups break up. The bulls go off alone or in the company of several younger bulls that follow them, and they remain this way through most of the summer. Cows stay with their yearlings. However, in a month or so, when the cow is about to give birth, she will drive away her yearling. In August, adult bulls leave the company of younger bulls and by September move about alone in search of mates.

Moose move during the winter to areas where there is a good supply of browse, shrubs, or sapling trees to feed on. In summer they may move to the edges of lakes to feed on aquatic vegetation, or to marshy meadows with lush grasses. In mountainous areas, movements may involve changes from high altitudes in summer to low altitudes in winter. Because of this movement, it is hard to define a moose's home range. It might be better to describe moose as having seasonal home ranges with an estimated size of 2 to 4 square miles.

In general, deep snow does not restrict the movement of moose as seriously as it does that of deer, for moose have longer legs and larger hooves. However, moose still have a tendency to use packed snow trails for easier walking. A group of moose restricted to one feeding area because of deep snow forms a network of trails through that area; this is called a moose yard.

For such large animals, moose move about surprisingly well. When alerted to possible danger, they can move almost silently through the woods. Bull moose have an amazing ability to keep their huge antlers from getting stuck in trees or brush. They can run at speeds of 35 miles per hour and can easily swim 8 to 12 miles. Mothers and new calves have been seen swimming back and forth across to islands in lakes.

| *Clues*: | Scats | Common | See page 58 |
| | Tracks | Uncommon | See page 16 |

Moose range map

Food and Feeding Habits

Moose are vegetarians. They eat large amounts of woody and herbaceous vegetation. Like deer, they do not have upper incisors. Their lower incisors bite against a callous pad in front of their upper jaw. Moose rip or tear off vegetation and then grind it with their back molars.

Moose have four different chambers in their stomach. They hastily tear off vegetation, which passes first to the chamber called the rumen, and then to a second chamber, where it is broken down into pellets, or the cud. Later, when the moose are at rest, they bring up the cud into their mouth and chew it; the food is then passed to the two other stomach chambers, where it is digested. This same digestive system occurs in white-tailed deer.

The moose diet is very varied. In the summer moose often eat aquatic vegetation, wading about in lakes and bogs. Sometimes they dive into the water, completely submerging themselves to get at the plants. They also eat leaves, twigs, and ground plants. To get at leaves they straddle saplings and walk forward, bending the tree until the leaves are within reach. Their favorite trees are willows, gray and white birch, quaking aspen, balsam poplar, and balsam fir. In the winter, moose eat the twigs and bark of the deciduous trees, conifers, and shrubs that are above the snow cover.

The body weight of moose fluctuates seasonally. They lose weight in winter and gain weight — sometimes amounting to a 55 percent increase — during the summer. Males weigh 900 to 1,400 pounds and females 700 to 1,100 pounds.

Clues:	Bark chewed off	Uncommon	See page 74
	Twig ends bitten	Uncommon	See page 80

Family Life

One conspicuous feature of the moose breeding cycle is the growth of antlers on the bulls. Antler growth starts in spring, continues through summer, and, for older bulls, is completed by August and September. When the antlers are mature, the velvet coating that nourished their growth dies and is shed. The bulls "spar" with shrubbery to aid in the removal of the velvet. The antlers themselves are shed between December and March. The older the bull, the earlier it sheds its antlers and the sooner it starts to grow new ones. Young bulls can be as much as 6 weeks slower than older bulls in growing and shedding their antlers.

There is no way to determine the age of a moose by counting the points on the antlers. The only clue that antlers give to age is the diameter at the base of the antlers, which gets larger each year. Bull calves have only short spikes their first fall. Yearling and 2-year-old bulls can have either simple spikes or branched antlers, but generally their antlers are not flattened like those of older bulls.

The breeding season begins in September when the mature bulls have left the company of their small summer groups of bulls and go out on their own. Their antlers are mature and free of velvet. They move to more open areas, where mating and courtship take place. Cows in estrus also move about more at this time, still accompanied by calves born in the summer. The cows give loud calls, probably to alert bulls to their presence, and when a bull hears a cow, he moves toward her, giving a continuous series of short grunts.

Once a cow in estrus and a bull have found each other, they stay

Young moose

together for 1 to 2 weeks. During this time there are three phases of behavior. In the first phase the bull simply stands sideways, several yards in front of the cow, for long periods. When she moves, he moves again to stand in front of her. In the next phase the bull follows a few steps behind the cow, moving when she moves. Finally, the female stands still and lets the bull mount and mate with her. They may mate several times over the course of a day or two. Following this, the bull leaves in search of another cow in estrus.

The wallow is another interesting aspect of moose courting and mating. It is an area of earth that the bull urinates on and then scrapes into a muddy hollow. The bull may repeatedly work on the wallow, and he will also lie down and roll about in it. The cow that has joined the bull will also lie down and roll in it, sometimes even joined by her calf. The function of the wallow is not known, but for many other mammals the scent of urine plays an important part in stimulating certain sexual behavior.

Other bulls or cows may show up during the courtship period. If another bull appears and challenges the courting bull, the two will engage in displays that may lead to fighting. These displays include circling the rival with antlers swaying from side to side, hitting shrubs and trees with their antlers, going up to the cow and sniffing her, and urinating in a wallow and then rolling in it. If the challenger does not leave, the two may engage in actual fighting, locking antlers and alternately pushing each other backward.

When another cow appears during courtship between a bull and cow, the courting cow will rush at her if she comes too close. If the two cows are near a wallow, both will try to claim it by lying down in it.

After a gestation period of about 8 months, the cow is ready to give birth. At this time she will be aggressive to her yearling calf and drive it away. She will then seek out a protected spot in which to give birth. Yearling females are able to mate, and in their first birth they have a single calf. Adult cows generally have single calves as well but may have twins. In areas with abundant food, a greater percentage of yearlings become pregnant and more adults have twins.

Calves are born in May or June. New calves are awkward and are kept hidden for 2 to 3 days. After this time they can easily follow their mother about through the woods. The calves have reddish brown, short, woolly fur, relatively long ears and legs, and a short body. They can give a high-pitched cry, to which the cow may respond with low-pitched grunts. Cows are very protective of their calves and will not let other moose or animals, such as humans, get near them.

Calves weigh 25 to 33 pounds, but grow rapidly, gaining 75 pounds in their first 9 weeks. A calf stays with its mother throughout its first year and is fully weaned by the time next calf is born.

Moose reach their prime when they are about 8 to 10 years old but may live as long as 23 years.

Clues: Scraped depressions   Uncommon   See page 92

Moose — Quick Reference

Habitat: Forests with lakes and swamps
Home range: 2 to 4 square miles, varying seasonally
Food: Woody, herbaceous, and aquatic vegetation
Mating: September to November
Gestation: 8 months
Young born: May to June
Number of young: 1 to 2
Number of litters: 1
Young independent: 1 year

Bibliography

BELOW ARE LISTED SOME of the references we used in researching this guide. First are listed the general texts. Of these, we found *Wild Mammals of North America: Biology, Management, and Economics*, edited by Joseph A. Chapman and George A. Feldhamer, the most useful for life history information and good bibliographies, and *A Field Guide to Animal Tracks*, by Olaus J. Murie, the most useful for animal tracks and signs. Following the general texts are specific articles and books for each species that were either of special interest or not included in the general texts.

GENERAL TEXTS

Brown, R. W., M. J. Lawrence, and J. Pope. 1984. *The Larousse Guide to Animal Tracks, Trails, and Signs*. New York: Larousse & Co.

Burt, W. H. 1952. *A Field Guide to the Mammals*. Boston: Houghton Mifflin Co.

Cahalane, V. H. 1961. *Mammals of North America*. New York: Macmillan Co.

Chapman, J. A., and G. A. Feldhamer, eds. 1982. *Wild Mammals of North America: Biology, Management, and Economics*. Baltimore and London: Johns Hopkins University Press.

Eisenberg, J. F., and D. G. Kleiman. 1972. Olfactory communication in mammals. *Ann. Rev. of Ecology and Systematics* 31: 1–32.

Fox, M. 1972. *Behavior of Wolves, Dogs and Related Canids*. New York: Harper and Row.

———, ed. 1975. *The Wild Canids, Their Systematics, Behavioral Ecology and Evolution*. New York: Van Nostrand Reinhold Co.

Godin, A. J. 1977. *Wild Mammals of New England*. Baltimore and London: Johns Hopkins University Press.

Hafez, E. S. E., ed. 1974. *The Behavior of Domestic Animals*. Baltimore: Williams and Wilkins Co.

Hazard, E. B. 1982. *The Mammals of Minnesota*. Minneapolis: University of Minnesota Press.

Johnson, R. P. 1975. Scent marking in mammals. *Anim. Behav.* 21: 521–35.

Murie, O. J. 1954. *A Field Guide to Animal Tracks*. Boston: Houghton Mifflin Co.

Palmer, L. E. 1949. *Fieldbook of Natural History*. New York: McGraw-Hill Book Co.

Rue, L. L., III. 1968. *Sportsman's Guide to Game Animals*. New York: Harper and Row.

Sebeok, T. A., ed. 1968. *Animal Communication*. Bloomington: Indiana University Press.

Smith, R. P. 1982. *Animal Tracks and Signs of North America*. Harrisburg, Penn.: Stackpole Books.

Stokes, D. W. 1976. *A Guide to Nature in Winter*. Boston: Little, Brown and Co.

Swartz, C. W., and E. R. Swartz. 1959. *The Wild Mammals of Missouri*. Columbia: University of Missouri Press.

Weir, B. J., and I. W. Rowlands. 1965. Reproductive strategies of mammals. *Ann. Rev. of Ecology and Systematics* 4: 139–64.

Whitaker, J. O., Jr. 1980. *The Audubon Society Field Guide to North American Mammals*. New York: Alfred A. Knopf.

VIRGINIA OPOSSUM

Hunsaker, D., II. "Behavior of New World Marsupials." In *The Biology of Marsupials*, edited by D. Hunsaker II. 279–348. 1977. New York: Academic Press.

Lay, D. W. 1942. Ecology of the opossum in eastern Texas. *J. Mamm.* 23: 147–59.

Shirer, H. W., and H. S. Fitch. 1970. Comparison from radio-tracking of movements and denning habits of the raccoon, striped skunk, and opossum in northeastern Kansas. *J. Mamm.* 51: 491–503.

SHREWS

Broadbooks, H. E. 1952. Nest and behavior of a short-tailed shrew, *Cryptotis parva*. *J. Mamm.* 33: 241–43.

Hamilton, W. J., Jr. 1930. The food of the *Soricidae*. *J. Mamm.* 11: 26–39.

Pearson, O. P. 1942. On the cause and nature of a poisonous action produced by the bite of the shrew. *J. Mamm.* 23: 159–66.

———. 1946. Scent glands of the short-tailed shrew. *Anat. Rec.* 94: 615–29.

Tomasi, T. E. 1979. Echolocation by the short-tailed shrew. *J. Mamm.* 60: 751–59.

MOLES

Arlton, A. V. 1936. An ecological study of the mole. *J. Mamm.* 17: 349–71.

Conaway, C. H. 1959. The reproductive cycle of the eastern mole. *J. Mamm.* 40: 180–94.

Godfrey, G., and P. Crowcroft. 1960. *The Life of the Mole*. London: Latimer, Trend, and Co., Ltd.

Hisaw, F. L. 1923. Observations on the burrowing habits of moles. *J. Mamm.* 4: 79–88.

Simpson, S. E. 1923. The nest and young of the star-nosed mole. *J. Mamm.* 4: 167–71.

Yates, T. L. 1983. The mole that keeps its nose clean. *Nat. Hist.* 92: 54–61.

EASTERN COTTONTAIL

Heinsinger, J. F. 1962. Periodicity of reingestion in the cottontail. *Am. Mid. Nat.* 67: 441–48.

Ingles., L. G. 1941. Natural history observations on the Audubon cottontail. *J. Mamm.* 22: 227–50.

Marsden, H. M., and N. R. Holler. 1964. Social behavior in confined populations of the cottontail and the swamp rabbit. *Wildl. Monogr.* 13: 1–39.

SNOWSHOE HARE

Keith, L. B. 1966. Animals using runways in common with snowshoe hares. *J. Mamm.* 47: 541.

Kuvelsky, W. P., Jr., and L. B. Keith. 1983. Demography of snowshoe hare populations in Wisconsin. *J. Mamm.* 64: 242–44.

O'Farrell, T. P. 1965. Home range and ecology of snowshoe hares in interior Alaska. *J. Mamm.* 46: 406–18.

EASTERN CHIPMUNK

Condrin, J. M. 1936. Observations on the seasonal and reproductive activities of the eastern chipmunk. *J. Mamm.* 17: 231–34.

Decker, D. J., and S. McCarthy. 1983. Chipmunks. *Conservationist* Nov./Dec.: 39–42.

Getty, T. 1981. Structure and dynamics of chipmunk home range. *J. Mamm.* 62: 726–37.

Schaffer, L. 1980. Use of scatterhoards by eastern chipmunks to replace stolen food. *J. Mamm.* 61: 733–34.

Tunis, E. 1971. *Chipmunks on the Doorstep.* New York: Thomas Y. Crowell Co.

Wishner, L. 1984. *Eastern Chipmunks: Secrets of Their Solitary Lives.* Washington, D. C.: Smithsonian.

Yahner, R. H. 1978. Burrow system and home range use by eastern chipmunks, *Tamias striatus*: Ecological and behavioral considerations. *J. Mamm.* 59: 324–29.
———, and G. E. Svendsen. 1978. Effects of climate on the circannual rhythm of the eastern chipmunk, *Tamias striatus*. *J. Mamm.* 59: 109–17.

WOODCHUCK

Bronson, F. H. 1964. Agonistic behavior in woodchucks. *Anim. Behav.* 12: 470–78.

Grizzell, R. A., Jr. 1955. A study of the southern woodchuck. *Am. Mid. Nat.* 53: 257–93.

Lloyd, J. E. 1972. Vocalization in *Marmota monax*. *J. Mamm.* 53: 214–16.

Merriam, H. G. 1971. Woodchuck burrow distribution and related movement patterns. *J. Mamm.* 52: 732–46.

Snyder, R. L., and J. J. Christian. 1960. Reproductive cycle and litter size of the woodchuck. *Ecology* 41: 647–56.

GRAY SQUIRREL

Horwich, R. H. 1972. The ontogeny of social behavior in the gray squirrel (*Sciurus carolinensis*). Berlin and Hamburg: Verlag Paul Parey.

Lewis, A. R. 1980. Patch use by gray squirrels and optimal foraging. *Ecology* 61: 1371–79.

Nichols, J. T. 1958. Food habits and behavior of the gray squirrel. *J. Mamm.* 39: 376–80.

Pack, J. C., H. S. Mosby, and P. B. Siegel. 1967. Influence of social hierarchy on gray squirrel behavior. *J. Wildl. Manage.* 31: 720–28.

Taylor, J. C. 1966. Home range and agonistic behaviour in the grey squirrel. *Symp. Zool. Soc. Lond.* 18: 229–35.

———. 1968. The use of marking points by grey squirrels. *J. Zool. Lond.* 155: 246–47.

Thompson, D. C. 1977. Diurnal and seasonal activity of the grey squirrel. *Can. J. Zool.* 55: 1185–89.

———. 1977. Reproductive behaviour of the grey squirrel. *Can. J. Zool.* 55: 1176–84.

———. 1978. Regulation of a northern grey squirrel population. *Ecology* 59: 708–15.

———. 1978. The social system of the grey squirrel. *Behaviour* 64: 303–28.

RED SQUIRREL

Layne, J. N. 1954. The biology of the red squirrel, *Tamiasciurus hudsonicus*, in central New York. *Ecol. Monogr.* 24: 227–67.

Smith, C. C. 1968. The adaptive nature of social organization in the genus of three squirrels. *Ecol. Monogr.* 38: 31—63.

———. 1970. The coevolution of pine squirrels (*Tamiasciurus*) and conifers. *Ecol. Monogr.* 40: 349–71.

———. 1981. The indivisible niche of *Tamiasciurus*: an example of nonpartitioning of resources. *Ecol. Monogr.* 51: 343–63.

BEAVER

Aleksink, M. 1968. Scent-mound communication, territoriality, and population regulation in beaver. *J. Mamm.* 49: 759–62.

Hediger, H. 1970. The breeding behavior of the Canadian beaver. *Forma et Functio* 2: 336–51.

Hodgdon, H. E., and J. S. Larson. 1973. Some sexual differences in behavior within a colony of marked beavers. *Anim. Behav.* 21: 147–52.

Lancia, R. A., W. E. Dodge, and J. S. Larson. 1982. Winter activity patterns of two radio-marked beaver colonies. *J. Mamm.* 63: 598–606.

Svendsen, G. E. 1978. Castor and anal glands of the beaver. *J. Mamm.* 59: 618–20.

Tevis, L., Jr. 1950. Summer behavior of a family of beavers in New York state. *J. Mamm.* 31: 40–65.

Wilsson, L. 1968. *My Beaver Colony*. New York: Doubleday and Co.

———. 1971. Observations and experiments on the ethology of the European beaver. *Viltrevy* 8: 115–266.

MICE

Abbott, H. G., and T. F. Quink. 1970. Ecology of eastern white pine seed caches made by small forest mammals. *Ecology* 51: 271–78.

Balph, D. F., and A. W. Stokes. 1960. Notes on the behavior of deer mice. *Utah Acad. Proc.* 37: 55–62.

Behney, W. H. 1936. Nocturnal explorations of the forest deer-mouse. *J. Mamm.* 17: 225–30.

Bowers, M. A., and H. D. Smith. 1979. Differential habitat utilization by sexes of the deer mouse. *Ecology* 60: 869–75.

Hall, E. R. 1928. Note on the life history of the woodland deer mouse. *J. Mamm.* 9: 255–56.

Huestis, R. R. 1933. Maternal behavior in the deer mouse. *J. Mamm.* 14: 47–49.

Jameson, E. W., Jr. 1952. Food of deer mice. *J. Mamm.* 33: 50–60.

King, J. A., ed. 1968. Biology of peromyscus. *Am. Soc. Mamm. Spec. Publ.* 2: xiii, 1–593.

Nicholson, A. J. 1943. The homes and social habits of the wood-mouse in southern Michigan. *Am. Mid. Nat.* 25: 196–233.

Sealander, J. A., Jr. 1952. Relationship of nest protection and huddling to survival of *peromyscus* at low temperature. *Ecology* 33: 61–71.

Vestal, B. M., and J. J. Hellack. 1978. Comparison of neighbor recognition in two species of deer mice. *J. Mamm.* 59: 339–46.

VOLES

Beer, J. R., and C. F. Macleod. 1961. Seasonal reproduction in the meadow vole. *J. Mamm.* 42: 483–89.

Berger, P. J., E. H. Sanders, P. D. Gardner, and N. C. Negus. 1977. Phenolic plant compounds functioning as reproductive inhibitors in *Microtus montanus*. *Science* 195: 575–77.

Cross, P. C. 1972. Observation on the induction of ovulation in *Microtus montanus*. *J. Mamm.* 53: 210–12.

Jannett, F. J., Jr. 1982. Nesting patterns of adult voles, *Microtus montanus*, in field populations. *J. Mamm.* 63: 495–98.

Madison, D. M. 1980. Space use and social structure in meadow voles, *Microtus pennsylvanicus*. *Behav. Ecol. Sociobiol.* 7: 65–71.

Owelette, D. E., and J. F. Heisinger. 1980. Reingestion of feces by *Microtus pennsylvanicus*. *J. Mamm.* 61: 366–68.

Pearson, O. P. 1959. A traffic survey of *microtus-reithrodontomys* runways. *J. Mamm.* 40: 169–80.

MUSKRAT

Errington, P. L. 1963. *Muskrat Populations*. Ames: Iowa State University Press.

MacArthur, R. A., and M. Aleksink. 1979. Seasonal microenvironments of the muskrat. *J. Mamm.* 60: 146–54.

PORCUPINE

Costello, D. F. 1966. *The World of the Porcupine*. Philadelphia: J. B. Lippincott Co.

Shadle, A. R. 1946. Copulation in the porcupine. *J. Wildl. Manage.* 10: 159–62.

———. 1947. Gestation period in the porcupine. *J. Mamm.* 29: 162–64.

———. 1951. Laboratory copulations and gestation of porcupine, *Erethizon dorsatum*. *J. Mamm.* 32: 219–21.

———. 1952. Sexual maturity and first recorded copulation of a 16-month male porcupine. *J. Mamm.* 34: 239–41.

———, and W. R. Ploss. 1943. An unusual porcupine parturition and development of the young. *J. Mamm.* 24: 492–96.

———, M. Smelzer, and M. Metz. 1946. The sex reactions of porcupines before and after copulation. *J. Mamm.* 27: 116–21.

COYOTE

Andelt, W. F., D. Althoff, and P. S. Gipson. 1979. Movements of breeding coyotes with emphasis on den site relationships. *J. Mamm.* 60: 568–75.

Bekoff, M., ed. 1978. *Coyotes: Biology, Behavior and Management*. New York: Academic Press.

———, and M. C. Wells. 1980. The social ecology of coyotes. *Sci. Am.* 242: 130–48.

Danner, D. A., and N. Dodd. 1982. Comparison of coyote and gray fox scat diameters. *J. Wildl. Manage.* 46: 240–41.

Green, J. S., and J. T. Flinders. 1981. Diameter and pH comparisons of coyote and red fox scats. *J. Wildl. Manage.* 45: 765–66.

Ryden, H. 1979. *God's Dog.* New York: Viking.

Weaver, J. L. 1979. Comparisons of coyote and wolf scat diameters. *J. Wildl. Manage.* 43: 786–88.

RED FOX

Burrows, R. 1968. *Wild Fox.* New York: Taplinger Publishing Co.

Henry, J. D. 1976. The use of urine marking in the scavenging behavior of the red fox. *Behavior* 61: 82–105.

———. 1985. The little foxes. *Nat. Hist.* 94: 46–56.

Lloyd, H. G. 1980. *The Red Fox.* London: B. T. Batsford Ltd.

Rue, L. L., III. 1969. *The World of the Red Fox.* Philadelphia: J. B. Lippincott Co.

Sheldon, W. G. 1949. Reproductive behavior of foxes in New York state. *J. Mamm.* 30: 236–46.

Storm, G. L., R. D. Andrews, R. L. Phillips, R. A. Bishop, D. B. Siniff, and J. R. Testes. 1976. Morphology, reproduction, dispersal and mortality of midwestern red fox populations. *Wildl. Monogr.* 49: 1–82.

Zimen, E., ed. 1980. *The Red Fox.* The Hague and Boston: Dr. W. Junk, Publishers.

DOMESTIC DOG

Bekoff, M. 1979. Accuracy of scent-mark identification for free-ranging dogs. *J. Mamm.* 61: 150.

———. 1979. Scent-marking by free-ranging domestic dogs. *Biology of Behavior* 4: 123–39.

Fiennes, R., and A. Fiennes. 1968. *The Natural History of Dogs.* New York: Natural History Press.

Fox, M. 1972. *Understanding Your Dog.* New York: Coward, McCann and Geoghegan.

Kleiman, D. 1966. Scent marking in the Canidae. *Symp. Zool. Soc. Lond.* 18: 167–77.

Lorenz, K. 1952. *Man Meets Dog.* London: Methuen and Co.

Shenkel, R. 1967. Submission: its features and fuction in the wolf and dog. *Am. Zoologist* 7: 319–29.

Sprague, R. H., and J. J. Ainsko. 1973. Elimination patterns in the laboratory beagle. *Behavior* 47: 257–67.

Trumler, E. 1973. *Your Dog and You.* New York: Seabury Press.

BLACK BEAR

Alt, G. L. 1984. Reuse of black bear dens in northeastern Pennsylvania. *J. Wildl. Manage.* 48: 236–39.

Garshelis, D., and M. R. Pelton. 1980. Activity of black bears in the Great Smoky Mountains National Park. *J. Mamm.* 61: 8–19.

Hamilton, R. J., and R. L. Marchinton. 1977. Denning and related activities of black bears in the coastal plain of North Carolina. Kalispell, Mont., *Proc. 4th Int. Conf. Bear Res. and Manage.*

Maehr, D. S., and J. R. Brady. 1984. Food habits of Florida black bears. *J. Wildl. Manage.* 48: 230–35.

RACCOON

Berner, A., and L. W. Gysel. 1967. Raccoon use of large tree cavities and ground burrows. *J. Wildl. Manage.* 31: 706–14.

Ellis, R. J. 1964. Tracking raccoons by radio. *J. Wildl. Manage.* 28: 363–68.

MacClintock, D. 1981. *Natural History of Raccoons.* New York: Scribner.

Ough, W. D. 1982. Scent marking by captive raccoons. *J. Mamm.* 63: 318–19.

Rue, L. L., III. 1968. *World of the Raccoon.* Philadelphia: J. B. Lippincott Co.

FISHER

Powell, R. A. 1982. *The Fisher: Life History, Ecology, and Behavior.* Minneapolis: University of Minnesota Press.

WEASELS

Erlinge, S. 1974. Distribution, territoriality, and numbers of the weasel, *Mustela nivalis*, in relation to prey abundance. *Oikos* 25: 308–14.

——. 1975. Feeding habits of the weasel, *Mustela nivalis*, in relation to prey abundance. *Oikos* 26: 378–84.

——. 1977. Agonistic behavior and dominance in stoats, *Mustela erminea. Z. Tierpsychol.* 44: 375–88.

——. 1977. Spacing strategy in the stoat, *Mustela erminea. Oikos* 28: 32–42.

Lockie, J. D. 1966. Territory in small carnivores. *Symp. Zool. Soc. Lond.* 18: 143–65.

Polderboer, E. B. 1942. Habits of the least weasel in northeastern Iowa. *J. Mamm.* 23: 145–47.

Quick, H. F. 1951. Notes on the ecology of weasels. *J. Mamm.* 32: 281–90.

Wright, P. L. 1942. Delayed implantation in the long-tailed weasel, short-tailed weasel and the marten. *Anat. Rec.* 83: 341–49.

——. 1948. Breeding habits of captive long-tailed weasels. *Am. Mid. Nat.* 39: 338–44.

——. 1948. Preimplantation stages in the long-tailed weasel. *Anat. Rec.* 100: 593–603.

MINK

Enders, R. K. 1952. Reproduction in the mink. *Proc. Am. Phil. Soc.* 96: 691–755.

Errington, P. L. 1954. Special responsiveness of minks to epizootics in muskrat populations. *Ecol. Monogr.* 24: 377–93.

Hansson, A. 1947. The physiology of reproduction in mink. *Acta Zool.* 28: 1–136.

Marshall, W. H. 1936. A study of the winter activity of the mink. *J. Mamm.* 17: 382–92.

Schladweiler, J. L., and G. L. Storm. 1969. Den-use by mink. *J. Wildl. Manage.* 33: 1025–26.

STRIPED SKUNK

Allen, D. L. 1939. Winter habits of Michigan skunks. *J. Wildl. Manage.* 3: 212–28.

——, and W. W. Shapton. 1942. An ecological study of winter dens with special reference to the eastern skunk. *Ecology* 23: 59–68.

Hamilton, W. J., Jr. 1936. Seasonal food of skunks in New York. *J. Mamm.* 17: 240–46.

Selko, L. F. 1938. Notes on the den ecology of the striped skunk in Iowa. *Am. Mid. Nat.* 20: 455–63.

Van De Graaff, K. M., J. Harper, and G. E. Goslow, Jr. 1982. Analysis of posture and gait selection during locomotion in the striped skunk. *J. Mamm.* 63: 582–90.

OTTER

Erlinge, S. 1967. Home range of the otter, *Lutra lutra*, in Sweden. *Oikos* 18: 186–209.
———. 1968. Food studies of captive otters, *Lutra lutra*. *Oikos* 19: 259–70.
———. 1968. Territoriality of the otter, *Lutra lutra*. *Oikos* 19: 81–98.
Greer, K. R. 1955. Yearly food habits of the river otter. *Am. Mid. Nat.* 54: 299–313.
Hamilton, W. J., Jr. and W. R. Eadie. 1964. Reproduction in the otter. *J. Mamm.* 45: 242–52.

BOBCAT

Johnson, M. K. 1982. Mammalian prey digestibility by bobcats. *J. Wildl. Manage.* 46: 530.
———, R. C. Belden, and D. R. Aldred. 1984. Differentiating mountain lion and bobcat scats. *J. Wildl. Manage.* 48: 239–44.
Rollings, C. T. 1945. Habits, foods and parasites of the bobcat in Minnesota. *J. Wildl. Manage.* 9: 131–45.
Ryden, H. 1981. *The Bobcat Year*. New York: Viking.
Young, S. P. 1958. *The Bobcat of North America*. Washington, D.C.: Wildlife Management Institute.

HOUSE CAT

Fox, M. W. 1974. *Understanding Your Cat*. Toronto: Bantam Books.
Leyhausen, P. 1979. *Cat Behavior*. New York: Garland STPM Press.
Palen, G. F., and G. V. Goddard. 1966. Catnip and oestrus behavior in the cat. *Anim. Behav.* 14: 372–77.

WHITE-TAILED DEER

Armstrong, E., D. Emler, and G. Racey. 1983. Winter bed-site selection by white-tailed deer in central Ontario. *J. Wildl. Manage.* 47: 880–84.
Atkeson, T. D., and R. L. Marchinton. 1982. Forehead glands in white-tailed deer. *J. Mamm.* 63: 613–17.
Hawkins, R. E., and W. D. Klimstra. 1970. A preliminary study of the social organization of white-tailed deer. *J. Wildl. Manage.* 34: 407–19.
Kile, T. L., and R. L. Marchinton. 1977. White-tailed deer rubs and scrapes: spatial, temporal and physical characteristics and social role. *Am. Mid. Nat.* 97: 257–66.
Richardson, L. W., H. A. Jacobson, R. J. Muncy, and C. J. Perkins. 1983. Acoustics of white-tailed deer. *J. Mamm.* 64: 245–52.
Sawyer, T. G., R. L. Marchinton, and C. W. Berisford. 1982. Scraping behavior in female white-tailed deer. *J. Mamm.* 63: 696–97.
Thomas, J. W., R. M. Robinson, and R. G. Marburer. 1965. Social behavior in a white-tailed deer herd containing hypogonadal males. *J. Mamm.* 46: 314–27.

MOOSE

Altmann, M. 1959. Group dynamics in Wyoming moose during the rutting season. *J. Mamm.* 40: 420–24.
Dodds, D. G. 1958. Observations of pre-rutting behavior in Newfoundland moose. *J. Mamm.* 39: 412–16.

Edwards, R. Y., and R. W. Ritcey. 1956. The migrations of a moose herd. *J. Mamm.* 37: 486–94.

Peterson, R. L. 1955. *North American Moose.* Toronto: University of Toronto Press.

Telfer, D. S. 1967. Comparison of a deer yard and a moose yard in Nova Scotia. *Canadian J. Zool.* 45: 485–89.

INDEX

References to illustrations are printed in boldface type.